COPING WITH GLOBALIZATION

I0125107

Coping with Globalization

Cross-National Patterns in Domestic Governance and Policy Performance

Edited by

STEVE CHAN

AND

JAMES R. SCARRITT

FRANK CASS
LONDON • PORTLAND, OR

First published in 2002 in Great Britain by
FRANK CASS PUBLISHERS
2 Park Square, Milton Park, Abingdon, Oxon, OX14 4RN

and in the United States of America by
FRANK CASS PUBLISHERS
270 Madison Ave, New York NY 10016

Transferred to Digital Printing 2005

Website: www.frankcass.com

British Library Cataloguing in Publication Data

Coping with globalization: cross-national patterns in
domestic governance and policy performance
1. Globalization 2. Political science
I. Chan, Steve II. Scarritt, James R.

ISBN 0 7146 5378 0 (cloth)
ISBN 0 7146 8313 2 (paper)

Library of Congress Cataloging-in-Publication Data

Coping with globalization: cross-national patterns in domestic governance and policy
performance / edited by Steve Chan and James R. Scarritt.
    p. cm.
Includes bibliographical references and index.
ISBN 0 7146 5378 0 (cloth) ISBN 0 7146 8313 2 (paper)
1. Globalization. I. Chan, Steve. II. Scarritt, James R.

JZ1318.C685 2002
320.9–dc21

2002073775

Typeset in 10/12pt Times by Vitaset, Paddock Wood, Kent

Contents

Notes on Contributors

Ross E. Burkhart is an assistant professor of political science at Boise State University. His research interests include cross-national democratization patterns, comparative political economy, human rights, and comparative public policy. His publications include articles in the *American Political Science Review*, *European Journal of Political Research*, and the *Journal of Politics*, as well as a forthcoming article in the *Social Science Journal*.

Steve Chan is a professor of political science at the University of Colorado at Boulder. His research addresses issues pertaining to military conversion, democratic peace, foreign policy decisions, international political economy, and the Asian newly industrializing countries. His most recent book, co-edited with A. Cooper Drury, is *Sanctions as Economic Statecraft*, published by Macmillan Press.

Karen Ferree is a PhD candidate in government at Harvard University. Her research interests include the political economy of elections; race and ethnicity; African politics (with a special focus on South Africa); and broad themes of economic and political development. Her contribution to this volume is part of a broader research project with Robert Bates and Smita Singh that examines economic development, political institutions, and civil conflict in Africa. In addition to this project, she is currently finishing her dissertation, which explores the question of how ethnic polarization shapes patterns of party behavior in South Africa.

Ronald D. Gelleny is an assistant professor at California State University at Fullerton. He is finishing his PhD at Binghamton University. His areas of research interest include European integration, globalization, political economy, and political behavior. His work has appeared in *European Union Politics*, *International Studies Quarterly*, and *Political Research Quarterly*.

David A. Leblang is an assistant professor of political science at the University of Colorado at Boulder. His research interests address issues of international financial markets broadly and especially the relationship between political information and market volatility. He is currently examining why politicians defend an exchange-rate peg in the face of a speculative attack. His prior work has appeared in a number of journals, including the *British Journal of Political Science*, the *American Journal of Political Science*, *International Organization*, and *International Studies Quarterly*.

Susan M. McMillan earned her PhD in political science at the University of Colorado, Boulder, and then took a position as assistant professor at Penn State University. She also has taught at the Ohio Wesleyan University and the Ohio State University. She is currently a senior researcher with Educational Data Systems in Morgan Hill, CA. Her publications include articles in *Comparative Political Studies, International Interactions,* and *Mershon International Studies Review.*

David L. Richards is an assistant professor of political science at Missouri Southern State College. His research interests include political violence, democratic institutions, measurement, and economic globalization within the context of government respect for human rights. His work in these areas has appeared in *International Studies Quarterly, Journal of Peace Research, Social Science Quarterly,* and several edited volumes.

Nita Rudra recently received her MA in economics and PhD in political economy and public policy from the University of Southern California. Currently, she is a visiting scholar at the University of California San Diego's Graduate School of International Relations and Pacific Studies and the University of Southern California's School of International Relations. Her research deals with the effects of international market forces on domestic politics, particularly with respect to labor policies and welfare spending.

James R. Scarritt is a professor of political science and faculty research associate at the Institute of Behavioral Science at the University of Colorado at Boulder. He is the author or co-author of articles appearing recently or forthcoming in *British Journal of Political Science, Comparative Political Studies, International Interactions, Journal of Commonwealth and Comparative Politics,* and *Nationalism and Ethnic Politics* and of a forthcoming book on Zambia. His research interests include African and comparative ethnopolitics, democratization, and human rights, and the effects of globalization on all of these topics.

Smita Singh is a scholar at the Harvard Academy for International and Area Studies, and a PhD candidate in government at Harvard University. She is currently working on a research project with Robert Bates and Karen Ferree that explores the interrelationships between economic performance, political transitions, and civil conflict in African countries in the post-World War Two period. Her chapter in this volume is part of this larger project. In addition to the political economy of African countries, Singh studies economic and political development in Southeast Asia. Her dissertation explores how the strategic organization of business communities structures the politics of economic policy-making in Nigeria and Indonesia.

Tables and Figures

FIGURES

Foreword

This volume is a welcome addition to the literature on globalization and its effects. To a distressing degree, that literature, both popular and scholarly, tends to be anecdotal in nature, devoid of comparative and systematic analysis, dependent on qualitative rather than quantitative methods, excessively deferential to disciplinary boundaries, and rife with ideological preconceptions, or some combination of these unfortunate characteristics. The scholarly community, as well as citizens and policy-makers in the United States and abroad, deserve and need better. Fortunately, a new scholarship is beginning to appear that brings the best tools, concepts, and theories in the social sciences to the task of understanding the globalization phenomenon and its implications. This volume, intelligently edited by Steve Chan and James R. Scarritt, is an exemplar of this new scholarship. Let me take the opportunity to describe why I believe this to be the case.

First, the volume comprises original chapters that examine globalization from an interdisciplinary point of view, with a particular emphasis on the interaction of economic and political factors to explain various aspects of globalization and its outcomes. Although each of the scholars represented herein comes from an identifiable discipline, none is lured by single-factor explanations, or is tempted, prior to his or her investigations, to privilege the economic, social, or political explanations that prevail in his or her own field. Each understands that globalization is a complex, multi-dimensional phenomenon that cannot be properly appreciated with the tools and concepts drawn from single disciplines.

The attention to the interaction of the political and the economic in these pages includes both methodological and substantive aspects. On the methodological front, the authors in this volume use research tools and concepts from economics, but also from political science and sociology. On the substantive front, the analyses of globalization in these pages are sensitive to the fact that economic, political, and social factors interact to shape how globalization is experienced in societies and among groups within societies. Thus globalization shapes who wins and who loses in particular societies, as well as what kinds of domestic policies governments choose, but governments also make policy decisions that determine how globalization works and how people within societies are affected by it.

Moreover, the editors include only work that meets the highest standards of systematic social science research. That is to say, each of the chapters reports research on globalization that is comparative rather than being

reliant on single case studies, that relies on quantitative data and sophisticated statistical techniques to identify tendencies and the conditions under
which these tendencies obtain across different kinds of societies, and that
both describes empirical reality and tests hypotheses about it.

The authors represented in this volume do not fall into the trap of
judging globalization from ideological points of view; rather, as suggested
above, they are one and all committed to systematic research and hypothesis
testing. All too often, even in some of the scholarly literature, analysts come
to globalization studies with preconceived notions about what it must look
like, and what its effects must be. To many breathless proponents, for
example, globalization is self-evidently good, leading to overall economic
growth in societies that tie their fates to it, to poverty reduction, to expansion of the middle class, and to the increasing probability of democracy. To
many fervent opponents of globalization, the increased permeability of
national and societal boundaries to products, production and distribution
facilities, capital, ideas, and people is a prescription for rising inequality
within and between countries, exploitation of poor societies by rich ones,
environmental degradation, and cultural violation. The authors of the
chapters in this volume, though often reaching firm conclusions about
aspects of globalization, and about how groups and societies cope with
them, do so only on the basis of evidence generated by systematic, empirical, comparative, and quantitative research. The purpose of their research
is not simply to embellish, or to build empirical foundations for, conclusions
drawn from ideological and political agendas.

Much to the editors' credit, the authors in this volume do not fall into
the common trap of assuming that globalization is a uniform process with
homogeneous effects across a wide range of societies. They are sensitive to
the fact that globalization is a complex process, involving flows of money,
products, production facilities, information, and people at various rates
across national and societal boundaries, and that these various globalization processes will affect societies and groups within societies in very
different ways, depending on the coping and adaptive resources available
to them. Societies and groups within societies vary in their degree of
vulnerability to globalization, and in their ability to take advantage of its
opportunities.

Nor do the editors assume *a priori* that globalization is an automatic,
inexorable phenomenon beyond human design and human intervention.
Although it is often cloaked in such language by proponents of globalization who celebrate its spread, as well as by opponents who lament the
same thing, the editors of this volume are sensitive to the fact that each and
every one of the processes that comprise economic, social, and political
globalization are the product of decisions by governments, international

agencies, and NGOs, and powerful private economic actors, all of whom have their own interests and perspectives when it comes to consequential decisions. Globalization does not fall fully formed from the sky; its form and overall course of development are the products of a myriad observable social choices. For example, globalization is shaped by, among many other things, the following: decisions of national governments about tariffs and non-tariff barriers to trade; the conditions placed on countries for financial help by the International Monetary Fund, the World Bank, and private banks; treaty agreements among governments on issues of the environment, immigration, and labor standards; international agreements on telecommunications and mass media practices; and decisions by global corporations about what products to produce, where and how to produce them, and where to market final products. More often than not, the key actors and institutions that decide the shape and progress of globalization are located in what some call the 'core' countries and others call the 'rich democracies'. As the editors note in their chapter, this suggests that what is happening in the world today is not so much globalization as what they call 'soft hegemony', the tool used by core societies to have their way and to gain disproportionate advantages. The authors represented in this volume are sensitive to this complexity.

The editors are also to be commended for including research that focuses on a wide range of globalization outcomes. Because they are primarily interested in encouraging and reporting research that asks under what conditions globalization might lead to improvements in human well-being, they are necessarily obliged to include research that goes beyond simple macroeconomic performances of national economies, the focus of much of the writing about globalization. Although the research reported in these pages does not ignore macroeconomic performance, it is striking how many other important and valued well-being outcomes are included: welfare provision and spending, education, democratic political processes, income and wealth equality, and human rights, all of which may be enhanced by globalization, diminished by it, or both, depending on circumstances.

What also characterizes this volume and distinguishes it from others in the field of globalization studies is that all of the substantive chapters are written by young and relatively junior scholars. What they have brought to this enterprise is top-notch training, enthusiasm for understanding globalization and its effects, and a freshness of vision and a perspective that illuminates complex problems, all of which are shown to good effect throughout the chapters.

Steve Chan and James Scarritt, then, have done their editorial job with consummate skill and judgment, bringing together a diverse set of young scholars who manage, in the end, to increase our understanding of globalization and how various societies and groups cope with it by reporting research that meets the highest standards in the social sciences and that recognizes the complexity of the phenomenon under study. In that sense, they have produced a work that will have an impact on globalization scholars and their students.

Edward S. Greenberg
Co-Director, Globalization and Democracy Program
Institute of Behavioral Science
University of Colorado, Boulder

List of Abbreviations

APEC	Asia-Pacific Economic Cooperation
ASEAN	Association of Southeast Asian Nations
FDI	foreign direct investment
GDP	gross domestic product
GNP	gross national product
GNPPC	gross national product per capita
GRO	grass roots organization
HDI	Human Development Index
IGO	intergovernmental organization
IMF	International Monetary Fund
LDC	less developed country
LIBOR	London Interbank Offer Rates
MAI	Multilateral Agreement on Investment
MNC	multinational corporation
NAFTA	North American Free Trade Agreement
NGO	nongovernmental organization
NIC	newly industrializing country
OECD	Organisation for Economic Co-operation and Development
PQLI	Physical Quality of Life Index
UNDP	United Nations Development Programme
WAEN	West African Enterprise Network
WTO	World Trade Organization

1

Globalization, Soft Hegemony, and Democratization: Their Sources and Effects

STEVE CHAN AND JAMES R. SCARRITT

INTRODUCTION

It is often said that in an age of globalization, national and local leaders and populations become increasingly subject to forces outside their domestic jurisdiction and popular control. The Westphalian tradition of territorially based and juridically autonomous states has supposedly come under the strain of a changing global economy and cultural shift. These changes challenge the capacity of national leaders to formulate and implement authoritative policy and that of people to hold them accountable for doing so. The massive and rapid exodus of speculative foreign capital was the proximate cause of the so-called Asian economic flu of the late 1990s. Adverse foreign reactions to domestic repression, whether in Tiananmen Square, Chechnya or Chiapas, illustrate possible constraints on domestic authoritarianism. Recent attempts by members of the European Union to influence the composition of Austria's coalition government (specifically to seek the exclusion of the Freedom Party with its neo-Nazi sympathies) furnish still another example of the putative influence of external political, economic, and cultural forces on domestic governance. World Trade Organization (WTO) regulations prohibit local communities from deciding to divest from countries that do not meet these communities' standards of democracy, wages and working conditions, or environmental protection.

In this volume, we seek to understand the extent, as well as the limits, of the influence of globalization processes. Unlike much of the existing scholarship, however, we rely on quantitative approaches to further this understanding. Case studies can offer profound insights. We choose instead to search for cross-national patterns. In particular, we seek to understand the nature and extent of global (or regional) influences on domestic political change and policy performance (such as economic growth, inequality, democratization, and the provision of basic human needs) and the domestic conditions that mediate this influence. This empirical undertaking is found mainly in subsequent chapters, although it begins in an illustrative way in a later section of this chapter. Our introduction begins with an exercise in conceptual clarification.

WHAT IS GLOBALIZATION?[1]

Webster's dictionary defines 'globalization' as the act or process 'to make worldwide in scope and application'. According to Randall and Theobald (1998: 235–42), Mittelman (1999: 5–7), Holton (1998) and Held *et al.* (1999), globalization has three central dimensions: economic, cultural, and political. The economic dimension is often viewed as having causal primacy. It involves 'the organization of production and consumption of goods and services at the global level ... achieved mainly through transnational corporations' (Randall and Theobald, 1998: 235). It involves substantial increases in trade and foreign investment. The cultural dimension has been, by and large, the result of 'developments in communication and information technology' (Randall and Theobald, 1998: 237). It reinforces the economic dimension through creating a consumer culture. Finally, the political dimension includes global awareness and networking around issues, 'a proliferation of international or governing regulatory organizations and of international regimes', and 'a trend toward the globalization of social classes and social movements' (Randall and Theobald, 1998: 239–40) and, one might add, nongovernmental organizations (NGOs), including those at the grass roots. In sharp contrast to definitions that conceive of globalization as a single smooth or cumulative process, these dimensions and their various aspects are in dialectical relationships with one another in which universalizing pressures trigger particularistic responses and vice versa. States, IGOs (intergovernmental organizations), NGOs, social movements, and local communities are not prisoners trapped in an intractable web of economic and cultural globalization. Including all of these at least partially contradictory processes in the concept of globalization makes it difficult to test the overall impact of this general phenomenon. Subsequent sections of this chapter, as well as the chapters that follow, test aspects of this impact, and we lay out a research agenda in the concluding section of this chapter for a more inclusive test.

Francis Fukuyama's (1992) philosophic celebration of the demise of totalitarian ideologies and the triumph of liberal ideals, and Samuel Huntington's (1991) historical analysis and Larry Diamond's (1999) more conceptual analysis of the 'third wave' show the increasing popularity of at least formal democratic principles and institutions in the world. The breakdown of trade and investment barriers and the concomitant rise of international capital and multinational corporations provide seemingly indisputable evidence of economic interdependence and globalization. 'Sovereignty at bay' (Vernon, 1971) appeals to many as an apt description of the political and economic reality that they, as public officials or private citizens, have to address – for better or worse. Few who suffered through East Asia's recent financial turmoil will doubt the impact of international capital, in the form of both investment funds and foreign debts, on their country's macroeconomic performance and their personal or corporate asset values (Jomo, 1999). Likewise, recent foreign interventions in Kosovo, Haiti and Iraq should convince even the most skeptical observers that international conventions and norms regarding aggression, ethnic cleansing, and human rights increasingly challenge the Westphalian tradition which buttresses each state's assertion of exclusive domestic jurisdiction. Of course, we are also told that advances in information technology and modern telecommunication have made the world 'a smaller place'. As inhabitants of this 'global village', we increasingly share the same thoughts, values, and habits – a cultural convergence, if you will.

Yet globalization is a dialectical rather than a cumulative process. Available statistics provide compelling evidence that the economic distance between the developed and underdeveloped economies and that between the privileged and disadvantaged classes are increasing rather than diminishing. The Matthew principle – the rich get richer, the poor poorer – underscores not only the widening income gap but also mounting discrepancies in life chances (such as access to education, health care and, yes, personal computers and the internet). From this perspective, globalization seems to be more of a codeword for the expanded opportunities of the more affluent segments of national and international society rather than a process that enriches all through accelerated growth. To those who are less fortunate (such as those poor Indonesians and Mexicans who had to bear the brunt of austerity programs), the same processes look more like a 'race to the bottom'.

Just as economic disparities and differences in life chances are not diminishing for the people of the world, one may also question whether the world has reached the 'end of history' for contending political ideologies. That various authoritarian regimes have met their demise does not in itself constitute proof that the relevant mass publics or elite circles have assimilated the democratic ethos. Although many countries have adopted formally democratic institutions in recent years, it remains quite problematic whether their political culture has undergone a concomitant change to promote and secure those civic values and political norms (e.g. social trust, civic mindedness, norms of diffused reciprocity, tolerance for dissent) that are critical for deepening, consolidating and sustaining democratic politics. Just recall that even in an established democracy such as the United States, voters have been known to reject the idea of affirmative action for minorities and equal-rights protection for gays and lesbians.

Accordingly, democratization as a globalization process, as the term is commonly used, seems to refer more to the wider geographic spread of certain forms of government, and less to the deeper cultural and institutional transformation of the relevant polities, what Diamond (1999: 49–60) calls the globalization of hollow democracy. As such, the political reforms of the recently proclaimed democracies in Eastern Europe and Latin America are fragile and vulnerable to reversal. There are ominous signs of political alienation and cynicism among the established democracies. The United States, for example, has suffered a sharp and persistent decline in the social capital and civic ethos necessary for securing democracy (Putnam, 1995).

Significantly, qualitative and quantitative studies of political change seem to agree that external influences are much less significant than internal ones – to the extent that they can be conceptually and operationally separated – in shaping a country's democratization (e.g. Hollifield and Jillson, 2000; Bratton and van de Walle, 1997). This view receives support from Ray's (1995) quantitative assessment of the relative role played historically by systemic-level and state-specific forces in motivating regime transformation. For each period studied by him, the former turned out to be much weaker than the latter. For instance, systemic-level forces were responsible for only 2.7 per cent (1865–1905), 1.4 per cent (1905–45), and 0.6 per cent (1945–85) of the changes in democratic scores for those countries included in his worldwide sample – compared to, respectively, 17.8 per cent, 29.3 per cent, and 28.5 per cent accounted for by country-specific forces. These results do not encourage optimism about the efficacy of external intervention to promote democratization and direct our attention instead to domestic conditions and processes.

Naturally, there is also the highly contentious matter of whether ideals such as liberal democracy are truly universal values shared by all people, or whether they are in fact parochial concerns shaped by different historical circumstances and perhaps employed to disguise and advance national or class interests. It does seem, however, that many proponents of liberal democracy as a globalization force tend to be more concerned about the protection of people's negative rights – that is, their right to be free from government interference and oppression – than about their positive rights – that is, the proposition that people everywhere are entitled to be free from the deprivations caused by hunger, disease, and poverty. A concern for procedural rights is often not matched by a comparable interest in substantive rights – in distributive justice if you will. However, a deeper democratization would probably result in a greater concern with substantive rights and thus a challenge to aspects of economic globalization.

Normative agreement or objection aside, the description of democratization as a globalization process seems unwise and unwarranted because it is likely to give short shrift to the cross currents pointing to the 'clash of civilizations' (Huntington, 1993). Islamic fundamentalism, Asian Confucianism, ethno-political violence in some African and Latin American countries, and the revival of ethnic and religious animosity in Eastern Europe belie the suggestion of universal values and political convergence. It is often difficult to tell whether the 'globalists' are advancing an ideal or offering a description or prediction; the distinction between 'ought' and 'is' (that is, between value and factual statements) tends to be all too often blurred.

There is of course a great deal of evidence suggesting certain convergences of popular and consumer culture. Children in Western Europe have increasing access to Netscape and CNN, those in Eastern Europe learn English at school, those in China are attracted to Coca-Cola and McDonald's, those in Latin America form fan clubs for *Star Trek* and *Star Wars*, and Michael Jackson and Michael Jordan become cultural icons for African children living in even very remote villages. One tends, however, to confuse rather than clarify matters when one refers to these phenomena as forces of globalization when they in fact represent signs of America's cultural hegemony. It is also a bit disingenuous to showcase a military campaign conducted by a Western alliance in Kosovo – a campaign that sought deliberately to bypass the authority of the United Nations – as a cause advancing globalization and 'world order'. Likewise, one wonders what analytical gains, and losses, follow when one attributes to international capital or international agencies such as the International Monetary Fund and the World Bank prominent roles as representing globalization without acknowledging the significance of US command of so many of the relevant financial, institutional and ideological assets, and its significant, if partial, control of the collective agenda.

The question can be put in another way. What value-added does one gain when one replaces pluralistic or state-centric views of international–domestic relations and a dialectical view of globalization with one that assigns particular importance to forces that are supposedly beyond the authority and power of states or other organizations, forces that are in some sense supposed to bring all the inhabitants of the world closer together – whether figuratively or literally? One may engage in 'concept stretching' when one combines a variety of heterogeneous phenomena and calls them by the same name (Sartori, 1970). One may choose to subsume under the concept of political participation nonviolent acts such as voting, making campaign contributions, attending rallies, writing to officials, and protesting, and violent acts such as rioting, plotting a coup, and joining a revolutionary war. But do the gains in connotative coverage justify the loss in denotative precision?

Globalization as a concept may imply the operation of powerful, impersonal, even natural, forces that are somehow independent of human agency. It also often implies some inevitable outcome regardless of our personal or collective preferences. As such, this perspective can shape subtly but profoundly the nature of not only academic scholarship but also social commentary and political discourse. Is one really to assume that the forces of globalization have nothing to do with statist, class or organizational agendas? Or is the truth of the matter closer to the other way round? That is, that 'globalization' forces are to a substantial degree produced by the actions and policies of states, MNCs (multinational corporations), social movements, and NGOs – the consequent pulling and hauling are the very substance of international relations and what statecraft is all about. Would it be more realistic to expect that states and NGOs in fact try to promote, bend, or forestall the forces of globalization even though, obviously, some are better at it than others? Is it not a big part of this game, if not the entire point, to shift onto others the burden of adjustment? Moreover, does not the nebulous term 'globalization' hide what is really happening – namely, a redistributive process that affects values, power, income, status, and life chances, a process whose consequences are hardly neutral for all concerned. Calling it 'globalization' may direct attention away from questions about national and organizational interests and responsibilities.

These points are illustrated by the controversy about the role of regionalism in globalization. Mittelman (1999: 111) asks 'Is regionalism merely a way station toward neo-liberal globalization, or a means toward a more pluralistic world order in which distinct patterns of socioeconomic organization coexist and compete for popular support?' His answer is that contemporary regionalism involves aspects of both of these directions due to the dialectical nature of what he calls the globalization syndrome. The varying regional impacts of globalization that are analyzed in subsequent chapters demonstrate the unevenness of economic globalization, but it is less clear that they demonstrate organized resistance to it.

WHO ADJUSTS?

If by globalization one means the increased flow of commerce, tourism, and ideas, then obviously countries have become more involved in such exchanges over time. The level of cross-border transactions, whether they be measured in trade volume, jet travel, or study abroad, has surely risen for all countries. There is hardly any surprise in discovering that over time all societies and economies have become more 'open' to foreign discourse, although the degree of 'openness' naturally varies from country to country (e.g. Burma versus Thailand, Chad versus Côte d'Ivoire, Cuba versus Jamaica).

Openness defined in terms of the extent of one's foreign involvement, however, does not quite get at the problem at hand which, as implied earlier, requires judgments about differential capacity to shape and influence terms of exchange. Some states are favored to be price-makers, while others are seemingly destined for the role of price-takers. Some states are better equipped to resist foreign dependency and penetration, while others appear to be far less prepared for such challenges. Finally, some may find ongoing trends to be rather congenial given their existing values or comparative advantages, while others are more likely to perceive these trends as discouraging and even threatening for the opposite reasons. An evolving situation may play into the strengths of some while forcing others to bear the burden of adjustment.

All of this goes to say that states and their economies and populations are positioned differently to address or adapt to the so-called forces of globalization (Waltz, 1999). Thus, Hong Kong and Singapore, to cite two obvious examples, are better prepared to take advantage of the liberalization of national financial regimes than Burma or Vietnam. Japan is better able to create and control production chains across national boundaries than China. Australia and New Zealand will find the promotion of liberal democracy and respect for human rights less disconcerting than, say, Indonesia.

To rephrase the preceding remarks, one may say that countries have different comparative advantages, or that they occupy different niches in the world political economy, or that they suffer from different degrees of sensitivity or vulnerability to external shocks. Alternatively, one may wish to argue that some states command greater cultural appeal or political reach so that they are in a better position to use their 'soft power' (Nye, 1990) to co-opt others. Similarly, some states – because of their larger or more autarchic economy, the homogeneity of their society, the consensus characterizing their elites, the cohesion among their bureaucrats, in short, their greater political capacity and social resilience – are better able to resist foreign political penetration and cultural domination than others. Therefore, while most indigenous people fell victim to colonialism by the end of the nineteenth century, a few did not. Although English, French, and Spanish have become the dominant languages in large parts of Africa and America, they hardly enjoy the same status in China and Japan as, say, in Malaysia, Morocco, and Mexico.

All things being equal, the larger economies are more self-sufficient. Given their sheer physical size, China, Brazil, and India have less need for foreign trade than, say, Singapore, Paraguay, and Bhutan. China's much larger domestic market makes a policy of import substitution more feasible and less costly. Conversely, for Singapore an export-oriented policy is not a matter of virtue but rather one of necessity. Differences in their tangible endowments expand the menu for choice for some and constrain the policy options available to the others (Russett and Starr, 1996). Small countries such as Singapore are more exposed to external influences and can do less to protect themselves against the unwanted effects of such exposure. They are therefore both more sensitive and vulnerable to the forces of 'globalization'.

Although size is certainly not everything, it makes the price of foreign attempts at assimilation – not to mention, conquest – prohibitively costly. It is difficult to imagine in today's world of 'trading nations' (Rosecrance, 1986) that anyone would want to follow Japan's disastrous example of seeking to seize physical control of China as it did during the first half of the twentieth century. China, Indonesia, or Russia offer three examples of states 'too big to swallow'. Security in their case need not come from an ability to project offensive force; their sheer mass deters any would-be aggressor by raising the prospect of protracted quagmire. From this per-spective, these countries are in a better position to resist foreign intervention in the name of professed global norms such as democracy, human rights, and collective defense. No one is going to mistake these countries for Haiti, Kuwait, or Kosovo.

History often comes with size. Longevity also has certain advantages. Here again, not all countries are alike. For example, some Asia Pacific countries are relatively recent creations of Europeans, whereas others have long traditions, deep cultures, and established identification. Foreign fads and fashions would have an easier time gaining 'cultural hegemony' in places where the local institutions are of recent vintage and subject to contestation by different communities. Therefore, one would expect a marked difference in popular adoption of Western ideas and practices between, say, Japan and Malaysia, or China and the Philippines. These countries accord-ingly differ sharply in their susceptibility to external cultural influences.

Different groups, regions and industries within the same country stand to benefit and suffer in different degrees from the so-called forces of globalization. In a world where barriers to transnational investment and manufacturing have fallen capital gains a significant advantage over labor, whose mobility faces much greater restrictions (Milner and Keohane, 1996: 249–51). Similarly, 'globalization' presumably means very different things to the competitiveness of companies such as Microsoft and Fruit of the

Loom and the personal fortunes of their employees. Surely, the North American Free Trade Agreement (NAFTA) has a differential impact on Tennessee than on, say, Texas. Therefore, national units of accounting may conceal rather than reveal sub-national differences in the distribution of the benefits and costs of globalization or regionalization. The costs of adjustment tend to fall disproportionately on some, whereas the benefits accrue to others.

WHICH EXTERNAL FORCES?

It should not be difficult to undertake empirical analyses seeking to determine the extent to which countries are sensitive to external developments. Indeed, much such research has been carried out to show how one country's arms spending 'stimulates' another country's arms spending. Likewise, other statistical studies demonstrate the degree to which the currency values, interest rates, or stock assets of one country rise or fall in tandem with the price fluctuations in foreign capital markets. There are still other analyses demonstrating 'contagion effects' such as when coups or democratic changes in one country 'diffuse' to its neighbors (Bratton and van de Walle, 1997). These studies suggest that the appropriate analytic question is not so much 'whether' one can escape from 'globalization' influences; it is rather 'how much' one is subject to such influences, to 'which' kind of influences, and from 'whom'.

As alluded to earlier, globalization is sometimes a euphemism for the soft power of hegemons or would-be hegemons and the MNCs that are based there. The cultural reach of these countries and corporations is reflected in the extent to which others adopt or emulate their ethos and institutions. To what extent have others assimilated the outlook, habit, and values of the US, Japan, Germany, India, or China? In a fundamental sense, competition for national influence revolves around the export of one's model of government, capital, business ethos, technical standards, and cultural practices. Whose ideas and institutions do others follow or adopt? Hegemony in Gramsci's sense very much requires and implies the power to shape or reshape others according to or in one's image. A hegemon's cultural reach is therefore in part reflected by its ability to recruit others to subscribe to its ideology and to accept its institutions as their own.

Fajnzylber (1990) argued that due to their very different histories and cultures, the US and Japan presented to their follower-nations two very different models of development. In the US, most firms have had an inward-looking tradition. Until relatively recently, their primary concern has been production to satisfy a large domestic market. Exports tended to be of secondary importance. Moreover, an abundance of natural resources has historically meant that much of the exports were in primary commodities (e.g. grain, cotton). The country's popular ethos professes profound misgivings about 'big government', and places a high value on individual freedom, exuberant consumerism, and equality of opportunity (coexisting with an acceptance of pronounced socioeconomic inequality in actual distributive outcomes). Public policy as well as mass culture tends to encourage consumption at the expense of savings.

In contrast, the core of Confucian economic philosophy advocates 'consume less, save more', and admonishes that the growth of a country's consumption must be kept within the limits of its productivity gain. The interests of Japanese producers have generally been favored at the expense of consumers. There has also been a much higher level of popular support for government intervention in the marketplace. The state is seen as a guardian of public trust and common welfare against particularistic interests. In fact, an ingenious system has seemingly evolved in which 'patronage politics' is limited to sectors not involved in international trade, such as agriculture and construction, while technocratic control over policy-making about major industries has been protected (Calder, 1988). Moreover, Japanese firms have always been outward-looking. Foreign exports are the central mission rather than a subsidiary concern of corporate executives. Being poor in natural resources and saddled with a relatively large population, manufactures with high added value are Japan's chief exports.

Concomitantly, cultural norms in Japan emphasize the virtues of group conformity, interpersonal collaboration, collective responsibility, and social integration at the expense of personal liberty. They also encourage frugality, savings, and distributive justice. Thus, Japan features more austere consumption patterns, higher rates of capital formation, and greater equity in income distribution than the US. Its public and private sectors both espouse fiscal conservatism.

Fajnzylber (1990) claimed that the Latin American and East Asian countries have been incorporated, respectively, into the US and Japanese spheres of formal and informal colonialism. This incorporation has influenced the peripheral countries' domestic patterns of authority, production, consumption, and interest alignment, patterns that have in turn limited profoundly their subsequent developmental possibilities. In Latin America, the relevant historical legacies and dense interactions with the US have produced a preference for producing for the domestic market, high consumption proclivities by the urban rich, and a heavy reliance on cash crops and minerals for export revenues. These tendencies have in turn led to an emphasis on import-substitution industrialization, and on foreign debts and budgetary deficits as ways for financing both public and private consumption, especially ostentatious consumption of luxurious imports by a small elite. These tendencies also foster an unequal distribution of income and a collective complacency (due to the 'easy' revenues from selling natural resources), creating vested interests that make graduation from commodity exports more problematic. Conversely, the newly industrializing East Asian countries have followed the Japanese model, which inclined them to pursue overseas businesses, practice fiscal conservatism, refrain from 'exuberant' consumption, and stress social integration (or 'harmony').

Fajnzylber's account shows that globalization forces are hardly impersonal processes that somehow materialize mysteriously. Instead, these forces often have definite national and organizational origins and promote specific social, economic, and political arrangements that work to the benefit of some and the disadvantage of others. These forces often become part of the 'deep' social structures, embedding themselves as entrenched interests and established institutions. They 'steer' subsequent course of events, making certain public policies and developmental paths more likely and attractive and other historical possibilities less so. At issue is the menu of choices available to national and organizational leaders. To what extent is this menu being expanded or constricted? That is, do these leaders have sufficient autonomy to select among alternative strategies or are they severely constrained by 'globalization' forces in making this selection? 'Globalization' forces exercise a profound and enduring impact because, quite separate from their overt influence, they play a subtle role in propagating ideas, shaping interests, promoting self-images, and fostering institutions that tend to define the policy agenda for national governance.

A SNAPSHOT OF 'SOFT' HEGEMONY

A very significant component of the dialectical conception of globalization presented in this chapter is the increased possibilities for major powers to exercise 'soft' hegemony. As demonstrated some time ago by Bruce Russett (1967), a systematic analysis of national attributes can offer meaningful and revealing maps of international regions and their memberships, which are defined as much by physical location and distance as by cultural, ideological, and institutional affinities. This insight has been applied in an initial probe to explore the similarities and differences in the 'profiles' of national political economies in the APEC (Asia-Pacific Economic Cooperation) region. Chan and Clark (1992) undertook a cluster analysis using aggregate data from the 1980s that were meant to capture the more salient aspects of the relevant political economies along the lines suggested by Fajnzylber. The variables used for their analysis included, for example, the rate of domestic savings, the rate of exports, the degree of equity in income distribution, and the level of consumption on 'transport and communication'.

The last variable was supposed to reflect a country's spending on personal motor vehicles and, as such, it provides a measure of its consumption habit for luxury goods in the context of the developing world. Fajnzylber (1990: 338) reported that although South Korea had become the leading automobile exporter among the developing countries, its per capita ownership of motor vehicles was only one-tenth to one-fifteenth of that of Latin American countries of comparable economic size.

Table 1.1 reproduces the cluster analysis in Chan and Clark (1992: 42). Cluster analysis is a method for sorting cases based on the proximity or similarity of their selected attributes. It has been used by social and natural scientists for a variety of purposes, such as to establish a numerical taxonomy of animal species, to create personality types, and to group cultural artifacts (Aldenderfer and Blashfield, 1984; Corter, 1996; Sokal and Sneath, 1963). The results in Table 1.1 are based on the so-called average linkage method for determining the distance between the various political economies named. They show, for instance, that if the reported cases were forced into two clusters, one of them would consist of Japan, South Korea, Taiwan, and Hong Kong and the remaining countries would belong to the other group. If three clusters were allowed, Indonesia would separate to become a class by itself. If the countries were allowed to break into four groups, the United States and the Philippines would become yet another separate category, and so on and so forth. As the number of clusters increases, finer and finer distinctions among the countries are being drawn.

TABLE 1.1
MODELS OF DEVELOPMENT: EAST ASIA, ca. 1980s

| | Number of clusters | | | | |
	6	5	4	3	2
Japan	1	1	1	1	1
South Korea	2	2	1	1	1
Taiwan	2	2	1	1	1
Hong Kong	2	2	1	1	1
Singapore	3	3	2	2	2
Malaysia	3	3	2	2	2
Australia	4	3	2	2	2
New Zealand	4	3	2	2	2
Canada	4	3	2	2	2
Thailand	4	3	2	2	2
United States	5	4	3	2	2
Philippines	5	4	3	2	2
Indonesia	6	5	4	3	2

Source: Chan and Clark (1992: 42).

When there are only two clusters, the most general typologies are being offered. At that most general level, the pattern revealed by Table 1.1 seems to make intuitive sense in terms of putative 'membership' in the US and Japanese cultural 'camps'.

The specific placement of individual countries also seems to make some intuitive sense. As one might have guessed, the Philippines, a former US and Spanish colony, has followed the American model most closely. As already noted, it and the United States formed a distinct cluster when countries were allowed to form four groups. With its traditional hacienda culture, agricultural exports (sugar and coconut), Catholicism, extended patronage system, and skewed socioeconomic distribution, the Philippines is also the most Latin American of the Asian countries (Hawes, 1987). Imitation of the 'American way of life,' from popular art to political campaigns, has gone the furthest in the Philippines in comparison to its regional neighbors. Although, in various ways, the political economies of Thailand and Singapore also exhibit features of the American model, the extent of this replication is much more limited in these countries than in the Philippines.

Also congruent with one's expectations, Table 1.1 shows that Taiwan and South Korea, two former Japanese colonies, most closely follow the Japanese model of development in terms of their patterns of economic production, consumption, and distribution. Hong Kong also belongs to this group, sharing with the other two a profile consisting of a large manufacturing sector, a heavy reliance on the export of consumer products, a high savings rate, a low tendency for luxurious purchases (especially for privately owned vehicles), and a comparatively egalitarian system of income distribution.

Table 1.1 also shows that, below the most general dichotomous categories, the other APEC countries, such as Indonesia, Singapore, Malaysia, Australia, and Thailand, 'belonged' to neither the US nor the Japanese cultural sphere. That is, their national profiles are more difficult to typecast, as they do not consistently feature those attributes exemplified by either the US or the Japanese political economies according to Fajnzylber. Indonesia presents an especially interesting and, among the countries studied, distinct case. As a relatively low income, oil exporting country with a heavy emphasis on import substitution, the military-dominated government in Jakarta (in the 1980s) presented a model of political economy that was substantially different from the rest of the countries in Table 1.1.

Interestingly, adoption of another country's model of political economy does not necessarily imply popular adoration of this country (Reich et al., 1997). The most notable example pertains to South Korea. Although public opinion in this country tends to present a rather negative image of Japan (Hastings and Hastings, 1996), its political and economic institutions have been deeply influenced by the legacy of Japanese colonialism (Cumings, 1984). Moreover, South Korea's elite ethos as well as popular culture continue to be influenced by Japan. Although the aggregate data used for the cluster analysis in Table 1.1 are relatively crude, the results show that in terms of these general characteristics South Korea is the country that is most similar to Japan in its macro-political economy. Thus, in this instance, popular sentiments do not necessarily reflect accurately Japan's soft power: sentimental affinity and institutional affinity do not correspond in this case. Yet, hegemons need not be loved; the durability of their influence depends instead on the extent to which their ideologies and institutions become deeply embedded in the 'follower' nations. This co-optation can take place in the absence of the latter's conscious awareness and, in the South Korea case just mentioned, apparently in the face of actual overt public (and possibly, elite) hostility directed against the hegemon.

That sentimental and institutional affinities need not correspond seems also to apply to some other cases. The mass public in Indonesia, Malaysia, and Thailand tend to hold generally favorable impressions of the US (Hastings and Hastings, 1996). These favorable sentiments, however, appear not to have produced behavioral patterns that mimic the American model. An interesting question then is whether popular sentiments are a leading or lagging indicator of aggregate behavior or institutional adoption, or whether their relationship implies reciprocal causality.

SOME FURTHER COMPARISONS

The illustration just provided, focusing on East Asia, is necessarily tentative, incomplete, and static. It may reflect selection bias both in terms of key countries omitted (e.g. China for which the relevant data were unavailable for the period studied) and specific variables employed. Moreover, the clustering patterns reveal similarities in political economic profiles at one time. One may therefore wish to inquire whether these patterns tend to endure over time (as one would expect from persistent hegemonic influence) or are subject to change. Moreover, it would be interesting to determine whether this approach has a broader applicability to other regions.

Using the same method of average linkage to determine the distance among cases as in Table 1.1, Table 1.2 reports the results of another cluster analysis using more recent data from the 1990s. While pursuing the generic ideas presented originally by Fajnzylber, this new analysis draws on a somewhat different set of operational indicators. Specifically, it is based on the following variables: the ratio of income share between the richest and poorest 20 per cent of population, merchandise trade as a per cent of gross national product (GNP), manufactures as a per cent of total exports, gross

TABLE 1.2
MODELS OF POLITICAL ECONOMY: APEC, ca. 1990s

	Number of clusters				
	6	5	4	3	2
Japan	1	1	1	1	1
China	1	1	1	1	1
South Korea	1	1	1	1	1
Taiwan	1	1	1	1	1
Thailand	1	1	1	1	1
United States	4	4	1	1	1
Philippines	4	4	1	1	1
Indonesia	3	3	3	1	1
Hong Kong	2	2	2	2	1
Singapore	2	2	2	2	1
Malaysia	2	2	2	2	1
Canada	5	5	4	3	2
Australia	6	5	4	3	2
New Zealand	6	5	4	3	2

domestic savings as a per cent of gross domestic product (GDP), general
government consumption as a per cent of GDP, and public spending on
education as a per cent of GNP. The World Bank (2000) and the United
Nations Development Programme (1999) were the sources for the relevant
data except for Taiwan (for which the data are from the Council for
Economic Planning and Development, 1999). In addition to employing
several different indicators, this new analysis also expanded the country
sample to include all the major members of APEC. Thus, it now has China,
Australia, Canada, and New Zealand among its cases.

What does one find in this new analysis? Despite changes in indicators
and sample, some of the 1980s patterns persist. When forced to form two
separate groups, Canada, Australia, and New Zealand coalesce into one
cluster while the remaining countries in the sample establish another. The
aforementioned three English-speaking countries are distinguished from
their other APEC counterparts by virtue of the relatively low content of
manufactures in their exports, by their relatively low savings rate, and by
their relatively high government consumption. Interestingly, the US did *not*
join its fellow English-speaking countries. The major distinguishing feature
that sets it apart from Canada, Australia, and New Zealand is its rather
high export of manufactures, an attribute that makes it more similar to the
East Asian economies. Whatever the merit of Fajnzylber's characterization
of the US as a major exporter of primary goods at one time, clearly this
attribution is no longer accurate for the 1990s.

Allowing the countries in Table 1.2 to split into three groups produces a new group of political economies dominated by overseas Chinese. Singapore, Hong Kong and Malaysia are united by their common deep involvement with foreign commerce, their high rates of domestic savings (two to three times the rate for the US), and the low level of government consumption in their economies. Compared to Canada, Australia, and New Zealand, for which a large portion of exports derives from agriculture or mining, these 'overseas Chinese' economies feature a rather high percentage of manufactured goods in their export portfolio.

Why are China and Taiwan, two other obviously Chinese economies, not part of this cluster? What, in other words, would distinguish China and Taiwan from Singapore, Hong Kong, and Malaysia? Significantly, the latter three were all one time British colonies and served as entrepots for regional/global trade. Although important differences exist among these three cases, they all tend to have relatively lopsided income distribution by regional standards. The ratio between the richest and poorest quintiles of population for Singapore, Hong Kong, and Malaysia were 9.6, 8.7, and 11.7 respectively. By comparison, these figures were substantially lower for Japan (4.3), China (8.6), South Korea (7.9), and Taiwan (5.4). As already mentioned, the latter two were Japanese colonies before World War Two. These economies as well as Japan and China featured high rates of domestic savings – about twice the level obtained for the US and the Philippines. They represent a core 'Confucian' area in East Asia, an area that also includes Thailand.

Indeed, as shown in the previous analysis focusing on the 1980s, the US and the Philippines demonstrated the greatest affinity in terms of the structure of their political economies. Besides relatively low savings rates, both were also characterized by a comparatively large public sector. General government consumption constituted 16 per cent of the US GDP and 13 per cent of the Philippine GDP. Only Canada (21 per cent), Australia (17 per cent) and New Zealand (14 per cent) indicated even higher demand by the public sector.

Finally, as in the case of the 1980s analysis, Indonesia presented a relatively unique case whose profile was rather different from the other APEC countries examined. Accordingly, under the column marked '4' in Table 1.2, this country formed a 'group of one'. Among all the APEC economies included in this analysis, Indonesia has had arguably one of the lowest rates of savings and government consumption. Moreover, in comparison with both its Asian neighbors and its North American counterparts, this country has committed a very low level of its economic resources to public education.

Mapping exercises such as the one just reported obviously cannot confirm or refute any specific proposition. As portrayals of political ecology, they can only be more or less intuitively satisfactory or disappointing. They can, however, present some broad geographic demarcation of hegemonic soft power and perhaps, if undertaken over time, give us a glimpse of the ebb and flow of such power. In some sense, East and Central Europe presents another region (as in East Asia) where hegemons might be expected to contest.

Table 1.3 reports the results of a cluster analysis that is based on identical variables and methodology as the analysis just presented for APEC in Table 1.2. The single most remarkable finding for East and Central Europe is that none of the countries included shared Russia's political economic profile. In the 1980s, all the countries in this analysis except Germany were Moscow's client states (and the German exception was only a partial exception at that). By the 1990s, however, *none* of them shared much in common with Russia in terms of the structural characteristics of their political economies – and *all* had aligned themselves more closely with Berlin than with Moscow. This situation is clearly shown in the furthest right-hand column in Table 1.3, where Russia received a score of '2' whereas all the other countries scored '1'.

What set Russia apart from the rest of East and Central Europe? The former's economy was much less exposed to foreign commerce and its exports consisted much less of manufactures. Moreover, income disparity in Russia was more severe than the other East and Central European countries, and government spending consumed a much smaller portion of its GNP. Indeed, Russia even spent a smaller percentage of its economic output on public education than most of its counterparts in Table 1.3. In these respects, Russia's political economy resembled that of a typical poor

TABLE 1.3
MODELS OF POLITICAL ECONOMY: EAST-CENTRAL EUROPE, ca. 1990s

	Number of clusters				
	6	5	4	3	2
Bulgaria	1	1	1	1	1
Romania	1	1	1	1	1
Hungary	4	4	1	1	1
Czech Republic	2	2	2	1	1
Poland	2	2	2	1	1
Slovakia	2	2	2	1	1
Slovenia	2	2	2	1	1
Germany	2	2	2	1	1
Estonia	3	3	3	2	1
Latvia	5	3	3	2	1
Lithuania	5	3	3	2	1
Russian Federation	6	5	4	3	2

developing country. If we had the data to include some of the former republics of the USSR in the analysis (e.g. Belarus, Ukraine, Moldava, Georgia, Kazakhstan, Turkestan), Russia's status would not have been so isolated.

Interestingly, when the countries in Table 1.3 break into three groups, we witness the emergence of a distinct group of three Baltic states which used to be part of the USSR. Estonia, Latvia and Lithuania demonstrate a close affinity in their political economy. They are distinguished by a relatively high turnover in foreign trade, high government consumption, and strong commitment to public education. They were, however, only marginally different from another group of countries that were even more similar to Germany's political economic profile. This latter group consisted of the Czech Republic, Poland, Slovakia, and Slovenia – countries that were under Germany's influence before World War Two. This group differed from the Baltic states mainly in their higher rates of domestic savings and in their greater proportion of manufactured exports.

Finally, while demonstrating certain affinities to the latter group, Romania, Bulgaria and, to a lesser extent, Hungary present similarities among themselves. These neighbors are connected by the Danube river. In a region with a historical ethos for egalitarianism and a proclivity for government provision of public services, Romania and Bulgaria ranked lowest among the group in Table 1.3 in terms of their comparative expenditure on public education.

As one more example of political geography, we repeat the same analysis (using the same method and variables) for the Western Hemisphere. The results are reported in Table 1.4, showing naturally that not all countries in this region are alike. Some are, however, more alike than others. One learns right away that the US, Canada, Brazil, and Mexico have more in common with each other than they have in common with the rest of their hemispheric neighbors. The commonality among the 'big four' cannot be their sheer size since that variable is not a part of the analysis. Rather, the US, Canada, Brazil, and Mexico differed from the rest of the region mainly because manufactures consisted of a much larger percentage of their exports. In contrast, the other countries reported in Table 1.4 relied on the foreign sale of minerals and cash crops to a much greater extent.

Surprisingly and significantly, the structure of the US political economy appeared to make it more similar to Brazil and Mexico than to Canada. In the next iteration of the cluster analysis, Canada split off to form a group all by itself. What characteristics differentiated Canada from its other two NAFTA partners and Brazil? Evidently, Canada had a much more egalitarian income distribution, a bigger governmental role in the economy, and a stronger commitment to public education. In these respects, the US

TABLE 1.4
MODELS OF POLITICAL ECONOMY: WESTERN HEMISPHERE, ca. 1990s

	Number of clusters				
	6	5	4	3	2
United States	1	1	1	1	1
Brazil	1	1	1	1	1
Mexico	5	5	1	1	1
Canada	2	2	2	2	1
Bolivia	3	3	3	3	2
Chile	3	3	3	3	2
Colombia	3	3	3	3	2
Costa Rica	3	3	3	3	2
Dominican Republic	3	3	3	3	2
Ecuador	3	3	3	3	2
Honduras	3	3	3	3	2
Paraguay	3	3	3	3	2
Peru	3	3	3	3	2
Venezuela	3	3	3	3	2
Panama	6	3	3	3	2
El Salvador	4	4	4	3	2
Guatemala	4	4	4	3	2

profile looked more 'Latin American' due its greater domestic income disparity, lower savings rate, and lower spending on public education. The latter two attributes, low savings and under funding of public education, particularly marked two poor Central American countries. El Salvador and Guatemala stood out as a separate group under column '4' by virtue of this dubious distinction. Further iterations to draw finer distinctions among the countries led to Mexico 'spinning off' under column '5' and then Panama doing the same under column '6'. Compared to its neighbors to the south, Mexico has exported proportionally far more manufactured goods and its economy has also been more oriented to foreign trade. As for Panama, its enclave economy (due to the Canal Zone) has produced relatively high government consumption and domestic savings in comparison to the other Latin American countries. Among all the countries in the Western Hemisphere listed in Table 1.4, Mexico and Panama are arguably the two with the strongest ties of historical interaction with the US. As just described, their political economies also appeared to depart most sub-stantially from the typical 'Latin American' patterns.

As already mentioned, the cluster results reported above are intended more for illustrative purposes than for the confirmation or refutation of specific propositions.[2] They provide some historical and contextual infor-mation for the argument that 'globalization' or 'regionalization' presents a two-way process. It is a process that consists of both an 'outside in' and an 'inside out' face. These two faces of the process are mutually constitutive.

Naturally, external forces challenge domestic governance and performance. These same external forces, however, also stem from domestic interests and power alignments that seek to project influence and control events abroad. Of course, as has been emphasized on several occasions already, states are not equally equipped to resist foreign penetration. Nor do they have the same capacity to shape others according to their own image. This latter capacity points to a power to co-opt and convert others and to control the rules of international exchange. This control over the 'intangibles' of international relations – setting norms, formulating agendas, defining problems, and transplanting institutional arrangements and cultural ethos – is indicative of a state's structural power. It represents a more far-reaching form of influence than the accounting of tangibles such as trade balance or investment flow. The very success in portraying ongoing social, economic and political changes as a matter of inevitable 'globalization' or 'regionalization' rather than as a matter of role adjustment or status mobility for different states and groups is in itself symptomatic of this power to dominate discourse.

SUMMARY AND PREVIEW

We have questioned the analytic utility of the popular concept of globalization as a homogeneous positive process. To what extent does this concept promise to illuminate rather than to obfuscate? Are we stretching this concept to include so many different phenomena that it loses empirical precision? By using this term, are we treating the relevant trends and processes as if they represent impersonal forces that somehow unfold naturally in the absence of human agency and partisan agendas? The term suggests that we are somehow all subject to some universal homogenization. It detracts attention from the question of which actors initiate, promote, and benefit from such forces, and which actors are on the receiving end of these forces and must bear most of the burden of adjusting to them.

It is of course a truism that states are becoming more sensitive to each other's policies. This is so simply because they engage in more external activities than before. It is quite a different matter, however, to determine whether they have become more vulnerable to each other's policies. Vulnerability – defined in terms of the net effects of other's actions on oneself after one has undertaken countermeasures to minimize the impact of these actions (Keohane and Nye, 1977) – differs sharply across states. Some states command tremendous resources to protect themselves against the unwanted consequences of others' actions, while others possess little means to resist foreign encroachment. Naturally, whether and, if so, how much do foreign influences matter for domestic governance or performance is an entirely different empirical matter.

Foreign encroachment is most effective when it is successful in co-opting the target's people and institutions. Put more positively from the point of view of the would-be hegemons, it exemplifies their soft power, cultural appeal, or political reach. The importance of such influence may exceed that of other more tangible or quantifiable indicators such as currency exchange rates, trade balance, investment flows, and even military interventions, although this 'soft' influence is usually positively correlated with the other 'hard' indicators. The influence of soft power comes from its control over ideas and institutions. From the perspective of southern states and their peoples and organizations, it embodies the legacies of past encounters with foreign interests. That foreign ideas and institutions continue to exercise a profound and pervasive influence even after direct, overt foreign control has been discontinued constitutes, after all, the main theoretical insight and policy implication of those whose writings stress neocolonialism. Foreign-inspired interests, ideologies, and institutions are the basis for hegemonic control. As alluded to earlier in the cluster analytic illustration, these inherited interests, ideologies, and institutions continue to determine a country's developmental path. Once launched on such a path, certain alternatives become more difficult and perhaps impossible to undertake or even imagine. It is in this sense that the power to co-opt (rather than to coerce) can be so influential as it helps to set the 'follower' nations' developmental trajectory, define their policy agenda, and shape their feasible options. 'Globalization' and national and organizational attempts to control its effects (if not to escape from its forces entirely) document what is after all the 'stuff' of international–domestic relations.

Taking an approach that is more in accord with Randall and Theobald's (1998) emphasis on the economic dimension of the globalization phenomenon, four of the essays in this volume focus on the domestic consequences of external trade and foreign investment. Does a country's level of economic involvement with others matter for the living conditions of its citizens and the political autonomy of its officials? Are the classical liberals right in claiming the economic benefits and political virtues of free trade and open market, or are the skepticisms voiced by the *dependentistas* closer to the mark?

These four chapters suggest that the answers to these questions are decidedly mixed. It depends on the nature of the putative impact of globalization, the time period, and the geographic region in question. In Chapter 2 Ross Burkhart shows that, after the introduction of appropriate statistical controls, globalization (measured according to a country's relative volume of trade flows, value of foreign direct investment, and number of telephones per capita) has had a generally favorable impact on economic growth but a minimal influence on a broader conception of human development which includes average life expectancy and literacy rate. Echoing a finding by other authors, he notes that the effects of 'economic globalization' tend to vary significantly across regions, so that any 'global' generalization about these effects can be highly misleading. The extent, and even the direction, of these effects are quite different in different parts of the world, especially in the core and the periphery.

In Chapter 3 David Richards and Ronald Gelleny focus on human rights instead of human development. They ask whether more extensive external trade and heavier dependence on foreign investors affect a government's respect for the physical integrity of its citizens (such that the people are free from torture, arbitrary imprisonment, and political murder). Their overall results indicate that 'in most times and places, economic globalization did not affect respect for human rights'. There are, however, again important regional variations. Although there is some evidence that a more open economy has promoted respect for human rights in Latin America, this effect has been absent in Asia and Africa. Furthermore, the overall effects of trade and foreign investment are not greater in the 'globalization era' of the 1990s than they were previously.

In Chapter 4 Karen Ferree and Smita Singh examine the effects of changes in the competitiveness of executive selection, a key aspect of change in democracy, on the economic growth of sub-Saharan African countries, once again employing appropriate controls. They find that negative changes in competitiveness, but not positive ones, are associated with large and immediate drops in growth performance. In addition, they find that countries with long periods of competitive multiparty elections experience higher growth rates over time, whereas countries with long periods of noncompetitive elections experience declining growth rates. They explain these findings in terms of the interaction among investors, voters, and political executives, who pursue high investment return, economic well-being, and various forms of power/personal utility respectively. The significance of investors, as well as external pressures to increase political competition, introduces globalization into their analysis.

In Chapter 5 Susan McMillan discovers variability also among her cases, the ASEAN Four (Malaysia, Indonesia, the Philippines, and Thailand, all members of the Association of Southeast Asian Nations). The focus of her analysis is on government policy rather than economic or social performance. Does deep involvement in the world economy constrain the officials' ability to undertake effective domestic policy to protect their countries against the risks of such involvement? Contrary to conventional wisdom, McMillan shows that in the ASEAN Four officials were able to increase public spending as a countermeasure against trade fluctuations and footloose investments. She rightly cautions that the ASEAN Four are not representative of the developing countries in general. Moreover, the empirical relationship in question – government fiscal freedom and foreign economic ties – tends to involve mutual influences that are subject to change over time and sensitive to cumulative effects.

In Chapter 6 Nita Rudra essentially reverses McMillan's focus and examines the effects of welfare expenditures and the consequent increase in labor costs on the competitiveness of the less developed countries to promote exports and seek investment capital. She presents the World Bank perspective that increased labor costs reduce competitiveness through the misallocation of resources, increased rent-seeking, and decreased productivity, and the competing International Labor Organization perspective that higher labor costs enhance productivity and thus competitiveness. She finds very little support for either of these perspectives. She also points out that some analysts emphasize the negative effect of increased labor costs on the pull factor of an attractive investment climate in the less developed countries, while others emphasize the push factor of international interest rates as the primary determinant of capital flows. In this case, she finds support for the latter hypothesis. She concludes that 'it is ultimately *not* economic necessity but the political choice of governments that has affected the globalization–welfare relationship in LDCs'.

In the final chapter David Leblang examines the relationship between political uncertainty and speculative attacks on formally pegged or de facto stable currencies in 87 developing countries. He hypothesizes that internal uncertainty will be perceived by global actors, who will then attack the currencies of those countries in which it exists. He first develops a multi-nomial logit model of the probabilities of leadership exit through constitutional and non-constitutional means (his measure of uncertainty), in which length of time in power, leader age, democracy, military regime, and the timing of elections are significant independent variables, and region and the number of prior leaders are control variables. He then includes leadership exit probabilities as independent variables in a probit model of speculative attacks, along with the control variables of real exchange-rate overvaluation, foreign interest rates, foreign exchange reserves, banking sector crisis, domestic monetary policy, and the number of prior crises. He finds that the probabilities of both types of leadership exit, but especially non-constitutional exit, are strongly positively associated with speculative attacks, as are most of his control variables. In a second model of attacks he adds several measures of external debt, and finds that these variables also have strong positive effects, but do not eliminate the effects of uncertainty.

FUTURE RESEARCH AGENDA

The empirical analyses presented in this book inevitably leave out many of the factors that we have included in our dialectical conception of globalization. We conclude this chapter by setting out a research agenda for placing the results of these analyses within this broader theoretical context. First, we attempt to list the major partially or fully unanswered questions about economic globalization that need to be answered in order to determine whether the optimists, pessimists or a middle position represented by the mixed findings presented here is right about the consequences of globalization. Second, we briefly discuss the need to examine more fully the relation between economic and cultural globalization. Third, we suggest how to determine whether the effects observed in this book and elsewhere are due to globalization, soft hegemony, or a combination of the two. Fourth, since full democratization or democratic consolidation is not an automatic consequence of globalization or soft hegemony, we attempt to indicate how the actual relationship between these processes might be effectively analyzed. Finally, we drop the assumption that the processes and relationships involved in globalization most broadly defined will continue to operate in the future without sharp disjunctions, and ask how the prospects for 'deglobalization' can be studied. We believe that all of these issues can be addressed through comparative, quantitative analysis if they are appropriately grounded theoretically, although this is not the place to discuss the complexities of research designs that will most adequately address them.

Consequences of Economic Globalization

If there is a single theme that emerges from this and the following chapters, it is that the effects of economic globalization vary but are shaped in a number of ways. They are shown to vary among issue areas (economic growth, human development, human rights, trade competitiveness, and welfare spending), between the core and periphery, across geographic regions, among countries in the same region, and over time. They are shown to be constrained by state policies and competitive national politics. (They are influenced as well by resistance from social movements and local communities, although we did not include this aspect in the empirical research in this book.) A recent broadly focused assessment suggests that these findings are very generally applicable (Keohane and Nye, 2000: 117). These findings call into question many of the assumptions of the extreme optimists and extreme pessimists regarding globalization. Although too incomplete to decisively disprove the polar positions of optimists and pessimists, the results reported in this volume do offer one compelling conclusion. It is that policies and politics do matter for normatively important outcomes. Officials, politicians, and ordinary people can make a difference through deliberate effort. The varying effects of globalization suggest that the impact of this process is not pre-ordained and that human agency and smart policy can influence outcomes. Waltz (1999: 694–5) points out that economic globalization has developed most fully in the core, and that the core countries can cope most effectively with its consequences. The motivation for this book is the need for more systematic research on how well various non-core countries cope. The findings presented in this book suggest some broader questions that need to be answered: Under what conditions could economic globalization become more strongly associated with improvements in human development and human rights than Burkhart's and Richards and Gelleny's findings indicate has been the case to date? Emizet (2000: 1064–7) suggests that human development suffers from a market economy in the middle-income countries, although it is enhanced by trade openness in most developing regions. These authors find different effects of trade and financial globalization. To what extent is this difference significant for other consequences of economic globalization? To what extent and how quickly will economic globalization facilitate or impede the creation of stable democracy throughout the developing world that Ferree and Singh find to be associated with economic growth in Africa? Rudra suggests that McMillan's finding about the ability of specific Southeast Asian governments to resist cuts in welfare spending in spite of globalization applies much more broadly because foreign direct investment (FDI) is driven most strongly by the push factor of interests in the developed world. Will this more general finding continue to hold, and within what limits? Finally, as Leblang says at the end of his chapter, 'a fascinating question concerns the conditions under which a politician is able and willing to defend a country's exchange rate in the face of a speculative attack'.

Other significant questions about the consequences of economic globalization are not addressed in this book. Among these are the exact effects of the greater mobility of capital in comparison to labor and the consequent potential for a 'race to the bottom' for wages and working conditions (Milner and Keohane, 1996: 249–51; Rodrik, 1997: 11–27; Spar and Yoffie, 1999), the likelihood that globalization will not create sufficient jobs to end the unemployment or underemployment crisis and the associated high level of poverty in many less developed countries with narrow economic bases (Dicken, 1998: 447–60), the importance of declining terms of trade for commodities produced by many developing countries, the role of debt in suppressing economic growth and human development, the possibilities for taxation of foreign direct investment and portfolio investment, the possible failure of structural adjustment programs in a number of the poorest countries, the degree and duration of the observed increase in inequality, and the degree to which the strength of domestic and international political institutions insulate developing economies from some or all of these problems. We especially need policy-relevant studies to inform us about the manner in which sound policy and effective institutions can help to mitigate or contain the adverse effects of economic globalization.

Economic and Cultural Globalization

Apart from Burkhart's inclusion of the number of telephones per 100 citizens in his measure of globalization, none of the chapters in this book deals with cultural globalization. To what extent is it an independent variable that could usefully be included in such analyses, and to what extent is it a mere corollary or reflection of economic globalization? It is certainly true that consumer culture, which is supportive of economic globalization, and popular culture, which is also supportive if less obviously so, comprise the major cultural content that has been globalized. In contrast, the increased ease of communications, especially through the internet – although falling far short of globalization apologist Thomas Friedman's characterization as the democratization of technology and information because of the cost of computers and the predominance of US and European web sites (2000: 46–53, 60–72) – provides important tools for resistance to some or all aspects of economic globalization. Systematic research is needed on the conditions under which these tools can be used effectively. Even Friedman (2000: 294) hopes 'that countries will ... learn to develop multiple filters to prevent their cultures from being erased by the homogenizing push and pull of global capitalism'. In the discussion that follows this statement (2000: 295–305), he suggests that some cultures can selectively adapt global elements without losing their integrity, but that others will need to enact laws protecting their educational systems and certain geographical areas from economic and cultural globalization, even in defiance of the market. Strong middle classes and mainstream politicians will have to take the lead in cultural protection. Systematic comparative research is needed on the conditions under which these actors will assume this role. Of course, these same actors may, under circumstances that need to be specified through systematic research, be motivated to promote nativist, revivalist, or fundamentalist movements – ostensibly in the name of cultural protection – in a reaction against perceived alien or atheistic influences.

Globalization versus Soft Hegemony

The analysis presented earlier in this chapter is only suggestive with regard to the existence of soft hegemony. A systematic test of whether globalization or soft hegemony is the dominant force in the contemporary world would be much more difficult because much of the empirical evidence that might be used tends to support both hypotheses. For example, William Robinson readily acknowledges that US soft hegemony is central to globalization (1996: 363–74). He suggests, however, that this hegemony is exercised on behalf of a transnational class rather than as a state, while acknowledging that members of this class have not fully escaped from their national identities. To avoid such confusion it would be necessary to focus on those data that support one hypothesis but not the other. We have suggested that globalization constrains some states substantially more than others. A finding, based on a systematic comparative study, that the United States, Japan, and other core countries are substantially less constrained than peripheral countries in a number of ways would lend considerable credence to soft hegemony, while a finding of relatively equal constraints would lend such credence to universalizing globalization. Another key question is whether multinational corporations are truly global or whether they are in important ways based in and responsible to their home states. The work of Doremus *et al.* (1998) suggests that the latter is the case, but more systematic comparative work needs to be done on this topic. Finally, do international institutions or regimes control the actions of potential hegemons as much as they control the actions of other countries, or are these institutions in fact primarily responsible to and under the control of the hegemons? Voting rights on the governing boards of the International Monetary Fund and the World Bank place these organizations firmly under the control of core countries, but the internationally diverse staff of the World Bank have demonstrated some ability to modify the bank's policies over the years. Other international institutions are more broadly controlled. In short, do international regimes and organizations discipline the behavior of hegemons as well as non-hegemons, and to what extent do they represent truly collective goods that facilitate common expectations and shared rules? This is another area in which more systematic comparative research is needed.

Economic Globalization and Democratization

We have suggested that economic globalization produces formal but often hollow democracy, but that democratic stability, consolidation (making democracy broadly legitimate and determinative of behavior, and thus likely to persist) and what Diamond (1999: 74–5) calls democratic deepening (making structures more liberal, accountable, representative, and accessible) are not automatic consequences or components of globalization. Democratic consolidation is very difficult to operationalize, so analysts have focused instead on democratic stability, which is necessary but not sufficient for consolidation. Emizet (2000: 1067–9) finds that a market economy and openness to trade have positive effects on democratic stability in most but not all regions, while human development and economic growth sustain democracy everywhere. Maxfield (1998: 1214–17) hypothesizes that the impact of capital flows on prospects for democracy and equity depends on how the flows are structured (with corporate bonds and equity being the most positive form), and that as financial internationalization continues investors will learn to place a premium on democratic institution building. A number of authors connect globalization to democratic stability through economic growth. Ferree and Singh find that stable democracy promotes growth in sub-Saharan Africa in the globalization era. Is stable democracy associated with human development and human rights as well as with economic growth, and do these relationships hold outside of Africa? Burkhart finds a positive relationship between democracy and human development (although not between democracy and growth) in his cross-regional sample, but he does not address the issue of long-term stable democracy. Richards and Gelleny find that democracy is positively associated with the protection of citizens' physical integrity in all non-core regions in the globalization era, and in some regions in the pre-globalization era. Emizet (2000: 1064–6) finds that democracy first enhances human development but over time hampers it. Gasiorowski (2000: 334–47) finds that both long-term and newly established democracies reduce growth and increase inflation. Therefore, there are contradictory and ambiguous findings about the globalization–democratization–development relationships, and systematic research is needed to clear up these contradictions and ambiguities. Diamond's concept of deepening should be incorporated into such research because its components are easier to operationalize than consolidation and more significant than mere stability. Deepened democracy is likely to be more effective in limiting the adverse effects of economic globalization, although research needs to be done on the relationships between specific components of deepening and responses to specific components of economic globalization.

Prospects for 'Deglobalization'

Pessimists about globalization are, if anything, even more pessimistic about soft hegemony exercised primarily by the United States. They disagree strongly with Friedman's statement (2000: 467) that 'America truly is the ultimate benign hegemon and reluctant enforcer', and most consider the concept of a benign hegemon to be an oxymoron. Thus, some may see that strategies for 'deglobalization' will also place limits on soft hegemony. Pessimists would point out that the findings of this book and other empirical research apply to the world as it is today (or, more accurately, as it was when the research reported in this book was carried out), and that less developed countries could be better off if that world were changed in fundamental ways. Yet some of these findings suggest possibilities for at least limited 'deglobalization'.

In a recent speech Walden Bello (2000) lists the components of 'deglobalization': reorienting economies from production for export to production for the local market; drawing most financial resources from within rather than being dependent on foreign investment and financial markets; carrying out income and land redistribution to create a vibrant internal market; de-emphasizing growth and maximizing equity to reduce environmental disequilibrium; making strategic economic decisions subject to democratic choice; subjecting the private sector and the state to constant monitoring by civil society; creating a production and exchange complex that includes community cooperatives, as well as private and state enterprises, but excludes multinational corporations; and encouraging production to take place at the community and national levels in order to preserve national and local communities. Although he does not discuss the means for attaining these goals in this speech, he and a large number of activists working within NGOs and social movements have developed a variety of means for attaining some of these goals, primarily through practice. Most of these activists are not motivated by an ideology of 'deglobalization', a socialist ideology, or any other all-encompassing ideology. Rather, they are working toward a variety of much more specific – and sometimes contradictory – goals. Along with (or sometimes instead of) working against specific components of economic globalization, many of these activists are working to contain aspects of cultural globalization, restructure political globalization, promote democracy, human development or human, women's or workers' rights, and/or assure environmental sustainability. They are not insensitive to the need to maintain sustainable growth, or to the importance of the market for attaining this goal. It can be argued that economic globalization is more vulnerable to a series of such goal-specific challenges from a number of directions than it would be to a coordinated ideological assault, and that the former are more likely to result in partial rather than total deglobalization. This is very different from Friedman's (2000: 101–11) assumption that globalization is a 'golden strait-jacket', from which a country can escape only with severe economic loss.

Of all of the topics discussed in this attempt to lay out a research agenda, this is the one on which systematic, comparative research is most needed. A number of promising hypotheses are presented in the relevant literature (Fisher, 1998; Haynes, 1997; Keck and Sikkink, 1998; McAdam *et al.*, 1996; Meyer and Tarrow, 1998; Mittelman, 2000: 179–202; and O'Brien *et al.*, 2000) but few have been tested quantitatively. For example, it is hypothesized that social movements and NGOs in developing countries need autonomy from the state, political parties and external organizations; strong and democratic organization; and an ability to work in broad coalitions with one another and with states and political parties if they are to be successful in limiting economic globalization. O'Brien *et al.* (2000) describe and analyze the extensive relationships that have been formed between global social movements and the World Bank and the IMF, and present hypotheses to explain the ambiguous results of these relationships. Protest is also a key tactic because it puts pressure on MNCs, states, and IGOs to make or accept changes, even though these changes are unlikely to be exactly the ones that the protesters are demanding. There are a number of testable hypotheses about the effectiveness of protest. Among NGOs, grass roots organizations (GROs) representing the interests of local communities and GRO networks are crucial for empowering ordinary people in the process of limiting the effects of economic globalization, and it is important to test hypotheses that attempt to explain their formation and effectiveness (Fisher, 1998).

In the attempt to limit the negative effects of globalization/soft hegemony, it is crucial for NGOs and social movements to interact with states as well as IGOs and local governments, and for these governmental levels to interact with one another. A number of hypotheses about these interactions are worth testing. States must also be strong and democratic, have some autonomy, and participate in effective interactions with one another (as well as with other levels of government). Economic globalization cannot weaken even peripheral states too much and may even strengthen some of them due to the 'orthodox paradox', the fact that a strong state is needed to successfully implement market economic policies. McMillan's and Rudra's findings that states can maintain welfare policies in the face of globalization and Ferree and Singh's finding that stable African democracies (which are the strong states in the region) produce more growth support this hypothesis. Nationalism is probably strengthened by economic globalization, and is also probably the most effective counter-ideology to it (Randall and Theobald, 1998: 262–4; Veseth, 1998: 35–9). The strength of nationalism sometimes hinders the formation of regional economic communities among less developed countries, which could be very important in attaining partial deglobalization. International regulatory organizations strengthen at least some states in some ways, although they may weaken other states in other ways (see the discussion under globalization versus soft hegemony above). Strong and partially autonomous local governments provide an additional possible arena for limiting the effects of globalization. Thus global networking around issues and subsequent actions on these issues can be facilitated by the multiplicity of relevant governmental levels.

A final set of hypotheses about possibilities for deglobalization that are important to test systematically concerns political learning. Over time individuals and organizations involved in the interactions that have been discussed will learn from this involvement. We need to discover the conditions under which this learning will be positive for attaining a consensus on managing the effects of globalization, and giving people an understanding of globalization's manifold distributive consequences for various actors, including both relative and absolute gains and losses.

NOTES

1. Parts of the following discussion are taken from Chan (2000) and Scarritt (2000).
2. Africa was not analyzed because only patchy data were available, and it is not clear that the same variables would be relevant.

REFERENCES

Aldenderfer, M.S. and Blashfield, R.K. (1984), *Cluster Analysis* (Beverly Hills, CA: Sage).

Bello, W. (2000), 'From Melbourne to Prague: The Struggle for a Deglobalized World', Speech delivered on the occasion of demonstrations against the World Economic Forum, Melbourne, Australia, 6–10 September.

Bratton, M. and Van de Walle, N. (1997), *Democratic Experiments in Africa: Regime Transitions in Comparative Perspective* (Cambridge: Cambridge University Press).

Calder, K.E. (1988), *Crisis and Compensation: Public Policy and Political Stability in Japan, 1949–1986* (Princeton, NJ: Princeton University Press).

Chan, S. (2000), 'Can Asia Pacific Escape the Impact of Globalization?', paper presented at the workshop on 'Twenty-First Century World Order and the Asia Pacific,' Lingnan University, Hong Kong, April.

Chan, S. and Clark, C. (1992), 'The Rise of the East Asian NICs: Confucian Capitalism, Status Mobility, and Developmental Legacy', in C. Clark and S. Chan (eds), *The Evolving Pacific Basin in the Global Political Economy: Domestic and International Linkages* (Boulder, CO: Lynne Rienner), pp. 27–48.

Corter, J.E. (1996), *Tree Models of Similarity and Association* (Beverly Hills, CA: Sage).

Council for Economic Planning and Development, *Taiwan Statistical Data Book* (Taipei, 1999).

Cumings, B. (1984), 'The Origins and Development of the Northeast Asian Political Economy: Industrial Sectors, Product Cycle, and Political Consequences', *International Organization* 38: 1–40.

Diamond, L. (1999), *Developing Democracy: Toward Consolidation* (Baltimore, MD: Johns Hopkins University Press).

Dicken, P. (1998), *Global Shift: Transforming the World Economy* (New York: Guilford Press).

Doremus, P.N., Keller, W.W., Pauly, L.W. and Reich, S. (1998), *The Myth of the Global Corporation* (Princeton, NJ: Princeton University Press).

Emizet, K.N.F. (2000), 'The Relationship Between the Liberal Ethos and Quality of Life', *Comparative Political Studies* 33: 1049–78.

Fajnzylber. F. (1990), 'The United States and Japan as Models of Industrialization', in G. Gereffi and D. Wyman (eds), *Manufacturing Miracles: Paths of Industrialization in East Asia* (Princeton, NJ: Princeton University Press), pp. 323–52.

Fisher, J. (1998), *Nongovernments: NGOs and the Political Development of the Third World* (West Hartford, CT: Kumarian Press).

Friedman, T.L. (2000), *The Lexus and the Olive Tree*, updated and expanded edition (New York: Anchor Books).

Fukuyama, F. (1992), *The End of History and the Last Man* (New York: Free Press).

Gasiorowski, M.J. (2000), 'Democracy and Macroeconomic Performance in Underdeveloped Countries', *Comparative Political Studies* 33: 319–49.

Hastings, E.H. and Hastings, P.K. (eds) (1996), *Index to International Public Opinion, 1994–1995* (Westport, CT: Greenwood).

Hawes, G. (1987), *The Philippine State and the Marcos Regime: The Politics of Export* (Ithaca, NY: Cornell University Press).

Haynes, J. (1997), *Democracy and Civil Society in the Third World* (Cambridge: Polity Press).

Held, D., McGrew, A., Goldblatt, D. and Perraton, J. (1999), *Global Transformations: Politics, Economics and Culture* (Stanford, CA: Stanford University Press).

Hollifield, J.F. and Jillson C. (eds) (2000), *Pathways to Democracy* (London: Routledge).

Holton, R.J. (1998), *Globalization and the Nation-State* (London: Macmillan).

Huntington, S.P. (1991), *The Third Wave: Democratization in the Late Twentieth Century* (Norman, OK: University of Oklahoma Press).

Huntington, S.P. (1993), 'The Clash of Civilizations?' *Foreign Affairs* 72: 22–49.

Jomo, K.S. (ed.) (1999), *Tigers in Trouble: Financial Governance, Liberalism and Crises in East Asia* (New York: St Martin's Press).

Keck, M.E. and Sikkink, K. (1998), *Activists beyond Borders: Advocacy Networks in International Politics* (Ithaca, NY: Cornell University Press).

Keohane, R.O. and Nye, J.S., Jr. (1977), *Power and Interdependence: World Politics in Transition* (Boston: Little, Brown).

Keohane, R.O. and Nye, J.S., Jr. (2000), 'Globalization: What's New? What's Not? (And So What?)', *Foreign Policy* 118 (Spring): 104–19.

Maxfield, S. (1998), 'Understanding the Political Implications of Financial Internationalization in Emerging Market Countries', *World Development* 26: 1201–19.

McAdam, D., McCarthy, J.D. and Zald, M.N. (eds) (1996), *Comparative Perspectives on Social Movements: Political Opportunities, Mobilizing Structures, and Cultural Framings* (Cambridge: Cambridge University Press).

Meyer, D.S. and Tarrow, S. (eds) (1998), *The Social Movement Society: Contentious Politics for a New Century* (Lanham, MD: Rowman & Littlefield).

Milner, H.V. and Keohane, R.O. (1996), 'Internationalization and Domestic Politics: A Conclusion', in R.O. Keohane and H.V. Milner (eds), *Internationalization and Domestic Politics* (Cambridge: Cambridge University Press), pp. 243–58.

Mittelman, J.H. (2000), *The Globalization Syndrome: Transformation and Resistance* (Princeton, NJ: Princeton University Press).

Nye, J.S. Jr. (1990), *Bound to Lead: The Changing Nature of American Power* (New York: Basic Books).

O'Brien, R., Goetz, A.M., Scholte, J.A. and Williams, M. (2000), *Contesting Global Governance: Multilateral Economic Institutions and Global Social Movements* (Cambridge: Cambridge University Press).

Putnam, R.D. (1995), 'Bowling Alone: America's Declining Social Capital', *Journal of Democracy* 6: 65–78.

Randall, V. and Theobald, R. (1998), *Political Change and Underdevelopment: A Critical Introduction to Third World Politics* (Durham, NC: Duke University Press).

Ray, J.L. (1995), *Democracy and International Conflict: An Evaluation of the Democratic Peace Proposition* (Columbia, SC: University of South Carolina Press).

Reich, S., Chan, S. and Bobrow, D.B. (1997). 'Exploring Cultural Power and Hegemony in the Asia-Pacific', paper presented at the annual meeting of the International Studies Association, Toronto, March.

Robinson, W.I. (1996), *Promoting Polyarchy: Globalization, US Intervention and Hegemony* (Cambridge: Cambridge University Press).

Rodrik, D. (1997), *Has Globalization Gone too Far?* (Washington: Institute for International Economics).

Rosecrance, R. (1986), *The Rise of the Trading State: Commerce and Conquest in the Modern World* (New York: Basic Books).

Russett, B.M. (1967), *International Regions and the International System: A Study of Political Ecology* (Chicago: Rand McNally).

Russett, B.M. and Starr, H. (1996), *World Politics: Menu for Choice* (New York: W.H. Freeman).

Sartori, G. (1970), 'Concept Misformation in Comparative Politics', *American Political Science Review* 64: 1033–53.

Scarritt, J.R. (2000), 'Globalization, Democratization, NGOs, and Social Movements: a Neo-Parsonian Perspective', in S.F. Krishna-Hensel (ed.), *The New Millennium: Challenges and Strategies for a Globalizing World* (Aldershot: Ashgate), pp. 47–69.

Sokal, R. and Sneath, P. (1963), *Principles of Numerical Taxonomy* (San Francisco: W.H. Freeman).

Spar, D. and Yoffie, D. (1999), 'Multinational Enterprises and the Prospects for Justice', *Journal of International Affairs* 52: 557–81.

United Nations Development Programme (1999), *Human Development Report 1999* (New York: Oxford University Press).

Vernon, R. (1971), *Sovereignty at Bay: The Multinational Spread of U.S. Enterprises* (New York: Basic Books).

Veseth, M. (1998), *Selling Globalization: The Myth of the Global Economy* (Boulder, CO: Lynne Rienner).

Waltz, K.N. (1999), 'Globalization and Governance', *PS: Political Science and Politics* 32: 693–700.

World Bank (2000), *World Development Report: 1999/2000* (New York: Oxford University Press).

2

Globalization, Regimes, and Development

ROSS E. BURKHART

INTRODUCTION

Does globalization lead to a higher quality of life? Or, does it lead to more difficult times? In what ways does globalization have its influence? Is it strictly through economic development, or by way of more broad-based human development? Or, perhaps in a flavor-of-the-month way, is globalization overrated in its impact, with other political, economic, social, and cultural factors better poised to provide us with a more complete understanding of the global development condition? To find answers to these questions, after a brief introduction and literature summary, I put forth in this chapter a measure of globalization based on an operational definition of it laid out in the opening chapter of this volume. I then subject the measure to statistical tests to ascertain more precisely whether or not it is an influential factor in enhancing or retarding development. The focus of the tests will be on explaining, through multivariate modeling, variance in two competing conceptions and measurements of development: economic (the more traditional approach), and human (a more current view that is quickly gaining adherents) as embodied in the United Nations Development Programme's (UNDP) Human Development Index (HDI).

If we use as a definition for globalization the ideas from the opening chapter (that is, globalization is characterized by an increasingly global scope for technological advances, international regimes, and trade flows), we find that this is an old phenomenon. Scholars such as Gilpin (2000), Held *et al.* (1999), Rodrik (1997), and Waltz (1999) all highlight and present convincing evidence that the world was more globalized at the end of the nineteenth century and the beginning of the twentieth century than it is today, paying particular attention to trade flows. However, at the end of the twentieth century and the beginning of the twenty-first century we find the world more globalized than during the middle of the twentieth century. With this increase comes an increased importance placed by scholars of international relations and comparative politics on the phenomenon.

'Globalization' has become both explanation and description of a whole host of events. These include the spread of multinational corporations, a greater devotion to the tenets if not actual practice of free trade, communications innovations (such as the internet and World Wide Web) producing the 'global village' phenomenon, and the proliferation of supranational organizations as a result of the blossoming of intergovernmental and nongovernmental organizations. By way of an increase of 'networks of interdependence at multicontinental distances' over the past three decades, globalization has arrived as a formidable presence in current international thought (Keohane and Nye, 2000: 105).

Globalization is credited with, and blamed for, much. Included among its advocates is Michael Porter (2000: 26–7), who argues that 'globalization provides a powerful discipline on unproductive behaviors; it is rewarding productive aspects of economic culture with unprecedented flows of capital, investment, technology, and economic opportunity ... [D]eveloping countries have unprecedented opportunities to enhance wealth.' Opposition to globalization has been voiced just as strongly. At the December 1999 World Trade Organization meeting in Seattle, the Reverend Christopher Laing (quoted in Sabatier, 2000: 31) summarized the mood among the anti-globalization protestors: 'We talk about globalization, but the truth is that we are witnessing an increasingly serious polarization.' Globalization has divided the scholarly and expert observer community into 'optimistic' and 'pessimistic' camps as to its eventual overall effect on societal well-being. The optimists retain the belief that globalization is beneficial. US Federal Reserve Board Chairman Alan Greenspan (2000:23) opined that: 'The bottom line of all the evidence we can marshal is that [globalization] has been a major force in increasing living standards [in the United States and around the world].' Greater global interconnectedness, it is thought, leads to more efficient economic transactions, greater convergence of beliefs in democracy and capitalism, and general societal progress (Friedman, 1999). The 'global village' cliché refers most prominently to more extensive exchanges of information by more people through increasingly accessible media: for example, stock market trades can now come from in-home personal computers worldwide. This democratization of information has the potential, according to the optimists, of unlocking the shackles of heretofore exploitive economic and cultural relationships.

The pessimists, on the other hand, view globalization as a predatory threat to lifestyles in both the global North and South. According to Vandana Shiva (2000),

Economic Globalisation has become a war against nature and the poor ... Globalisation is the rule of commerce and it has elevated Wall

Street to be the only source of value. As a result, things that should have high worth – nature, culture, the future are being devalued and destroyed.

Like an economic ball-and-chain, it is additionally believed, globalization drags down workers' employment prospects in the industrialized countries when multinational corporations spurn high-wage workers in the global North in an attempt to take advantage of the cheap labor in the global South. Yet the workers in the global South gain only marginally from these employment opportunities, as their wages remain low given competitive labor markets. Thus, according to this perspective, overall standards of living decline with globalization. This trend is exacerbated by a global trade policy that treats all countries the same, regardless of their ability to profit from comparative advantage (Greider, 1997). Aghion and Williamson (1998: 170–2) further demonstrated that wealth inequality increased within countries that had an abundance of resources but a shortage of labor during the globalization period of the late nineteenth century. The pessimist is wary of promises of abundance, and instead predicts a world of unequal wealth and knowledge distribution.

While there is plausible truth in both the optimist and pessimist world-views, both cannot be entirely correct. Assessment of these worldviews is critical to the current debate. A preliminary question confronting scholars is whether or not globalization can be validly captured. While it is true that globalization 'describes a bewildering number of relationships and arrangements that are inevitably subject to strategic, political, social, and cultural – as well as "purely economic" – influences', scholars have developed a common understanding of the core relationships and arrangements involved in globalization (Tonelson, 1997: 355). As alluded to in the opening chapter, these relationships and arrangements involve international trade through multinational corporations, a greater ability to communicate information through technological advances, and wider participation in international regimes.

What do these relationships and arrangements have to do with development? Globalization is more than a construct in the forefront of current capitalist economic thought. It is also proposed by its most strident advocates as nothing short of a way of life in and of itself. To achieve this hegemony, globalization must have enough converts. To accomplish a critical threshold of acceptance, it has to appeal to people like any other social system by promising a better quality of life. Thus, the current debate becomes: Does globalization enhance development, if development can be equated with quality of life?

ANALYTIC FRAMEWORK

Diametrically opposing perspectives, played out in academic settings and in the media, guarantee spirited debate on the effects of globalization. Managing this debate in order to determine the effect of globalization on development demands from the analyst a sound analytic framework, one that is fair to both sides. A cross-national, quantitatively based methodology has the potential to provide such a framework. Objectively measuring globalization and performing a comprehensive modeling exercise on this measure as well as other well-measured variables can shed light on the accuracy of claims made by the optimists and pessimists.

In creating this framework, I first discuss a measure of globalization. I then present models of development in which globalization is hypothesized to have both a direct and indirect impact. I include both measures of economic and human development in the modeling exercise, as dependent variables and as proxy independent variables in each other's models. I then estimate the models and draw some conclusions about the impact of globalization on different conceptions of development.

Measuring Globalization

A major source of the fuel for the globalization debate comes from different ways to measure this concept. Some scholars, as alluded to earlier, focus on trade flows as a summary measure. Other analysts examine the process of de-industrialization in the global North (e.g. Alderson, 1999; Beenstock, 1984; Wood, 1994). Still others focus on foreign direct investment as a summary measure (e.g. Dixon and Boswell, 1996; Firebaugh, 1992; de Soysa and Oneal, 1999). However, there is less focus on unifying the different measures in a quantitative fashion, and not all globalization is economic. The definition from the opening chapter proposes three dimensions of globalization: economic, cultural, and political. There could very well be other 'globalizations' as well. Three that come to mind are the uniting of international trade union and labor migration movements, the increased overlapping of IGO and NGO (intergovernmental and nongovernmental organizations) environmental agendas to combat global warming and acid rain, and the recent international conferences to combat diseases such as AIDS (acquired immune deficiency syndrome). Any or all of these dimensions may overlap. Yet combining them into an index creates a more inclusive operationalization of a concept that has suffered in the past from narrow or imprecise definition. An index of globalization seems to be a useful way to broaden our conception of globalization as well as a useful way to measure it.

There are many plausible variables that can comprise a globalization index. First, I use both foreign trade flows and foreign direct investment in tandem with one another. In addition, I take advantage of the availability of data on telephone use to include that variable in the index. Each variable can fit plausibly within the three globalization dimensions suggested in this volume's opening chapter. Foreign trade flows are at some level a political decision, choosing either to disengage from global trade relations for the sake of economic autarchy or trade protection, or to put into practice the tenets of free trade by increasing foreign commerce. These choices correspond respectively to the pessimist and optimist school of globalization. Foreign direct investment measures the economic activity of multinational corporations. Telephone use is a measure of the global culture of advanced technology, especially of the ability of citizens to gain access to the internet and World Wide Web.

I measure foreign trade flow for each country and year by adding exports to imports and dividing the resulting sum by gross national product. These data were taken from the *International Financial Statistics Yearbook* series published by the International Monetary Fund. Data on foreign direct investment were based on the *International Financial Statistics Yearbook* and were per capitalized. I measure telephone use by the number of telephones per 100 citizens. These data came from various editions of the *Statistical Yearbook* published by the United Nations. The globalization index is an annual measure for years 1990–95, and covers roughly 85 to 90 developed and developing countries. This index is based on the difference between the observed minimum and maximum scores across all countries in the sample, and over all included time points for the number of telephones per 100 citizens (68.7 maximum, 0.0 minimum), foreign trade as a percentage of GNP (334 per cent maximum, 0.31 per cent minimum), and foreign direct investment per capita in US dollars (3607.10 maximum, 0.0 minimum).

Globalization is thus calculated using the following formula:

Globalization = $(X_{phone} + X_{trade} + X_{FDI}) / 3$
Where
X_{phone} = (telephones per 100 citizens) / (68.7),
X_{trade} = (foreign trade – 0.31) / (334.76),
and
X_{FDI} = (foreign direct investment) / (3607.10)

The Look of Globalization

Where has globalization taken place over the past few years? Below are three tables that present the mean scores of globalization. Table 2.1 categorizes the world by region, Table 2.2 by world-system position (core, semi-

TABLE 2.1
MEAN GLOBALIZATION SCORE BY WORLD REGION

Region	Mean globalization score	Number of cases
OECD	0.348	201
Eastern Europe	0.220	44
Caribbean	0.219	73
East Asia	0.201	86
North Africa & Middle East	0.197	93
Oceania	0.163	34
Central & South America	0.144	165
Sub-Saharan Africa	0.130	276
South & Central Asia	0.116	55
Global mean	0.199	1036

peripheral, and peripheral countries), and Table 2.3 by level of democracy. World-system position is represented by dummy variables according to Burkhart and Lewis-Beck (1994: 908–9) and Burkhart (1997: 61), while levels of democracy are determined by summing the scores for political rights and civil liberties as reported in various editions of *Freedom in the World* (albeit reversing the scales used in this source).

The tabular results reveal a few surprises. From Table 2.1, the Caribbean, not commonly thought of as a standard-bearer in the globalization debate, proves to be a strongly globalizing region. Along with the OECD (Organisation for Economic Co-operation and Development) countries, Eastern Europe, and East Asia, its value on the globalization index is higher than the global mean. Analyzing each of the index components, the high number of telephones in the Caribbean proved to be decisive in its high rank on the globalization index. The Caribbean's high rank corresponds with the tendency for its colonizers (Britain, France, and the Netherlands) to be also highly globalized. It is reflected in such forms as the communications intensive tourism and banking industries. Successful exports of Caribbean culture, such as 'world music', could also have encouraged this region's globalization (Holton, 1998: 180–1). Scoring surprisingly low in globalization is the Central and South American region, despite the broad publicity given to it for its recently democratizing polities, more open economies, and

TABLE 2.2
MEAN GLOBALIZATION SCORE BY WORLD-SYSTEM POSITION

World-system position	Mean globalization score	Number of cases
Core	0.364	141
Semi-periphery	0.237	233
Periphery	0.150	662
Global mean	0.199	1036

TABLE 2.3
MEAN GLOBALIZATION SCORE BY LEVEL OF DEMOCRACY

Level of democracy	Mean globalization score	Number of cases
2 (dictatorship)	0.116	51
3	0.133	50
4	0.147	44
5	0.134	77
6	0.183	53
7	0.154	69
8	0.151	61
9	0.139	74
10	0.142	79
11	0.147	91
12	0.207	74
13	0.256	137
14 (democracy)	0.351	176
Global mean	0.199	1036
Global median	0.156	1036

free-market politicians anxious to promote external trade. This region ranks below the global mean on all components of the globalization index, a status it shared only with the sub-Saharan African countries and the Central and South Asian countries. The low degree of globalization for Central and South America could perhaps be explained by the residual tendency toward statist political economy in this region.

If world-system position can be considered a proxy for economic development (in this sample, it correlates with GNP per capita at 0.81, N = 1,323), then in a broad sense globalization is a creature of economic status. The core countries are one and a half times more globalized than the semi-peripheral countries, and nearly two and a half times more globalized than the peripheral countries. Meanwhile, the semi-peripheral countries are one and a half times more globalized than the peripheral countries. While the basic relationship between economics and globalization is clear, the regional breakdown reported above provide some appropriate nuances.

Finally, there may be some question as to whether globalization is associated with regime type. According to Table 2.3, there does seem to be an association between rising levels of globalization and rising levels of democracy. However, this relationship appears to present an 'N curve' as globalization actually declines within the middle stages of democratic development. This non-linearity was first observed by Lipset *et al.* (1993) in the relationship between democracy and economic development. It is interesting to see this pattern occur again in regard to globalization. The countries scoring in the middle of the democracy scale are also the least politically stable countries. This tendency may contribute to both low economic development and low globalization, as the business climate in those countries may be more ambiguous than in politically stable democracies and dictatorships.

Measuring Development

We now turn from bivariate to multivariate analyses of globalization, regimes, and development. The quantitative work on development is extensive, and is concentrated on economic rather than human development. The most popular focus is on the determinants of economic growth (see Barro, 1997; Kurzman *et al.*, 2000; Siermann, 1998). A close cousin of human development, the Physical Quality of Life Index (PQLI), has received some attention from scholars (e.g., Moon, 1991; Pourgerami, 1991; Emizet, 2000). Scholarship on human development presents the most recent phase in the evolution of developmental studies (see Ivanova *et al.*, 1998; Ranis *et al.*, 2000). For economic development and growth, the relevant literature suggests standard variables such as human capital stock (for example, literacy rates), democracy (conducive to those economic policies that promote economic growth desired by the population), government expenditure (which, if excessive, discourages business enterprise and thus development), initial levels of wealth, investment, political stability (growth is made more difficult when the regime and thus rules of conduct change) and population growth. Economic development and growth are thus associated with higher levels of capital stock and flow (human and physical) and political stability, and lower levels of public spending, population growth, and initial wealth (in the familiar convergence thesis of the endogenous growth theory).

The PQLI and human development approach, while less advanced than that of economic development and growth, has its central set of variables as well. It includes, as facilitators of PQLI and human development, democracy (the electorate is likely to choose policies enhancing its quality of life), economic development, government expenditures (especially for social welfare programs), public investment in human capital (especially in school and hospital construction), and urbanization (since human resources such as education and health care are more readily available and more easily delivered in an urban setting). Conversely, population growth is supposed to inhibit PQLI and human development.

The relevant literature tends to take into account regional and world-system influences which are often presented as dummy variables. Regions that are outside the core of the world-system are presumed to have lower levels of development, regardless of how it is measured, while core countries have a developmental advantage.

OPERATIONAL PROCEDURES

Model Specification

I propose models of development that incorporate the standard determinants just mentioned as well as the globalization index as independent variables. I use GNP per capita (GNPPC), in constant 1995 US dollars, to represent economic development. Data for this variable are from the United States Arms Control and Disarmament Agency (1997). For human development, I adopt the HDI as reported in the *Human Development Report* published by the United Nations Development Programme. The HDI readings are for the 1990–95 time period, with each annual reading actually based on the observed values of this index's three components from three years prior to publication of the *Human Development Report*. The three components are education (tertiary school enrollment and literacy rates), health (life expectancy), and income (gross domestic product per capita). Therefore, the HDI incorporates more information than does GNPPC. It is increasingly advocated as the 'proper' measure of development.

I modify the HDI somewhat in this analysis. I create an additive index of the literacy rate, life expectancy, and GNPPC (in lieu of gross domestic product per capita). I do this for two reasons. The first is data comparability. The income data presented in the *Human Development Report* are not comparable across the years, and the school enrollment data are not available across all the years. Additionally, since the index is scaled for each year during the 1990s, the index numbers are not strictly comparable from year to year as the upper and lower limits change each year (the 'shifting goalpost' phenomenon). Second, these modifications come without statistical cost. The modified HDI measure across the 1987–95 period correlates at 0.91 (N=1,323) with the unmodified measure of HDI, and at 0.98 (N=935) with its sister measure, the Physical Quality of Life Index. Instead of statistically duplicating results with these highly related measures, I use the modified HDI measure alone as a dependent variable in the following analysis. To make the HDI comparable across countries and years, I use the constant GNPPC variable. The modified HDI is based on the observed minimum and maximum scores for life expectancy (22.6 years and 80 years, respectively), adult literacy rate (12 per cent and 99 per cent), and constant GNPPC ($57 and $48,720).

Modified HDI is thus calculated using the following formula:

Modified HDI = $(X_{life} + X_{lit} + X_{GNP}) / 3$
Where
X_{life} = (Life Expectancy – 22.6) / (80 – 22.6),
X_{lit} = (Literacy Rate – 12) / (99 – 12),
and
X_{GNP} = (GNPPC – 57) / (48,720 – 57)

But why a focus on the HDI? The dominant conception of development has been oriented, since World War Two, around economic growth. However, with the slowdown in economic growth in the 1970s, and a concern with the environmental impact of economic growth, 'the first doubts began to appear about the sufficiency of economic growth as a solvent of social problems' (Desai, 1991: 351). The HDI built upon the work by scholars interested in basic human needs beginning in the 1970s. This work laid out a separate framework for fulfilling development aspirations more applicable to populations in the less developed countries (e.g., Morris, 1979; Shaefer, 1992; Streeten *et al.*, 1981). The HDI is meant to suggest an alternative and preferred measurement of quality of life and thus of development. Its advocates even posit that public policy should raise the HDI to the highest levels possible, at the expense, if necessary, of economic development as measured by GNP per capita. They contend that the 'good life' should not be represented solely by dollars, but rather, in addition, by increases in education and health that permit people to better pursue personal and societal betterment. In the view of these critics, 'commodity fetishism' is misguided if 'the objective of the development effort is to provide all human beings with the *opportunity* for a full life' (Streeten *et al.*, 1981: 21).

Concerns for human development lead to a political conception of society that is far different from the one based on an exclusive focus on maximizing economic growth. For instance, 'The Human Development Index advances the task of thinking more holistically about social health' (Miringoff and Miringoff, 1999: 31).

As in the work of development scholars such as Gustav Ranis, I allow for the highly plausible possibility that human and economic development can have reciprocal influence on each other. Rather than adding human and economic development variables directly to each model and thus running the danger of biasing the parameter estimates, I account for the possibility of reciprocal causality by introducing a proxy variable for each type of development. In the economic development model, I use the literacy rate as a proxy variable for human development. There is a high correlation between literacy rate and human development. In the human development model, I use world-system position as a surrogate for economic development. These two variables are also highly correlated.

My final model for explaining economic development is as follows.

Logged GNPPC = f (Initial Level of Logged GNPPC, Gross Direct Investment, [Gross Direct Investment × Political Stability], Population Growth, Adult Literacy, Democracy, Central Government Expenditure, [Central Government Expenditure × Semi-peripheral World-System

Position], [Central Government Expenditure × Peripheral World-System Position], Protestant Population, Logged Globalization, [East European Country × Globalization], [North African/Middle Eastern Country × Globalization], [Sub-Saharan African Country × Globalization], [Central/ South American Country × Globalization], [Caribbean Country × Globalization], [South/Central Asian Country × Globalization], [East Asian Country × Globalization], [Oceania Country × Globalization])

The model for explaining human development is specified slightly differently from the economic development model, and takes the following form in accordance with the prior research discussed above:

Modified HDI = f (Democracy, Gross Direct Investment, Central Government Expenditure, [Central Government Expenditure × Semi-peripheral World-System Position], [Central Government Expenditure × Peripheral World-System Position], Population Growth, Urbanization, Logged Globalization, [East European Country × Globalization], [North African/ Middle Eastern Country × Globalization], [Sub-Saharan African Country × Globalization], [Central/South American Country × Globalization], [Caribbean Country × Globalization], [South/Central Asian Country × Globalization], [East Asian Country × Globalization], [Oceania Country × Globalization]).

Globalization is logged to the base 10 in each model in order to approximate the assumption of linearity. The analyses cover the years 1990–95. Gross direct investment is measured as a percentage of gross domestic product (a stock measure), and the relevant data are drawn from various editions of the *Human Development Report.* The democracy variable is computed by adding the national scores for political rights and civil liberties reported in the annual publication *Freedom in the World.* The coding, however, is reversed so that the highest score of 14 is associated with the highest level of democracy, and the lowest score of 2 is associated with the lowest level of democracy. Political stability is indicated by the standard deviation of the democracy scores for each country during 1990–95, with a high score suggesting an unstable polity. Population growth is measured by the annual rate of increase in population, and is based on the *Statistical Yearbook* published by the United Nations. Central government expenditure is expressed as a percentage of GNP and drawn from various editions of the *Human Development Report.* The percentage of Protestants for each national population (logged to the base 10 after adding one to the variable) comes from D. Barrett's (1982) *World Christian Encyclopedia.* Urbanization as a percentage of total population comes from various editions of the *Human Development Report.*

Methodological Caveats

The pooled cross-sectional, time series data set is unbalanced, which constricts the econometric tools available for statistical estimation. I use TSP Version 4.4 for model estimation. Since the pooled data are cross-sectionally dominant (85–90 countries and up to six time points), I am more concerned with panel heteroskedasticity than with autocorrelation. The VARCOMP procedure in TSP is a GLS variance components random effects estimator, which is an efficient estimator designed to alleviate panel heteroskedasticity (Stimson, 1985: 929). I employ it as the estimator of choice. Parenthetically, I performed a check of the VARCOMP results against those from the AR1(TSCS) procedure, which models an AR(1) process in these admittedly limited time-series data. I found little substantive difference between the two sets of results, and thus present only the model estimates by VARCOMP.

A separate issue, multicollinearity, is in moderate evidence in each of the following model estimates. Roughly one-quarter of the independent variables had Variance Inflation Factors (VIFs) greater than five, a sign of multicollinearity (Studenmund, 1992: 275). However, the VIFs were not outrageously high (with none of them reaching above ten), and multicollinearity remedies are few in the face of a well-specified model. The danger is in removing a variable that should be included in the model. Because I believe that there is a strong theoretical reason for including all the independent variables stipulated above, I tolerate these parameter estimates but counsel caution in their interpretation due to the presence of multicollinearity.

STATISTICAL RESULTS

Table 2.4 reports the parameter estimates for each development model: 99 per cent of the variance in the model for economic development and 84 per cent of the variance in human development are accounted for by the independent variables. Many of the coefficients appear to be in the theoretically correct direction, thus lessening the concern stemming from multicollinearity. The results for economic development, especially when the globalization index interacts with the regional dummy variables, present some intriguing questions. As noted earlier, the optimist and pessimist camps promote mutually contradictory yet seemingly persuasive arguments for their respective positions.

Turning attention first to the determinants of economic development, several prior expectations appear to be validated even after the introduction of a strong control variable in the form of a country's initial level of economic development. According to the rationale presented by Emizet (2000) and Romer (1989), a positive coefficient for the initial level of

TABLE 2.4
PARAMETER ESTIMATES FOR DEVELOPMENT MODELS
[( ) = ABSOLUTE t-RATIOS, *=p<0.10]

Independent variable	Economic development	Human development
Initial Economic Development	0.98* (40.35)	
Gross Direct Investment	0.005* (6.05)	0.0005 (1.42)
Gross Direct Investment × Political Stability	−0.0008* (1.86)	
Population Growth	−0.00002 (0.03)	0.0009* (2.12)
Adult Literacy Rate	0.0002 (0.49)	
Democracy	0.003 (1.48)	0.004* (4.01)
Central Government Expenditure	−0.0006 (0.87)	0.0009* (1.67)
Semi-peripheral World-System Position × Central Government Expenditure	0.0004 (0.61)	−0.001* (1.80)
Peripheral World-System Position × Central Government Expenditure	0.0002 (0.23)	−0.002* (2.87)
Protestant Population	−0.0006* (1.70)	
Urbanization		0.002* (5.13)
Globalization	0.20* (3.04)	0.04 (0.79)
East European Country × Globalization	0.09 (1.44)	0.04 (0.83)
North African/Middle Eastern Country × Globalization	−0.03 (0.52)	0.17* (3.26)
Sub-Saharan African Country × Globalization	−0.07 (1.25)	0.32* (7.55)
Central/South American Country × Globalization	−0.03 (0.62)	0.14* (3.32)
Caribbean Country × Globalization	−0.06 (0.71)	0.15* (1.79)
South/Central Asian Country × Globalization	−0.10* (1.67)	0.32* (6.38)
East Asian Country × Globalization	−0.09* (1.67)	0.07 (1.59)
Oceania Country × Globalization	−0.11 (1.20)	0.23* (2.53)
Constant	0.11 (1.08)	0.71* (19.36)
Adjusted R-squared	0.99	0.84
Standard Error of Estimate	0.07	0.08
Number of Cases	346	353

economic development coefficient tends to refute the convergence theory of economic development. This pattern implies that those with a low economic base would subsequently perform less well than those who started with a high economic base. Cumulative economic advantage tends to accrue to those countries already ahead. Stated alternatively, economic development should not be expected in poor countries simply because they are poor and have the room to develop economically.

Gross direct investment exercises a very positive influence on economic development as shown in prior research. However, as commonly speculated, this influence is mitigated by political instability. Investment in unstable polities actually leads to a decline in economic development. Perhaps this tendency is due to a correlation between regime instability and official corruption. Political instability tends to discourage investment although it is neither necessary nor sufficient for official corruption. In the case of human development, gross direct investment is not a statistically significant determinant. This result confirms a finding by Moon (1991: 125) that government spending on health and education was not a statistically significant predictor of PQLI.

Neither population growth nor adult literacy seems to be crucial for economic development, ceteris paribus, although each coefficient is signed in the correct direction. Their weak effects seem to warrant encouragement for those developing countries that lack human capital or are under population pressure. Also, the failure of adult literacy to reach statistical significance tends to undermine the expectation of reciprocal causality between human and economic development.

Democracy fails to have a significant impact on economic development. This finding is similar to the conclusion reached by Burkhart and Lewis-Beck (1994: 907) that democracy did not 'Granger cause' economic development during 1972–89. If the strength, leftist ideology, and domestic reach of a state are represented by a large public sector as measured by the central government's expenditures, then strong leftist states with considerable reach are not better able to achieve economic development. Our results also show that unfavorable positions within the world economic system, either in the semi-periphery or the periphery, are not conducive to economic development.

Finally, there is scant support for Max Weber's (1958) thesis that the Protestant work ethic promotes economic development. Given the recent economic rise of the Catholic and Orthodox countries in the south Mediterranean, the Islamic countries in North Africa and the Middle East, and the Buddhist countries in East Asia, the *negative* coefficient of the relative size of the Protestant population in a country on its economic development is unsurprising.

Those in the optimist camp have some reason to be pleased with the model estimates. Globalization's direct impact on economic development is positive and is convincingly significant in statistical terms. There are regional caveats to this conclusion (and one needs to be reminded about the multicollinearity caution), but for the most part it seems secure. For instance, since the OECD countries are the baseline countries for interpreting the interaction effects of the regional dummy variables and globalization index, the implication is that globalization will help the OECD countries to achieve higher levels of economic development.

There is weak evidence that globalization has harmed economic development in Asia, whether in South/Central or East Asia, albeit not enough to make the net impact of globalization on these regions negative. One can infer this net impact by subtracting the South/Central and East Asian coefficients, respectively, from the OECD baseline. This finding for the East Asian countries is somewhat surprising, since countries such as Singapore are among the most globalized in the world.

Accounting for and interpreting this statistical tendency leads us down a couple of paths. This tendency cannot be attributed to a lumping together of countries from the region with disparate economic performance. As noted in the Appendix to this chapter, the East Asian countries encompassed in this data set include China (for one year only), Indonesia, South Korea, Mongolia, Myanmar (for one year only), the Philippines, Singapore, and Thailand. Nevertheless, the negative coefficient featured by the interaction of globalization and East Asian regional effects does not lend strong support for the pessimist camp. It is statistically weak ($p=0.094$). Subtracting the coefficient from the OECD baseline still produces a net positive impact of globalization on East Asia's economic development. From the perspective of the pessimists, however, the argument that the semi-peripheral and peripheral countries do not benefit from globalization as much as do the core countries is supported by the evidence presented here. The overall positive effect of globalization on economic development is attenuated by the developing regions' generally negative relationship with economic development once globalization is taken into account. The Matthew principle seems to hold, albeit weakly. This principle claims that the wealthy countries tend to benefit more directly from globalization while most poor countries are hurt by it, with the result that the economic gap between these two classes of countries widens.

The globalization pessimist camp has some additional reasons for satisfaction in accounting for human development as opposed to economic development. There is no direct impact of globalization on human development. Moreover, since the OECD countries are the baseline countries for understanding the interaction effects between the regional dummy variables and globalization index, our result implies that globalization will not help these countries to achieve higher levels of human development. The reported statistical relationship, however, is not significantly negative. In addition, most of the regional–globalization interaction terms prove to be statistically significant and positively signed. This pattern holds for nearly all the non-OECD regions. Only the East European countries and the East Asian countries do not receive a boost from globalization to enhance their respective human development. All other regions show such a positive effect from globalization. These results correspond to repeated observations that, overall, the quality of life in developing countries has improved during the post-World War Two period. Combining that argument with the ceiling effects of using 0–100 percentages in the HDI adds resonance to the arguments made by globalization optimists.

Five conclusions seem warranted in interpreting the other parameter estimates in the human development model. First, state strength, leftist ideology, and governmental reach – as represented by the size of public spending – have at least a marginally positive, direct impact on human development. However, for the non-core countries, these factors appear to work against their efforts to increase human development. Second, the statistical significance of the interaction terms for central-government expenditure and world-system position support the view that there is a reciprocal causality between economic development and human development. In juxtaposition with other statistical tendencies noted earlier, the collective evidence from this set of analyses is therefore rather ambiguous regarding the possibility of mutual influence between the two alternative visions of development (note, however, that the HDI does include as one of its components, GNPPC). Third, democracy reaches statistical significance in explaining human development. Fourth, population growth has a rather strong, positive impact on human development. This relationship therefore again lends hope to those countries facing strains of demographic burden since it suggests human development is possible in such an environment. Fifth, as hypothesized, urbanization is a most potent force for promoting higher levels of human development.

In comparing the impact of globalization on human development versus economic development, it is important to note that the statistical model did not include the initial level of human development as one of its predictors. The 'quality of life convergence' hypothesis has not been advocated by development scholars at this point. This may be due to the lower profile of human development research, as opposed to the high-profile economic development scholarship. This may offer a worthwhile topic for future research.

What is the average amount of globalization and development extant in

FIGURE 2.1
GLOBALIZATION AND ECONOMIC DEVELOPMENT

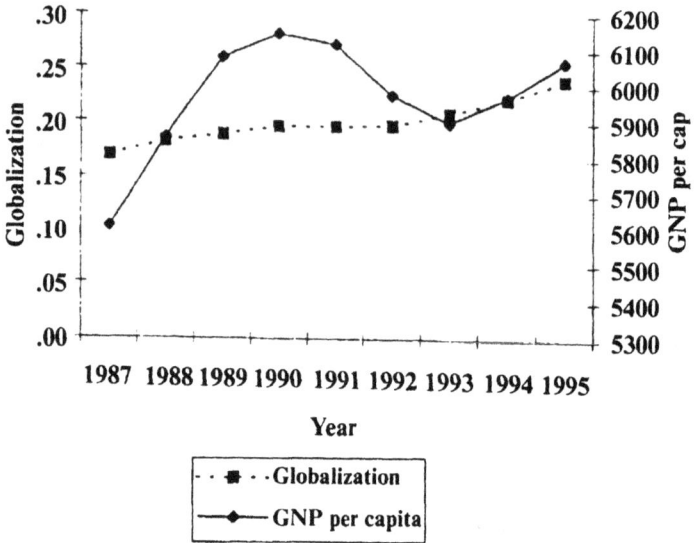

FIGURE 2.2
GLOBALIZATION AND HUMAN DEVELOPMENT

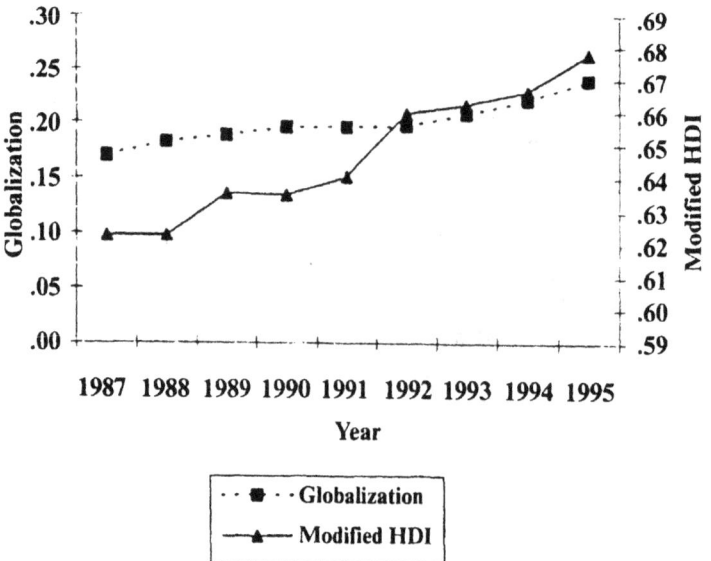

the world? I have computed the average scores for globalization, economic development, and human development, and plotted them for the 1987–95 period, with an average number of 107 valid cases for each year.

Globalization, rather than being an exploding phenomenon, has risen in a fairly steady if unspectacular fashion in recent times. Both economic development and human development seem to have undergone more dramatic fluctuations, even after allowing for scaling differences on the two figures. The apparent N-curve of economic development should caution against too much emphasis being placed on the positive and statistically significant coefficient for globalization in the economic development model being presented as the basic story of this relationship. If anything, the rise in levels of globalization and economic development appear to be long-term trends, while in the short term regional economic fluctuations (especially during the recessionary times of the early 1990s) may dampen the impact of globalization on economic development.

CONCLUSIONS

I conclude this empirical exercise by returning to the questions that began it. Does globalization lead to a higher quality of life? How does globalization have its influence, if any? What other political, economic, social, and cultural factors are relevant in explaining development? The answers to these questions are mixed, defying easy polemical statements on their behalf by either the optimists or the pessimists. Globalization by itself has a strong effect on economic development, but a minimal impact on human development. At the same time, globalization has had a demonstrable positive influence on human development in the world's poorer regions, while this is not at all the case with economic development. Investment, especially in politically stable regimes, enhances development, while higher levels of democracy and urbanization help to bring about more human development. Those who argue that development has different meanings receive some support from the evidence presented in this study.

While the evidence should be interpreted with caution, it implies that the decision on whether to seek further globalization opportunities for the sake of promoting a higher quality of life will not be easy. If globalization is here to stay, at least for the foreseeable future, then officials should as a general rule try to take advantage of its apparent direct, positive contribution to economic development, but be wary of high expectations of its effects in enhancing human development. They should be especially cognizant of the regional interaction effects that can shape, even overwhelm, the 'global' impact of globalization.

Finally, the geography of globalization is a potent element in the public mind. Globalization is supposed to spread inexorably to all parts of the globe, so the story goes. The evidence presented here suggests that the spread will be slower and less even than commonly anticipated, and that the benefits may not accrue in the developing world at the rate suggested by its most hopeful advocates. The counsel by the United Nations (2000: 2) in its *Millennium Declaration* seems particularly appropriate: 'We believe that the central challenge we face today is to ensure that globalization becomes a positive force for all the world's people.' While globalization is hardly an impossible task, more than half of the world's population still has never made or received a telephone call (Annan, 2000: 15). The call for countries to globalize should thus be issued with the full realization that there are considerable challenges to face and obstacles to overcome along the way.

APPENDIX—COUNTRIES AND YEARS USED IN THE DEVELOPMENT MODELS

Argentina (1990–91)
Australia (1990–93, 1995)
Austria (1990–93)
Bangladesh (1990–91)
Belgium (1990–93)
Bolivia (1990–95)
Botswana (1990–94)
Brazil (1990–95)
Burma (1992)
Cameroon (1990–94)
Canada (1990–91, 1993)
Central African Republic (1993)
Chad (1991–93)
Chile (1990, 1993–95)
China (1993)
Colombia (1990–91, 1994–95)
Costa Rica (1990–95)
Côte d'Ivoire (1991–92)
Denmark (1990–93, 1995)
Dominican Republic (1990–92, 1994–95)
Ecuador (1990–95)
Egypt (1990–91, 1993–94)
El Salvador (1990–95)
Finland (1990–93, 1995)
France (1990–93, 1995)
Gabon (1990–93)
The Gambia (1994–95)
Germany (1990–93, 1995)
Greece (1991–93)
Guatemala (1990–91, 1994)

Guinea-Bissau (1991)
Hungary (1991–92)
India (1990–95)
Indonesia (1990–95)
Ireland (1990–93, 1995)
Israel (1990–93, 1995)
Italy (1990–93, 1995)
Japan (1990–92)
Jordan (1990–95)
Kenya (1990–95)
Kuwait (1993–95)
Madagascar (1991–95)
Malawi (1990–92)
Malaysia (1990–95)
Mali (1990)
Mauritania (1990)
Mauritius (1990–95)
Mexico (1990–92, 1995)
Mongolia (1993–94)
Morocco (1992, 1994)
Namibia (1990–94)
Nepal (1990–93)
Netherlands (1990–93, 1995)
New Zealand (1990–93, 1995)
Nicaragua (1990–95)
Norway (1990–92, 1995)
Oman (1990–91)
Pakistan (1990–95)
Panama (1990–94)
Papua New Guinea (1990, 1992–95)

APPENDIX cont.

Paraguay (1990–94)
Peru (1990–95)
Philippines (1990–95)
Poland (1990, 1995)
Portugal (1990–93, 1995)
Romania (1991–93, 1995)
Rwanda (1992–93)
Sierra Leone (1990–94)
Singapore (1990, 1992–95)
South Africa (1990, 1992–95)
South Korea (1990–95)
Spain (1990–93, 1995)
Sri Lanka (1990–95)

Sweden (1990–93, 1995)
Switzerland (1995)
Syria (1990–93, 1995)
Thailand (1990–95)
Tunisia (1990–94)
Turkey (1990–95)
United Kingdom (1990–93, 1995)
United States (1990–93, 1995)
Uruguay (1990–95)
Venezuela (1990–95)
Zambia (1990–91)
Zimbabwe (1990–93)

REFERENCES

Aghion, P., and Williamson, J. (1998), *Growth, Inequality, and Globalization: Theory, History, and Policy* (Cambridge: Cambridge University Press).

Alderson, A. (1999), 'Explaining Deindustrialization: Globalization, Failure, or Success?', *American Sociological Review* 64: 701–21.

Annan, K. (2000), *We the Peoples: The Role of the United Nations in the 21st Century* (New York: United Nations).

Barrett, D. (ed.) (1982), *World Christian Encyclopedia: A Comparative Study of Churches and Religions in the Modern World, AD 1900–2000* (Nairobi: Oxford University Press).

Barro, R. (1997), *Determinants of Economic Growth.* (Cambridge: MIT Press).

Beenstock, M. (1984), *The World Economy in Transition*, 2nd edn (London: Allen and Unwin).

Burkhart, R. (1997), 'Comparative Democracy and Income Distribution: Shape and Direction of the Causal Arrow', *Journal of Politics* 59, 1: 148–64.

Burkhart, R., and Lewis-Beck, M. (1994), 'Comparative Democracy: The Economic Development Thesis', *American Political Science Review* 88, 4: 903–10.

Desai, M. (1991), 'Human Development: Concepts and Measurement', *European Economic Review* 35: 350–57.

Dixon, W. and Boswell, T. (1996), 'Dependency, Disarticulation, and Denominator Effects: Another Look at Foreign Capital Penetration', *American Journal of Sociology* 102: 543–62.

Emizet, K. (2000), 'The Relationship between the Liberal Ethos and Quality of Life: A Comparative Analysis of Pooled Time Series Data from 1970 to 1994', *Comparative Political Studies* 33: 1049–73.

Firebaugh, G. (1992), 'Growth Effects of Foreign and Domestic Investment', *American Journal of Sociology* 98: 105–30.

Freedom House (various years), *Freedom in the World* (New York).

Friedman, T. (1999), *The Lexus and the Olive Tree* (New York: Farrar, Straus & Giroux).

Gilpin, R. (2000), *The Challenge of Global Capitalism: The World Economy in the 21st Century* (Princeton, NJ: Princeton University Press).

Greenspan, A. (2000), US Congress, House of Representatives, Committee on Banking and Financial Services, *Hearing on the Conduct of Monetary Policy*, 106th Cong., 2nd sess., 25 July.

Greider, W. (1997), *One World, Ready or Not: The Manic Logic of Global Capitalism* (New York: Simon & Schuster).

Held, D., McGrew, A., Goldblatt, D. and Perraton, J. (1999), *Global Transformations: Politics, Economics and Culture* (Stanford, CA: Stanford University Press).

Holton, R. (1998), *Globalization and the Nation-State* (New York: St Martin's Press).

International Monetary Fund (various years), *International Financial Statistics Yearbook* (Washington, DC).

Ivanova, I., Arcelus, F. and Srinivasan, G. (1998), 'An Assessment of the Measurement Properties of the Human Development Index', *Social Indicators Research* 46: 157–79.

Keohane, R. and Nye, J. (2000), 'Globalization: What's New? What's Not? (And So What?)', *Foreign Policy* 118: 104–19.

Kurzman, C., Werum, R. and Burkhart, R. (2000), 'Democracy's Effect on Economic Growth: A Pooled Time Series Analysis, 1951–1980', unpublished paper.

Lipset, S., Seong, K. and Torres, J. (1993), 'A Comparative Analysis of the Social Requisites of Democracy', *International Social Science Journal* 45: 155–75.

Miringoff, M. and Miringoff, M-L. (1999), *The Social Health of the Nation: How America is Really Doing* (New York: Oxford University Press).

Moon, B. (1991), *The Political Economy of Basic Human Needs* (Ithaca, NY: Cornell University Press).

Morris, M. (1979), *Measuring the Condition of the World's Poor: The Physical Quality of Life Index* (London: Frank Cass).

Porter, M. (2000), 'Attitudes, Values, Beliefs, and the Microeconomics of Prosperity', in L. Harrison and S. Huntington (eds), *Culture Matters: How Values Shape Human Progress* (New York: Basic Books), pp. 14–28.

Pourgerami, A. (1991), *Development and Democracy in the Third World* (Boulder, CO: Westview Press).

Ranis, G., Stewart, F. and Ramirez, A. (2000), 'Economic Growth and Human Development', *World Development* 28, 2: 197–219.

Rodrik, D. (1997), *Has Globalization Gone Too Far?* (Washington, DC: Institute for International Economics).

Romer, P.M. (1989), 'Endogenous Technological Change', *Journal of Political Economy* 98: 71–102.

Sabatier, P. (2000), 'Five Americans at War with Globalization', *World Press Review* 47, 2 (February): 31.

Shaefer, G. (ed.) (1992), *Basic Human Needs: An Interdisciplinary and International View* (Frankfurt: Peter Lang).

Shiva, V. (2000), 'Poverty and Globalisation', *BBC Reith Lectures 2000*, website http://news.bbc.co.uk/hi/english/static/events/reith_2000/lecture5.stm, accessed 27 July.

Siermann, C. (1998), *Politics, Institutions and the Economic Performance of Nations* (Cheltenham: Edward Elgar).

Soysa, I. de and Oneal, J. (1999), 'Boon or Bane? Reassessing the Productivity of Foreign Direct Investment', *American Sociological Review* 64: 766–82.

Stimson, J. (1985), 'Regression in Space and Time: A Statistical Essay', *American Journal of Political Science* 29, 4: 914–47.

Streeten, P., Burki, S., Ul Haq, M., Hicks, N. and Stewart, F. (1981), *First Things First: Meeting Basic Human Needs in Developing Countries* (New York: Oxford University Press).

Studenmund, A. (1992), *Using Econometrics: A Practical Guide,* 2nd edn (New York: HarperCollins).

Tonelson, A. (1997), 'Globalization: The Great American Non-Debate', *Current History* 96, 613: 353–9.

United Nations (2000), *The United Nations Millennium Declaration* (New York, United Nations, 6 September).

United Nations (various years), *Statistical Yearbook* (New York).

United Nations Development Programme (various years), *Human Development Report* (New York: Oxford University Press).

United States Arms Control and Disarmament Agency (1997), *World Military Expenditures and Arms Transfers, 1996* (Washington, DC).

Waltz, K. (1999), 'Globalization and Governance', *PS* 23, 4: 693–700.
Weber, M. (1958), *The Protestant Ethic and the Spirit of Capitalism*, T. Parsons (trans.) (New York: Scribner).
Wood, A. (1994), *North–South Trade, Employment, and Inequality* (Oxford: Oxford University Press).

3

Is it a Small World after All?: Globalization and Government Respect for Human Rights in Developing Countries

DAVID L. RICHARDS AND RONALD D. GELLENY

INTRODUCTION

In the autumn of 1999 and the spring of 2000, the world witnessed large-scale demonstrations in the United States against the World Trade Organization (WTO), the World Bank, and the International Monetary Fund (IMF). These demonstrations were an angry manifestation of one side of what has become a bitter debate over what is popularly called 'economic globalization'. 'Economic globalization' is a term used to represent the increasingly dynamic forces of international trade and finance, and it implies a continuing growth over time in the volume of international trade and transnational capital movement, the number of countries engaging in these activities, and an increase in the politico-economic interdependence of participating nations. While economic globalization is a rather recent buzz-word, the basic phenomena it represents have existed for some time. Chase-Dunn *et al.* (1998: 2) point out that:

> The degree of international connectedness of economic and political/military networks was already important in the fourteenth and fifteenth centuries. The first 'transnational corporations' were the great chartered companies of the seventeenth century [which] organized both production and exchange on an intercontinental scale.

At the end of the twentieth century, multinational corporations (MNCs) 'control almost 80 per cent of international trade and a large portion of flows of foreign investments' (World Trade Organization, 1999a: 4).

Trade openness, the classic indicator of economic liberalization (the decision by political elites to engage in free-market reforms), is a critical element to economic globalization, but is no longer the sole vehicle of economic interdependence. Rather, the integration of financial markets has come to dominate the current globalization process, which, as we will later argue, began in earnest in the early 1990s. Unlike past surges of global capital, the 1990s witnessed an expansion in the variety of both financial instruments and investment recipients. Capital flows have taken the form of not only foreign direct investment (FDI), but also of instruments such as equity and portfolio investments. Furthermore, capital flows have found their way to non-traditional venues, with developing countries receiving about two-thirds of the growth in FDI worldwide since the early 1990s (World Bank, 1999). Additionally, unlike past years, governments in developing countries have encouraged both trade and financial integration.

During the current globalization era, political elites have accepted that an increasingly integrated global economy necessitates, to some degree, reduced political sovereignty of individual countries in the arena of economic policy-making. Indeed, during the recent era of economic globalization, intergovernmental organizations overseeing the world economy are, to all appearances, more powerful than were their predecessors. The WTO, for instance, is empowered to override domestic laws in member states (136 countries as of April 2000) where such laws contradict WTO trade policy. The hotly contested Multilateral Agreement on Investment (MAI), first proposed by the OECD (Organisation for Economic Co-operation and Development) and now elsewhere, seeks rigid, centralized controls on the policy options of even local governments in subscriber states. Some feel that the economic growth associated with globalization negates the decline in domestic political sovereignty, while others feel that globalization undermines the capacity of governments to pursue social and economic objectives that will benefit the citizens of developing countries.

The proponents of economic globalization (neo-liberals) stress that, ultimately, an interdependent world economy will bring economic growth and democratic political stability to those nations currently lacking these characteristics (particularly those countries labeled as 'developing nations'), thus increasing the ability of their governments to respect a broad array of human rights at an acceptable level. The opponents of economic globalization (who subscribe to a school of thought we call 'post-dependency') charge that the current structure of the global economy implies a forfeit of personal freedoms and national political sovereignty, increased economic disparity among countries, and environmental disaster.

At the end of the day, both camps base their arguments regarding economic globalization on the basis of social rather than economic utility. While supporters openly posit that increased personal wealth and macro-economic development are the 'good ends' of economic globalization, their underlying logic is that these things are good because they bring with them a higher probability of democratic political stability and an increased standard of living, allowing for a life of human dignity. Critics of economic globalization are more direct about their interest in social utility when they assert that globalization leads instead to economic inequality and external dominance, impeding a life of human dignity.

Although the effects of globalization are hotly disputed, there is little disagreement that economic globalization has intensified. Thus, the debate over its social utility is important. The core question in this debate is, 'To what extent are foreign economic power and domestic political power intertwined, and, to what social ends?' In this chapter we address that question empirically, as we examine the relationship between the globalization of economies in the developing world and the level of respect afforded to citizens' human rights by governments in those countries. We use a subset of internationally recognized human rights known as 'physical-integrity rights' as our indicator of the social utility of economic globalization, as these rights are tools for attaining a life of human dignity.[1]

First, we briefly discuss what discernible phenomena are implied when the term 'economic globalization' is invoked. Next, we visit two competing views that offer hypotheses about the nature of the relationship between economic globalization and government respect for human rights in developing countries. Third, we conduct a region-specific empirical examination of the relationship between economic globalization and government respect for human rights in 43 developing countries, 1981–96. For our analyses, we conceptualize and operationalize economic globalization as two-dimensional, consisting of both financial globalization and trade globalization. To address globalization as a distinct era, all of our regional analyses are subdivided into pre-globalization and globalization eras.

ECONOMIC GLOBALIZATION: WHAT IS IT?

The term 'globalization', as commonly used, is a slight misnomer, as globalization is not only the process of making a commodity or relationship truly spatially global in availability (as the name implies): it is also the process of increasing the interdependence and the volume of international economic activity among those entities where a commodity or relationship already exists. This spatial spread, increased interdependence, and increased level of economic activity are all assumed to take place over time. Thus, three elements are involved in the single term 'globalization': spatial globalization (an increase in the number of countries and/or regions participating in international activity); what we call 'volumization' (an increase in the level of international activity); and time. These three elements apply to any type of globalization: economic, political, cultural, or technical.

Earlier, we defined economic globalization as a continuing increase over time in the volume of international trade and transnational capital movement and investment as well as an increase in the politico-economic interdependence of nations. Let us examine economic globalization in light of the three elements of the globalization paradigm introduced above. We will see that the elements of quantity, space, and time are interrelated.

Economic globalization invokes a more dynamic and varied process than the type of foreign economic investment dealt with in classic dependency and neo-liberal studies of the relationship between foreign economic penetration and the social and economic welfare of citizens in developing countries. First, economic globalization requires net growth over time in the use of the various elements of globalization, although this increase need not be monotonic. Classic dependency and neo-liberal studies examined the effect of foreign investment on various social phenomena, but these theories did not place this investment in a structure of necessary growth, as does the globalization paradigm.

Second, the globalization paradigm implies that there is a past era we can call the 'pre-globalization era' and a current era we can call the 'globalization era'. These two eras are separated by a point in time at which there was a significant shift in both external economic actors' interest in investing in developing countries and in the willingness of the latter's political elites to facilitate the interests of these external forces. The globalization paradigm also requires an increase from the pre-globalization era to the globalization era in the volume of foreign economic activity in developing economies (volumization) and the diversity of economic tools used.

Third, the 'global' element of economic globalization requires that at the same time the purported shift in behavior (resulting in quantity increase) occurred between those countries and investors already economically related to some degree, an increase also occurred in the number of developing countries willing to participate in the new system of increased mutual economic reliance. Hence, the 'global' in globalization. This spatial increase was not, and is not assumed to be, uniform, however. Some regions of the world, such as Africa, climbed on the bandwagon later than did others, as differences in the willingness and ability of countries to take part in the global economy were made clear.

Thus, by definition, economic globalization requires increases in the volume of economic exchange, the receptivity of domestic political authorities to these changes, and an increase in spatial scope (so far as the sheer number of countries or regions involved). In addition, it implies both net growth in these factors over time, and a particular point in time at which this growth increased noticeably.

WHEN DID WE BECOME GLOBALIZED?

The preceding section posits that the term 'globalization' includes a temporal element such that recent history may be divided into two eras at a point in which some significant shift in behavior occurred. The first is the 'pre-globalization era' in which some of the elements of economic globalization may be in place and functioning, but a significant shift in behavior regarding these elements has not yet occurred. Second is what we call the 'globalization era', in which a shift in behavior has occurred such that the volume and interdependence of the global economy has significantly increased from the preceding era. Given these designations, we must ask ourselves, 'When did the shift from the pre-globalization era to the globalization era occur?' We assert that the globalization era began in 1990 for Asia, Latin America, and the Middle East, and in 1993 for Africa.

Financial capital flows are one marker that differentiates the era of globalization from the pre-globalization era. Prior to the end of the late 1980s and early 1990s many developing countries imposed capital restrictions to limit international financial transactions (Tamirisa, 1999). However, the political environment began to change in the 1980s. The debt crisis of the 1970s and early 1980s caused private bank lending to drop dramatically. Thus, other venues of cash for governments and private firms in developing countries were needed. Furthermore, one implication of the end of the Cold War was the dominance of the liberal market system. Thus, existing financial support from Soviet-bloc countries dried up, with no legitimate alternative to market liberalization in order to generate economic growth.

By the 1990s, governments in developing countries recognized that protectionism was not working. Countries with policies that imposed protectionist measures were not performing as well as those that had adopted more liberal policies. Consequently, many developing countries liberalized their capital and merchandise markets (Heredia, 1997; United Nations, 1999; World Bank, 1999). The WTO points out that by the beginning of 1996, of the 900 existing bilateral investment treaties (at that time), over 60 per cent had been negotiated since 1990 (WTO, 1996). Moreover, until the 1990s, portfolio and bond investment in most developing countries was non-existent. However, the last decade of the twentieth century witnessed a boom in such investments. For example, portfolio investment to developing countries jumped from $3.4 billion during the period of 1983–88 to over $44 billion during 1989–95 (Singh and Weisse, 1998). Bond investment in developing countries soared from $1.2 billion in 1990 to over $11 billion dollars in 1992 (World Bank, 1999). Similarly, developing countries experienced a remarkable surge in FDI in the 1990s.

FDI grew 'more than sixfold from 1990 to 1998, and their share of global FDI flows has risen from 25 per cent in 1991 to an estimated 42 per cent in 1998' (World Bank, 1999: 48).

In addition to financial liberalization, expanding world trade has been considered an important part of the dynamics of the radically changing world economy. Indeed, since the beginning of the 1990s the volume of world trade has undergone rapid growth (United Nations, 1995). Bergsten and Schott (1997) note that Mexico began to liberalize trade and finance policies in the early 1990s in preparation for the North American Free Trade Agreement (NAFTA) negotiations. Between 1990 and 1998, Latin American countries expanded their volume of merchandise trade exports by over 8 per cent annually (WTO, 1999b). Schott and Watal (2000) argue that the continued opening of industrialized markets through successive trade negotiations significantly contributed to economic growth in developing nations, especially those in Asia and Latin America.

Most regions of the world, including Asia, Latin America, and the Middle East, experienced rising capital flows. However, the continent of Africa was the one exception to the trend. Africa did not experience significant increases in FDI and portfolio investments until around 1993 (Bhattacharya et al.,1997; World Bank, 1999). Instead, Africa continued to account for the largest share of official development aid (ODA) during the same period rather than attracting much needed financial capital. Additionally, many African countries were slow to achieve significant growth in export and import markets. In fact, it was not until the beginning of 1994 that African countries increased their volume of international trade (United Nations, 1998). One reason was the slow and erratic pace of economic liberalization of many African countries until the early 1990s (World Bank, 1995; Pill and Pradhan, 1997). Moreover, through the 1980s and the start of the 1990s Africa was considered a greater political and economic risk than the other regions. Good government is said to be extremely important for international investors. That is, investors want a predictable investment environment that includes a stable rule of law, protection of property rights, and limits on government corruption (World Bank, 1997a). Clearly, many African countries lacked basic economic and political stability, and thus had great difficulty in attracting investors to the region.

However, many African countries began to loosen trade policies and financial capital restrictions around 1993–94. For example, Kenya, Malawi, Mauritius, Tunisia, and Zimbabwe increasingly enacted liberal economic policies designed to attract foreign investors (United Nations, 1995). In the private sector, African entrepreneurs have increasingly called for market reforms to encourage economic growth. In 1992, the West African

Enterprise Network (WAEN) was formed by entrepreneurs from 12 West African countries who advocated the position that modern private business practices were the key to economic growth. National authorities have increasingly turned to the WAEN for economic advice and have implemented market reforms (Courcelle and de Lattre, 1996). For example, with consultation with national WAEN members, Ghana loosed rules on interventions by foreign firms on the local stock exchange, thereby increasing available capital resources for local firms. African countries have begun to adopt more 'sound' macroeconomic policies, including lowering government spending and opening their doors to private investors (United Nations, 1996). As a result, total private capital flows to sub-Saharan Africa grew from less than one billion dollars in 1991 to over five billion in 1994 (World Bank, 1997a). Additionally, Africa began to export a larger volume of goods internationally, expanding from $95,600,000 in 1992 to $123,600,000 in 1996 (United Nations, 1996; Rocard, 1999; WTO, 1999b). Therefore, Africa has increasingly experienced the effects of economic globalization, albeit from a lower initial base than the other developing regions.

ECONOMIC GLOBALIZATION: BOON OR BANE FOR HUMAN RIGHTS?

The point of contention surrounding economic globalization, however, is not how globalized the world has become, but rather, what the consequences of this situation are. Below, we outline two differing positions about the effect that economic globalization has on government respect for human rights in developing countries.

Boon: The Neo-Liberal Argument

From the neo-liberal perspective, economic globalization is seen as a matter of vital importance to the economic growth and consequent social development of developing countries. That is, those developing countries that embrace economic globalization will be launched toward modernity and affluence, and those that fail to attempt to reap the benefits of globalization will be left behind and continue to stagnate in terms of economic and social growth.

The neo-liberal globalization argument contends that developing countries must open their borders to foreign investment in order to achieve economic growth. The opening of borders to financial flows enhances economic growth, since capital is attracted to the most efficient or productive investments, which in turn helps to boost productivity. Hence, for developing countries to realize the full potential benefits of economic globalization, they must be receptive to FDI and portfolio investment. In fact, studies have shown a strong association between economic growth in developing countries and inward financial flows (Eichengreen, 1997; World Bank, 1997b). For example, Chile, Spain, and Taiwan have all experienced economic growth that is credited to open economic policies. Even India, traditionally skeptical of open markets, has recently experienced greater economic growth while embracing global investment.

At a seminar in 1996, Renato Ruggierio, then WTO director-general, reiterated 'There can be no doubt that FDI has joined international trade as a primary motor of globalization' (WTO, 1996: 1). FDI consists of building plants or acquiring a controlling interest (more than 10 per cent of outstanding stock) in a foreign enterprise. Such investment provides developing countries with access to sophisticated technology, management and marketing skills, creates more jobs than domestic firms, and often pays higher wages than normally found in the domestic market (see Spar, 1998). For example, MNCs in Turkey pay domestic workers on average 124 per cent more than local firms do (*The Economist*, 2000).

In addition to FDI, portfolio investment is a critical component in the globalization process. The liberalization of portfolio investment allows firms in developing countries to access surplus capital beyond the home market. The use of equity capital rather than debt financing allows host firms to avoid fixed loan payments, thereby enabling them to take advantage of long-term opportunities rather than being hamstrung by relying on internal sources of finance and short-term credit (Caprio and Demirguc-Kunt, 1998). Moreover, developing countries are able to draw upon international sources to finance state ventures, such as public enterprises and infrastructure projects. Thus, the liberalization of portfolio investment provides developing countries with more ample sources of revenue to support economic growth.

Increased trade interdependence is also seen as applying additional disciplinary pressure on government economic policy. As with capital liberalization, trade integration establishes direct ties between national economies and the world system. In this case, governments are not confined by short-run fluctuations, but rather by the long-run competitiveness of national producers in global markets (Garrett, 1995; Sachs and Warner, 1995). For a country to generate high income and employment levels, national producers must be able to compete effectively against foreign firms in the domestic and international markets. Thus, as governments are dependent on investment to increase economic growth, they must be willing to implement policies that foster a friendly business environment. As with FDI, trade liberalization destroys vested protectionist interests inclined to impede economic competition. Indeed, Norton (2000) argues that free trade has done more to lower poverty than any law, regulation, or social policy.

Mitchell and McCormick (1988) present three hypotheses about the relationship between economic development and human rights violations. The only one of these hypotheses which held up to empirical scrutiny was what they call the 'simple poverty thesis'. This hypothesis posits a linear, inverse relationship between 'the wealth of a society and its human rights violations' (Mitchell and McCormick, 1988: 478). This thesis rests on the argument that economic scarcity will drive political instability, and governments will engage in repression reactively. The inverse of this relationship, of course, is that economic prosperity will minimize human-rights violations; and this proposition presents the core of the neo-liberal perspective on economic globalization and government respect for human rights.

Yet, what is the process by which economic development ameliorates human rights violations? Supporters of the neo-liberal perspective associate economic development with the growth of a middle class. In turn, a growing middle class is seen as conducive to democratic political liberalization, which is reliably associated with increased government respect for human rights (Lerner, 1958; Lipset, 1959; Nelson, 1987; Dahl, 1989; Huntington, 1991; Helliwell, 1994; Henderson, 1991; Poe and Tate, 1994). That is, as the middle class grows and modernizes, citizens increasingly participate, or demand participation, in the political system and become more willing to challenge the status quo enforced by political elites. For example, as citizens become wealthier and better educated, they will demand greater political equality for all, and exhibit less tolerance of political violence and repression. Therefore, a significant segment of the society is likely to demand social and economic reforms that take into account the concerns of not only the middle class, but more importantly, also those at the lowest economic levels, as it is they who are most at risk of human rights abuse (Clark and Clark, 1993; Richards, 1999a).

Neo-liberals would point out that MNCs often educate and train their employees, provide housing and health benefits, and enact labor standards where few, if any, previously existed. These conditions reduce the stress that leads to the kinds of domestic unrest or even political violence known to be associated with human rights violations. Moreover, MNCs and trade agreements act as agents of change by eliminating the power of local elite monopolies, as well as altering traditional value systems and social attitudes in developing countries (Diebold, 1974; Biersteker, 1978). MNC investment disrupts traditional policies designed to benefit local interest groups at the cost of less influential groups. That is, in order to induce and maintain FDI, governments must meet certain fundamental requirements, including setting up a foundation of law, establishing a nondiscriminatory policy environment, and investing in social services and infrastructure (Chhibber, 1997; Spar and Yoffie, 1999). Therefore, MNCs contribute to tearing down local elite interests and raising social conditions to a higher level in developing countries.

Taiwan is a commonly invoked example of the globalization process ensuring economic growth as well as political and social stability. For some time, Taiwan has adopted liberal economic policies, and as a result, experienced greater government respect for human rights. Much of Taiwan's early economic growth was due to MNC investment (Chang, 1998). Furthermore, as Taiwan's economy grew, so too did its middle class. Over time, the middle class increasingly called for greater political participation as well as the suppression of domestic political violence (Clark and Clark, 1993). Consequently, the Taiwanese government consistently both improved its respect for the physical-integrity rights of its citizens and reaffirmed the value of conducting free and fair elections. Indeed, even the financial turbulence of the late 1990s failed to prevent the 2000 presidential election.

Bane: The Post-Dependency Argument

Of course, neo-liberals are not the only people with an opinion on how economic globalization affects the welfare of citizens in developing countries. Others, who subscribe to a school of thought we label 'post-dependency', view the effects of globalization on government respect for human rights differently. As the moniker 'post-dependency' implies, many criticisms leveled toward foreign investment in developing countries are not new. Most criticisms targeted at FDI and MNCs, in particular, have their roots in 'dependency theory'. While accounts of the dependency argument are diverse, all share the understanding that international capitalism depends upon the exploitation of the less developed by the more developed. This is done through the corruption of local elites by external economic forces. Once 'bought', local elites bow to the desires of foreign economic interests, despite the cost to their own citizens. Rather than expanding economic growth as posited by the neo-liberals, MNCs (in particular) prevent it. Commonly, MNCs are seen to extract more money from developing countries than they invest, displace crucial indigenous capital, and contribute to local unemployment rates by promoting capital-intensive production (Gilpin, 1987; Spero and Hart, 1997).

Post-dependency differs from its predecessor both in the increased degree of threat it sees, and in the variety of manners in which this threat is posed. Threats now come not only in the form of FDI, but also bond and equity investments, collective free trade agreements governed by the developed countries, and 'hot' lending by foreign banks. Surges of international investment are not unprecedented. However, the sustained breadth, mobility, and diversity of the instruments of economic globalization presently witnessed are clearly unrivaled. Because of financial instruments such as portfolio investment, developing countries are particularly vulnerable to economic and political shocks that can cause a quick and massive outflow of capital. Capital flight is now possible with a speed and volume never seen before. This flight occurs as investors lose confidence in a country's ability to maintain stability. Stability is very important, as foreign investors are attracted to markets that exhibit sound economic and political stability. Studies have consistently shown that foreign capital tends to flow to countries with stable political environments (Maxfield, 1998; World Bank, 1999).

Because in the globalization era foreign capitalists are increasingly able to use the threat of suddenly leaving the markets of developing countries, they can extort beneficial tax and labor policies as never before. Thus, policy independence is eroded if government leaders in developing countries wish to maintain the high level of investment necessary to satisfy the domestic economic elites whose support is necessary for their persistence in power. The result is political elites being held hostage to market forces in a competitive 'race to the bottom' regarding policies on taxes, labor, and social welfare (Haggard and Maxfield, 1996; Spar and Yoffie, 1999). Prime Minister Mahathir of Malaysia, in the midst of the 1997 Asian economic crisis, railed against the ability of speculators to move 'hot' or portfolio money in and out of countries without regard to the social consequences in the crisis-burdened developing country. For instance, Mahathir's government was forced to abandon several large infrastructure projects in the face of an economic crisis and ensuing demands to reduce government spending in order to re-establish economic stability for foreign investors and IMF assistance loans. Consequently, unemployment rates continued to rise and social demands to ease the economic plight could not be met. The result was increased social unrest.

As a response to unrest, governments can resort to political repression or human rights violations. In 1994, the Venezuelan government suspended certain constitutional rights in order to deal with an internal banking crisis that threatened the economic stability of the country. Bangladesh frequently makes use of laws that permit the government to jail those deemed as terrorists or enemies of the state. This approach conveniently allows for the imprisoning of political opponents who threaten economic and political reforms implemented to attract foreign investors.

Sometimes, MNCs may even be directly pro-active in the maintenance of stability. Shell Oil has been accused of complicity with the Nigerian government in the execution of writer and activist Ken Saro-Wiwa. Shell was allegedly unhappy with Saro-Wiwa's campaign against its purported environmental devastation of the country. Public Broadcasting Service (PBS) reports that 'Human rights activists have accused Shell of paying one of Nigeria's most vicious security units to protect its interests. Earlier, Shell denied the charge, but not now' (Public Broadcasting Service).

To post-dependency adherents, political stability and economic stability are interrelated in an unfortunate manner and the drive to preserve stability is a large part of the story of globalization-induced human rights violations. Investors favor developing countries where governments implement policies that include budgetary control and cheap labor costs. The result of the restrictions necessary to produce the desired objectives is that developing countries are prevented from implementing economic and social policies designed to help their less fortunate citizens. Much-needed health and education reforms in developing countries are extremely expensive to implement. Thus, programs designed to help the masses and the poor must often be sacrificed. This situation creates a tinder-box for the abuse of human rights, as previous research has consistently shown domestic conflict to be a reliable predictor of such abuse by governments. As mentioned earlier, economic scarcity may very well drive domestic conflict or even rebellion, which must be doused in order to maintain the political and economic stability required by investors. In a circular fashion, the forced cessation of domestic conflict produced by policies designed to promote economic stability is often accompanied by an array of human rights abuses by government agents in the name of preserving political stability.

Mexico, with its membership in NAFTA, its globalization-era economic reforms, and its gross poverty and history of human rights violations, may be the best natural laboratory in which to view the post-dependency argument. Chomsky (1995: 176–7) points out:

> In the past decade of economic reform, the number of people living in extreme poverty in rural areas of Mexico has increased by almost a third. Half of the country's total population lacks resources to meet basic needs, a dramatic rise ... Following World Bank–IMF prescriptions, agricultural production was shifted to export and animal feeds—a policy that benefited agribusiness, foreign consumers, and affluent sectors in Mexico at the expense of the general population ... [A]gricultural employment declined, productive lands were abandoned, and Mexico began to import massive amounts of food. Real wages in manufacturing fell sharply. Labor's share in the gross domestic product, which had risen until the mid-seventies, has declined by well over a third. These are standard concomitants of neoliberal reforms.

These conditions, along with the privatization of communal lands for NAFTA and the resulting inability of average Mexican farmers to compete with their US and Canadian counterparts under the NAFTA guidelines, added much fuel to the fire of the 1994 Chiapas uprising. In response to this uprising, the Mexican government mounted an intense campaign of terror, resulting in widespread human rights violations such as extra-judicial killings, disappearances, imprisonment, and torture. For the post-dependency adherent, the route from economic liberalization to rebellion to repression is clear.

Mexico is not the only example, however, as in order to attract and maintain FDI, developing countries everywhere often feel the necessity to maintain a heavy hand over indigenous labor. Such policies may include curtailing union activities to keep wages low and pre-empt work stoppages. Clashes between South Korean unions and authorities have centered on such issues (Pion-Berlin, 1983; Rodrik, 1997). Frundt (1987) describes how Guatemalan authorities resorted to the systematic harassment, and even murder, of 'problematic' unionized employees and their representatives at the behest of a Texas based Coca-Cola franchisee who owned a bottling plant in Guatemala.

Three Pertinent Considerations

The arguments above leave us with three things to consider when engaging in an empirical analysis examining the relationship between economic globalization and government respect for human rights. First, the neo-liberal and post-dependency schools of thought both assume that economic globalization will affect government respect for human rights in developing countries in some manner. Second, the neo-liberal school asserts that this effect will be to increase respect for human rights, while the post-dependency school posits economic globalization will decrease respect for human rights. Third, the globalization paradigm, within which these schools of thought are couched, additionally declares that should economic globalization indeed affect government respect for human rights, its effect will be stronger in the globalization era than in the pre-globalization era. As a corollary, should the posited effect of economic globalization be found in only one era, it should be during the globalization era. Consequently, in the analysis that follows, these issues form the core of our empirical agenda.

DATA, MODEL, AND METHODS

This study uses a data set containing information about 43 developing countries for the years 1981, 1984, 1987, 1990, 1993, 1995, and 1996. We study these countries and years due to the availability of general data for our dependent variable. Because of major source biases in human rights reports, information about government respect for human rights is unreliable before 1981, thus explaining the starting point of our time series.

The actual number of cases for our analysis is reduced somewhat by missing data, as the economic data required for operationalizing our conceptualization of economic globalization are not systematically recorded across time and space for many developing countries. However, the loss of some cases for analysis is worth the sacrifice in favor of a broad conceptualization of economic globalization.

Below is our basic model for testing the effect of economic globalization on government respect for human rights in developing countries. Our analyses will include spatial and temporal variations of this model:

Government Respect for Physical-Integrity Rights = – Level of Domestic Conflict – Presence of Interstate War + Level of Democracy + Level of Economic Development – Population Size +/– Financial Globalization +/– Trade Globalization

Note that all variables are additive. Theoretically, a case could be made for including interaction effects, especially between globalization and economic development, or between globalization and domestic conflict. However, using joint F tests and calculating what Jaccard *et al.* (1990) call an 'eta squared' index, we found no evidence in our sample that interaction effects (of the types tested for) were present. Consequently, the model we present is additive.

In addition to interaction effects, there exists the possibility that government respect for physical-integrity rights is a predictor of a country's level of economic globalization. That is, an environment of government respect for human rights is a stable environment, and investors will be attracted to this atmosphere as they will feel more secure in their investments. As Minister Peter Hain of the United Kingdom Foreign and Commonwealth Office told the UN Commission on Human Rights, 'Countries which protect and advance human rights and pursue good governance win international confidence. They attract both greater international development assistance and greater foreign private sector investment' (Foreign and Commonwealth Office, 2000: 72). Although we are specifically concerned in this chapter with the relationship between human rights and economic globalization in the direction that globalization affects government respect for these rights, we need to be aware, for both theoretical and statistical reasons, that the relationship may be two-way. Thus, we used three-stage-least-squares estimation to examine this possibility. We found that in our data, government respect for physical-integrity rights was not a significant predictor of a country's level of economic globalization.

All signs for the variables in the model above are those that previous research would lead us to expect. A (+) indicates that we expect a variable to *increase* government respect for physical-integrity rights. A (–) indicates that we expect a variable to *decrease* government respect for these rights. Our variables for economic globalization, however, have been assigned a (+/–) as the two schools of thought reviewed earlier present divergent expectations.

Government Respect for Human Rights

In looking for an appropriate yardstick to measure the performance of political systems, we should look toward the effect of governments on their citizens' quality of life. In this study, we focus on government respect for physical-integrity rights, one category of internationally recognized human rights. Physical-integrity rights include the rights against torture, disappearance, extrajudicial killing, and political imprisonment. To this point, almost all existing scientific studies of government respect for human rights have focused on physical-integrity rights. The duty of governments to respect physical-integrity rights is laid out in the Universal Declaration of Human Rights (1948), The International Covenant on Civil and Political Liberties (1966), and many regional and other pacts.

We use Cingranelli and Richards's (1999a) measure of government respect for physical-integrity rights as our dependent variable. While the Political Terror Scale (PTS) is the most widely-used indicator of this phenomenon, Cingranelli and Richards show that the PTS suffers from an *a priori* asserted pattern of respect for rights that does not hold up to empirical testing, and that it is also constructed in such a way that human rights conditions cannot be differentiated from the human rights practices of governments. This latter problem is the more important of the two: while nongovernmental actors can affect human rights conditions in a country, we are interested here only in the practices of governments.

Cingranelli and Richards's (1999a) indicator is a nine-point additive scale derived from a Mokken scale analysis of four ordinal indicators of government respect for physical integrity – the rights against torture, extrajudicial killing, disappearance, and political imprisonment. This index ranges from zero (no respect for any of the four physical-integrity rights) to eight (full respect for all four physical-integrity rights). These scores, indicating the level of government respect for physical-integrity rights, are based on information about government respect for these rights found in both Amnesty International's *Annual Report* and the US State Department's annual *Country Reports on Human Rights Practices*.

Measuring Economic Globalization

We employ a two-dimensional operationalization of economic globalization. We do so because globalization really affects developing economies on two different fronts, finance and trade. Thus, we assert the existence of two separate dimensions of economic globalization: financial globalization and trade globalization. Financial globalization is exerted in two primary ways. First, through FDI, MNCs wield influence within a developing country by maintaining a controlling stake in a local operation.[2] Moreover, FDI tends to represent a long-term commitment to local markets. Second, foreign investors also exert influence by investing in a developing country's assets for dividend earnings. This is portfolio investment.[3] Portfolio investment, unlike FDI, is often associated with short-term financial commitment in developing countries. Trade globalization is exerted in developing countries by exposing domestic enterprises to international competition. Local firms that are unable to compete successfully fall by the wayside while successful firms become more efficient and find new markets for their products.

In creating our indicators of economic globalization for the analysis, there are two primary dimensional concerns. First, our conceptualization of economic globalization demands that our indicator of financial globalization can be shown to occupy a separate dimensional space from our indicator of trade globalization. Second, our conceptualization of financial globalization incorporates two phenomena, net inflow of FDI and net inflow of portfolio investment. Thus, combining these two instruments assumes that they both can be shown to belong to a unidimensional space that we call financial globalization.

We can use a single principal-components analysis to demonstrate that FDI and portfolio inflows can be shown to be unidimensional and that they occupy a dimension separate from trade globalization. Our FDI and portfolio investment flow data are in 1987 US dollars and were drawn from the World Bank's *World Development Indicators on CD-ROM* (1997c). Trade globalization is measured as the level of trade openness for our developing countries. Openness is typically operationalized in the literature as the sum of the value of imports and exports of goods and services of a country, measured as a percentage of that country's gross domestic product (Sachs and Warner, 1995). The data used to compute this measure of openness were taken from the IMF's *Direction of Trade Statistics* (various years).

Our principal-components analysis found that the two financial variables, FDI and portfolio investment flows, were closely related enough to be called unidimensional when combined. Their factor loading scores were 0.913 and 0.911, respectively. As expected, trade openness was not dimensionally related to the two financial variables. Indeed, its factor loading score was only 0.024.

These similarities and differences having been demonstrated, our indicator of financial globalization is a principal-component factor score representing a country-year's net FDI and portfolio investment flows. Our indicator of trade globalization is the trade-openness variable as operationalized above. The correlation between financial globalization and trade globalization is a slight 0.018.

Alternative Explanations

Four studies (Mitchell and McCormick, 1988; Henderson 1991, 1993; Poe and Tate, 1994) are primarily responsible for introducing a set of variables, now commonly included in quantitative analyses of human rights, that serve as controls for phenomena other than factors of immediate interest (such as economic globalization, here) that may influence government respect for physical-integrity rights. The most commonly used indicators are level of economic development, level of domestic conflict or presence of civil war, interstate war or level of external conflict, level of democracy, and population size. The reliability of these indicators as predictors of government respect for physical integrity rights has been further established by subsequent studies such as Poe *et al.* 1999; Camp Keith 1999; Richards 1999a, 1999b; and Richards *et al.* 2001. We follow the lead of these studies, and drawing on this previous research, we use Freedom House's political-rights index as our indicator of level of democracy; logged gross national product per capita in thousands of dollars as our indicator of level of economic development; and the log of total population to measure population size.

The indicator of domestic conflict used in this study is the same one employed by Cingranelli and Richards (1999b). It is a logged, weighted index based on seven event-count variables (assassinations, general strikes, guerrilla warfare, major governmental crises, riots, revolutions, and anti-government demonstrations) culled from Arthur Banks's *Cross-Polity Time-Series Data* (1971).[4] Our indicator of external conflict, also the same as that employed by Cingranelli and Richards (1999b), is a dichotomous variable indicating whether or not a country is militarily involved in an interstate militarized action. Some examples of this would be war, sending peacekeeping troops into hostilities, or border skirmishes with a contiguous country. This indicator is adapted from the 'Hostility Level' variable contained in version 2.10 of the Militarized Interstate Dispute (MID) data collection compiled by the Correlates of War (COW) Project.[5]

ANALYSIS RESULTS

We depart from the tradition of studies in this area as we eschew pooling our cases on a global basis. Instead, we conduct separate analyses for four regions: Africa, Asia, the Middle East, and Latin America. Table 3.1 shows the countries, grouped by region, included in our analyses. The cases selected were among those on a list of developing countries published by the World Bank (1997c). They were also picked randomly from a sample of 80 countries for which we had data available for the dependent variable. We conduct separate regional analyses because we are concerned that global pooling could conceal important variations of interest to us.

TABLE 3.1
COUNTRIES INCLUDED IN EMPIRICAL ANALYSES, BY REGION

Africa	Asia	Latin America	Middle East
Benin	Burma (Myanmar)	Argentina	Algeria
Burkina Faso	India	Bolivia	Egypt
Burundi	Indonesia	Brazil	Iran
Cameroon	Laos	Chile	Jordan
Chad	Malaysia	Colombia	Morocco
Ethiopia	Pakistan	Costa Rica	Syria
Ghana	Thailand	El Salvador	Tunisia
Malawi		Guatemala	Turkey
Mali		Haiti	
Mauritania		Mexico	
Niger		Paraguay	
Nigeria		Peru	
Tanzania		Uruguay	
Uganda			
Zambia			

Changes From One Era to the Next

Despite differences of opinion on whether economic globalization will increase or decrease the level of government respect for physical-integrity rights in developing countries, there is general agreement that some change has occurred in respect for these rights from the pre-globalization era to the globalization era. Accordingly, we will first seek to determine the validity of the latter proposition. As already noted, for Asia, Latin America, and the Middle East, we define the pre-globalization era as 1981–89 and the globalization era as 1990–96. In contrast, Africa's pre-globalization era is defined as 1981–92 and its globalization era as 1993–96.

Table 3.2 shows the level and change in level of government respect for physical-integrity rights, financial globalization, and trade globalization in the pre-globalization and globalization eras. From Table 3.2 Section A, we see that in two of our four regions, the level of respect for physical-integrity rights has decreased. While the Middle East demonstrates the greatest decrease in respect for these rights, Asia is not far behind. None of these decreases, however, are statistically significant. Most noticeably in Table 3.2 Section A, government respect for these rights in Latin America manifested

TABLE 3.2
PRE-GLOBALIZATION ERA AND GLOBALIZATION ERA LEVELS AND
CHANGE IN LEVELS OF:

A. Government respect for physical integrity rights

	Pre-globalization level	Globalization level	Change
Africa	4.28	4.53	+0.25
Asia	3.20	2.75	-0.45
Latin America	3.00	4.04	+1.04*
Middle East	3.70	3.22	-0.48

B. Financial globalization

	Pre-globalization level	Globalization level	Change
Africa	-0.36	-0.28	+0.08*
Asia	-0.22	0.60	+0.82*
Latin America	-0.15	0.80	+0.95*
Middle East	-0.31	-0.17	+0.14*

C. Trade globalization

	Pre-globalization level	Globalization level	Change
Africa	39.42	44.39	+4.97
Asia	34.98	44.17	+9.19
Latin America	29.67	35.72	+6.05*
Middle East	42.50	46.28	+3.78

* $p < 0.05$.

a statistically significant increase of an entire scale score.[6] Cingranelli and Richards (1999a) point out that a change from a scale score of three to a scale score of four represents a decline in the number of confirmed instances of torture by government agents. This is intuitively appealing in the Latin American case, as what we refer to here as the 'pre-globalization era' represents a time when autocratic regimes in places such as Chile and Argentina had come to an end, and turmoil in countries such as El Salvador and Guatemala had also decreased greatly. Table 3.2 Section A also shows what global pooling can hide. Were we to pool all our regions, we would see that government respect for physical-integrity rights in all the developing countries during the pre-globalization era averaged 3.5, and it averaged 3.6 during the globalization era for an overtime change of +0.10 between the two periods (statistically insignificant). These figures conceal important regional differences.

We posited a pre-globalization era and a globalization era, with economic globalization increasing significantly between these two periods. Our next task is accordingly to determine whether there is a marked overtime difference in the observed levels of economic globalization (in terms of both finance and trade) as hypothesized. Table 3.2 Section B shows the level of and change in the factor score for indicating a country-year's level of financial globalization (the combined level of FDI and portfolio investment) in the pre-globalization and globalization eras. We present factor scores rather than real dollar amounts because of the unwieldy nature of the rather large sums involved. What is really sought here is a comparison in relative terms, which the factor scores allow us to do. In order to understand what these scores represent in some real sense, however, one should keep in mind that the lowest score in Table 3.2 Section B, -0.36, represents a combined level of FDI and portfolio investment of about $66,638,370. An example of this would be Niger in 1987. The highest score in Section B, 0.80, represents a combined level of FDI and portfolio investment of about $5,500,000,000. An approximate (slightly higher) example of this would be India in 1995.[7] Note that a negative factor score does not necessarily indicate a loss in combined investment.

Table 3.2 Section B tells us that all four regions evidenced a statistically significant increase in their level of financial globalization from the pre-globalization period to the globalization period. The largest increase was seen in Latin America, with Asia a close second. Increases in the Middle East and Africa were much less than in Latin America and Asia.[8] That Africa evidenced the smallest increase is not surprising, given its late start and low initial base. Were we to view the relative level of financial globalization as a hierarchy, we would see that nothing has changed between the two eras. That is, Latin America began and ended with the highest levels of financial globalization while Africa began and ended with the lowest levels. Asia and the Middle East remained in their intermediary positions.

Table 3.2 Section C shows the level and change in level of trade globalization for our four regions. In our data set, these values, indicating the 'openness' of a country with regard to trade, range from a low of 1.73 (Burma, 1996) to a high of 157.88 (Malaysia, 1996). We see in Table 3.2 Section C that while all four regions experienced an increase in trade globalization, only one of those regions, Latin America, experienced statistically significant growth.[9] In addition, the regional hierarchy of trade globalization is different from that for financial globalization. In our data, the Middle East manifests, on average, the most 'open' economic environment regarding trade, while Latin America, although significantly improved, offers the least open environment. This may change over time, however, as Latin American nations may follow Mexico's lead in entering bilateral trade agreements with countries outside of the Americas. In recent years, Mexico has forged important trade agreements with the United States and Canada (NAFTA), and most recently at the time of writing, with Israel and the European Union.

Table 3.2, Sections A, B and C, show us that Latin America has been the most dynamic of our four regions with regard to change, evidencing a statistically significant increase in its average level of government respect for physical-integrity rights, average level of financial globalization, and average level of trade globalization. All regions demonstrated a statistically significant increase in their average level of financial globalization. Asia and the Middle East showed a decrease (statistically insignificant) in their average level of government respect for physical-integrity rights, and an increase (statistically insignificant) in their average level of trade globalization. Africa showed insignificant increases in both respect for human rights and trade globalization.

Economic Globalization and Government Respect for Human Rights

Our next line of inquiry concerns how well our indicators of financial and trade globalization serve as predictors of the level of government respect for physical-integrity rights in developing countries. We are looking to answer three questions in this section of our inquiry: First, does economic globalization actually have any statistically significant effect on government respect for physical-integrity rights? Second, if any type of globalization does manifest an impact, is this effect positive or negative? And third, are the expected effects stronger in the globalization era than in the pre-globalization era? Any effect can be positive (increased respect for human rights) or negative (decreased respect for human rights). As in the previous section, we pursue a separate comparison of the pre-globalization and globalization eras for each region.

Following Richards *et al.* (2001), we employ ordered-logit maximum-likelihood analysis to estimate our models, as our dependent variable is ordinal. Ordinary least-squares (OLS) regression, the most commonly used technique in human rights research, requires data to be distributed with an error term of zero mean and constant variance. The variance of probability models, however, is heteroskedastic (bow-shaped), rendering the use of OLS on ordinal dependent variables a violation of the constant error-variance assumption of OLS. Consequently, ordered-logit is a more suitable estimation technique, as it takes into account the particular error distribution of ordered dependent variables. To address the threat of heteroskedasticity, we report robust standard errors.

Table 3.3 shows the results of two ordered-logit estimations for the region of Africa. One set of results is for the pre-globalization era, and the other set is for the globalization era. Chi-squared tests indicate that both of these models are significant improvements upon their null counterparts. Typically, the first question to ask at this point in an analysis is 'How do these results compare with what past research would lead us to believe?' Since the analysis of the globalization variables is new, this question then

TABLE 3.3
AFRICA: ORDERED-LOGIT ESTIMATIONS OF THE EFFECT OF ECONOMIC
GLOBALIZATION ON GOVERNMENT RESPECT FOR PHYSICAL-INTEGRITY
RIGHTS IN THE PRE-GLOBALIZATION AND GLOBALIZATION ERAS

Variable	Pre-globalization	Globalization
Domestic conflict	-0.34** (0.11)	-0.34** (0.20)
External conflict	-0.92 (0.89)	-0.18 (1.32)
Democracy	0.64 (0.55)	0.78** (0.34)
Economic development	0.54 (0.60)	0.29 (0.74)
Population size	-0.02 (0.62)	-0.27 (0.41)
Financial globalization	11.35 (7.74)	0.65 (0.91)
Trade globalization	-0.02 (0.03)	0.03 (0.02)
N	54	34
Prob > X.	0.00	0.00
Log likelihood	-92.90	-55.66

Figures in parentheses are heteroskedasticity-corrected robust standard errors.
 * $p < 0.10$.
 ** $p < 0.05$.

concerns our control variables. It should be noted that unlike previous research based on cross-regional (or global) pooled analyses, our study is regionally specific. Thus, we may reasonably expect some differences from the results reported by prior research.

We see in Table 3.3 that in Africa, a country's level of domestic conflict was found to decrease government respect for human rights in both eras, although it is a less statistically significant predictor in the globalization era. Chi-squared tests indicate that both of these models are significant improvements upon their null counterparts. Democracy is a strong predictor of respect for human rights in the globalization era. That is, increases in a country's level of democracy are associated with increases in government respect for human rights. With the end of the Cold War and the beginning of the globalization era in Africa only a few years apart, this result supports Cingranelli and Richards's (1999b) similar finding. The signs for both statistically significant indicators are as previous research would have us expect. The major finding from Table 3.3, however, is that neither financial nor trade globalization turns out to be statistically significant predictors of the level of government respect for physical-integrity rights in Africa, in either era.

TABLE 3.4
ASIA: ORDERED-LOGIT ESTIMATIONS OF THE EFFECT OF ECONOMIC
GLOBALIZATION ON GOVERNMENT RESPECT FOR PHYSICAL-INTEGRITY
RIGHTS IN THE PRE-GLOBALIZATION AND GLOBALIZATION ERAS

Variable	Pre-globalization	Globalization
Domestic conflict	-0.03	-0.14
	(0.32)	(0.30)
External conflict	-0.43	-1.59
	(1.72)	(1.18)
Democracy	1.67**	0.69*
	(0.72)	(0.42)
Economic development	-1.37	1.23
	(4.05)	(1.04)
Population size	-1.80**	-2.14**
	(0.74)	(0.93)
Financial globalization	2.62	0.70
	(4.06)	(0.93)
Trade globalization	0.01	-0.02
	(0.11)	(0.02)
N	20	23
Prob > X.	0.00	0.00
Log likelihood	-21.59	-30.39

Figures in parentheses are heteroskedasticity-corrected robust standard errors.
  * $p < 0.10$.
 ** $p < 0.05$.

Table 3.4 shows the results of two ordered-logit estimations for Asia. Chi-squared tests indicate that both of these models are significant improvements upon their null counterparts. We see that in Asia, democracy has had a statistically significant and positive effect on government respect for human rights in both eras, although the effect has declined in the globalization era. Population size, however, has had a statistically significant and negative effect on government respect for human rights in both eras, although in this case the effect has been enhanced in the globalization era. Both of these effects are as we would be led to expect by previous research. As for Africa, however, neither financial nor trade globalization was a statistically significant determinant of the level of government respect for physical-integrity rights in Asia during either era.

Table 3.5 shows the results of two ordered-logit estimations for Latin America. Chi-squared tests indicate that both of these models are significant improvements upon their null counterparts. We see that in this region, democracy has a statistically significant effect, increasing respect for human rights in both eras, with the effect being larger in the globalization era. Domestic conflict is a statistically significant predictor of decreased

TABLE 3.5
LATIN AMERICA: ORDERED-LOGIT ESTIMATIONS OF THE EFFECT OF
ECONOMIC GLOBALIZATION ON GOVERNMENT RESPECT FOR PHYSICAL
INTEGRITY RIGHTS IN THE PRE-GLOBALIZATION AND GLOBALIZATION ERAS

Variable	Pre-globalization	Globalization
Domestic conflict	-0.61**	-0.21
	(0.16)	(0.21)
External conflict	-0.74	-0.44
	(1.07)	(0.84)
Democracy	1.02**	1.18**
	(0.25)	(0.32)
Economic development	-0.21	-0.00
	(0.67)	(0.72)
Population size	-0.01	-1.56**
	(0.48)	(0.42)
Financial globalization	-1.22	0.44**
	(1.48)	(0.21)
Trade globalization	0.04	-0.00
	(0.03)	(0.02)
N	38	46
Prob > X.	0.00	0.00
Log likelihood	-58.89	-76.44

Figures in parentheses are heteroskedasticity-corrected robust standard errors.
 * $p < 0.10$.
** $p < 0.05$.

respect for human rights in the pre-globalization era, but not in the globalization era. This result makes some sense, as the transition into the globalization era coincided with the end of several bitter and long domestic conflicts in Latin America, particularly in Central America. There is no doubt that these conflicts were the fuel on which the fire of gross human rights violations in the region fed. In addition, the globalization era began at about the same time as the end of the Cold War, when superpower funding for these conflicts dried up. Table 3.5 also shows that in the globalization era, population size is a statistically significant predictor of decreased government respect for physical-integrity rights. Previous research anticipates this result, given the high rate of population growth in Latin America, especially in the urban areas.

The most interesting finding in Table 3.5 is that financial globalization is a statistically significant predictor of increased government respect for human rights in the globalization period. This tendency lends some support to the neo-liberal argument outlined earlier. The fact that financial globalization goes from being statistically insignificant to statistically significant is worth noting.

TABLE 3.6
THE MIDDLE EAST. ORDERED-LOGIT ESTIMATIONS OF THE EFFECT OF
ECONOMIC GLOBALIZATION ON GOVERNMENT RESPECT FOR PHYSICAL-
INTEGRITY RIGHTS IN THE PRE-GLOBALIZATION AND GLOBALIZATION ERAS

Variable	Pre-globalization	Globalization
Domestic conflict	-0.38	-0.47**
	(0.32)	(0.18)
External conflict	-6.96**	-0.57
	(1.41)	(0.98)
Democracy	-0.89	0.72*
	(0.58)	(0.45)
Economic development	-3.61*	-4.49**
	(1.93)	(1.42)
Population size	6.31**	-2.11*
	(1.54)	(1.26)
Financial globalization	-19.13**	3.41**
	(8.22)	(1.41)
Trade globalization	0.25**	0.02
	(0.05)	(0.03)
N	23	27
Prob > X.	0.00	0.00
Log likelihood	-21.17	-27.51

Figures in parentheses are heteroskedasticity-corrected robust standard errors.
 * p <0.10.
 ** p <0.05.

Table 3.6 shows the results of two ordered-logit estimations for the
Middle East. Chi-squared tests indicate that both of these models are
significant improvements upon their null counterparts. The results for the
Middle East are unique among our four regions. First, we see that domestic
conflict is statistically significantly associated with decreased government
respect for human rights in the globalization period only. This phenomenon
is seen in Turkey, Egypt and, to some extent, Jordan and Algeria. Next, we
see that external conflict is statistically significantly associated with
decreased government respect for human rights in the pre-globalization
period only. The pre-globalization period averaged twice as many country-
years showing a significant level of external conflict than the globalization
era.

Table 3.6 shows democracy reliably associated with increased government respect for physical-integrity rights in the globalization period only.
This result does not mean that there was a significant trend toward
democratization in this period; it rather reflects how some short-term
democratic concessions in the early 1990s in countries such as Turkey and
Jordan produced modest improvements in government respect for physical-

integrity rights. One surprising result in Table 3.6 is that a country's population size is statistically significantly associated with respect for human rights in both eras, positively in the pre-globalization era and negatively in the globalization era. It is a more reliable predictor in the pre-globalization era. Although there were only modest gains in population size in our Middle East sample from one era to the next, there were some noticeable declines in respect for human rights (see Table 3.2 Section A). That is, in the pre-globalization era, respect for human rights was at a higher level, and population growth was modest. In the globalization era, respect for human rights declined noticeably, but population growth was more modest than in the preceding era, thus accounting for the smaller, less statistically significant, negative coefficient.

Concerning the relationship between economic globalization and government respect for physical-integrity rights, Table 3.6 provides some interesting results. Financial globalization is a statistically significant predictor of government respect for human rights in both eras, but the effect (sign) changes from negative in the pre-globalization era to positive in the globalization era. This change seems reasonable. Table 3.2 Section B shows that the average level of financial globalization in our Middle East sample was higher in the globalization era than in the pre-globalization era. Examining the data in more detail, we see that for most of these countries, the level of financial globalization in 1996 is the same or slightly lower than the level in 1981. So how then can the globalization era average be higher? The higher average is because the level of financial globalization in many of these countries declined after 1981 (sometimes precipitously), only to rebound and stabilize in the globalization period. At the same time, remember that on average, respect for human rights was higher in the pre-globalization era than in the globalization era. Thus, we have a situation in the pre-globalization era where there are declining levels of financial globalization, and stable, but relatively high, and sometimes increasing levels of respect for human rights. Consequently, there is a statistically significant, negative coefficient.

A few examples help to shed light on the statistical patterns for the Middle East. Tunisia, while encountering a rise in financial globalization, saw its level of respect for human rights rise from a four (full respect for the rights against disappearances and extrajudicial killings) to a six (full respect for the rights against disappearances and extrajudicial killings and partial respect for the rights against torture and political imprisonment). Iran and Syria, also experiencing increases in financial globalization, saw their levels of respect for human rights rise from one to two and from two to three, respectively. As mentioned before, however, a positive coefficient can also indicate mutual decline. For instance, Turkey's level of financial globalization fell from 1993 to 1996; its level of respect for human rights also fell. Egypt experienced a decline in financial globalization from 1990 to 1993, and this drop was accompanied by a loss in respect for human rights. The level of government respect for human rights in Jordan fell from six to four as the level financial globalization fell from 1993 to 1995.

Table 3.6 shows that in our Middle East sample, trade globalization is statistically significantly and positively associated with government respect for human rights, but only in the pre-globalization period. This is one of those instances where the positive coefficient is certainly driven by mutual decline. That is, reductions in trade globalization are associated with reductions in the level of government respect for physical-integrity rights. As shown in Table 3.2 Section A, it is true that on average, the level of respect for human rights was higher in the pre-globalization era than in the globalization era. However, averages can be deceiving. Many countries in our Middle East sample experienced a decline in their level of respect for human rights during the pre-globalization period. Despite this occasionally steep decline, however, the initial level of government respect in these countries was so much higher than what they fell to in the globalization period that the average level of this variable remained higher. Algeria experienced a decline in trade globalization from 58 to 24 in the pre-globalization period, accompanied by a drop in respect for human rights from a near-perfect seven to a five. In this same era, Jordan's level of trade globalization fell from 111 to 59, and Egypt's from 49 to 15. Consequently, both of these countries experienced a loss in respect for human rights from a five to a four.

DISCUSSION AND CONCLUSION

In this chapter, we sought to discover the nature of the relationship (if any) between economic globalization and government respect for human rights in developing countries. First, we outlined two schools of thought with differing opinions about the nature of this relationship. We then tested this relationship using summary statistics and maximum-likelihood ordered-logit analyses on a data set comprising 43 developing countries. Our analyses were divided by era and region. We examined two eras: pre-globalization (1981–89) and globalization (1990–96); and four regions: Africa, Asia, Latin America and the Middle East. Our findings indicate significant differences among the four regions that would have been masked had we used pooled analyses.

In Latin America, financial globalization was found to be reliably associated with increased government respect for human rights in the globalization era. Many Latin American countries chose to pursue import substitution for much of the 1970s and 1980s. Thus, macroeconomic conditions were not favorable to attracting foreign investment until they began to adopt neo-liberal economic principles. In addition, the globalization era saw the end of many domestic conflicts that were previously associated with gross violations of human rights. There can be no doubt that the end of these conflicts increased the attractiveness of the region to investors. Investors require incentives other than low labor costs and tax incentives. They are also concerned over the existence of a legal and regulatory structure to ensure property rights and the operation of an efficient economy. In order to attain this environment, governments must implement the necessary and appropriate institutional foundations for a market economy. An efficient market requires the rule of law, transparent regulations, and the free movement of production factors. Therefore, economic globalization promotes domestic change, including the enhancement of the citizens' political rights. Indeed, Latin America evidenced not only the largest increase in the volume of financial globalization from one era to the next, but also the highest absolute score for this variable among the four regions in the globalization era.

In the Middle East, both financial and trade globalization were reliably associated with government respect for human rights. In the pre-globalization era, financial globalization was associated with decreased respect for human rights, while trade globalization was associated with increased respect. In the globalization era, however, financial globalization was associated with increased respect for human rights, and trade globalization was not reliably associated with respect for human rights at all. As in Latin America, most countries in the Middle East did not begin to open their doors to financial globalization until the beginning of the 1990s. Consequently, we see a dramatic reversal in effect, from hurting human rights to helping them.

In Africa and Asia, neither financial nor trade globalization manifested a statistically significant relationship with government respect for human rights, in either era. This finding should not be surprising for Africa, as its countries have only relatively recently opened their borders to the process of globalization. It was not until 1993 that most African nations began to become more receptive to FDI and portfolio investment. Conversely, the same null result for Asia is somewhat surprising, especially concerning financial globalization. Table 3.2 Section B shows that Asia experienced a statistically significant increase in financial globalization from one era to the next, and that it was second only to Latin America in its level of financial globalization.

So, who are right, neo-liberals or post-dependency adherents? Both schools are correct in their shared proposition that economic globalization has some effect on government respect for human rights in developing countries. This proposition, however, appears to be true only at some times and in some places. Our analyses included two economic globalization components for two eras in four regions. Thus, our analyses contained 16 coefficients representing the relationship between economic globalization and respect for human rights. Only four (or 25 per cent) of these coefficients were reliably associated with government respect for human rights. Thus, in most times and places, economic globalization did not affect government respect for human rights. In addition, its effects in Latin America and the Middle East varied by the type of economic globalization (finance versus trade).

Of the four statistically significant coefficients representing the relationship between economic globalization and respect for human rights, three pertained to financial globalization. It seems accordingly that financial globalization has had a larger role in government respect for human rights in the developing countries than trade globalization. There are several possible reasons why trade globalization proved to be relatively ineffective. Developing countries have gradually reduced tariffs for many years. In fact, non-tariff barriers may simply be replacing tariffs. Furthermore, many developing countries are joining (and emphasizing) regional trade blocs. It is possible that members of regional trade organizations are discriminating against non-member countries, thus limiting the benefits of multilateral trade (World Bank, 1997). A recent study suggests that countries that emphasize broad liberalization grow faster than countries that join regional trade blocs (Vamvakidis, 1999).

The acid test of which school of thought is 'correct', however, lies in the signs of the statistically significant globalization coefficients. Of these four coefficients, three are positive, indicating a reliable association with increased government respect for human rights. They offer some degree of support for the neo-liberal argument that economic globalization works for, and not against, the social benefit of citizens in developing countries. These results also corroborate similar findings by Richards et al. (2001). The only negative coefficient represented financial globalization in the Middle East in the pre-globalization era. Given the Middle East's statistically significant increase in financial globalization (see Table 3.2), however, coupled with the fact that financial globalization is associated with increased respect in the globalization era, this negative coefficient does not appear to harm the neo-liberal argument.

Earlier, we maintained that the globalization paradigm asserts that any effect of economic globalization found in the globalization era should be greater than in the pre-globalization era. Or, as a corollary, if effects were to be found in only one era, it should be the globalization era. We found no strong support for these arguments. In the Middle East, the financial globalization coefficient was significantly larger in the pre-globalization era. While in Latin America financial globalization was significant in the globalization but not pre-globalization era, the opposite was true for trade globalization in the Middle East.

Our most general conclusion is that in those developing countries where it has an effect, economic globalization is reliably associated with increased government respect for human rights. Given that economic globalization is a phenomenon on the increase, this generalization bodes well for many. There is a serious caveat, however, in that economic globalization does not significantly promote respect for human rights in all regions or at all times. The results for Africa and Asia caution us against over-generalization.

Our findings have significantly contributed to the research program on the determinants of government respect for human rights. They indicate that the control variables commonly employed in large cross-national pooled analyses are pertinent factors for understanding government respect for human rights, although they do vary by region and era in both their predictive ability and the direction (positive or negative) of their impact. While all of the control indicators employed here were statistically significant indicators of government respect for human rights, they were so only in some eras and countries. Moreover, some indicators, such as democracy, population size and democracy, featured coefficient signs that appear occasionally counter-intuitive in view of the results reported by previous research.

Several interesting questions are raised by the association between economic globalization and government respect for human rights found in our study. Perhaps the most interesting is, 'Why did economic globalization (especially the financial dimension) not affect government respect for human rights in Asia and Africa?' Another question is 'Through what processes did economic globalization affect government respect for human rights?' That is, what political changes produced by economic globalization were responsible for the increase in government respect for human rights in those cases where such an effect was evident? A third question is 'Why does financial globalization affect government respect for human rights so much more significantly than trade globalization?' We have engaged in some preliminary speculation regarding these questions, but they truly require a more case-intensive approach than is possible in this chapter. Finally, we end with another caveat. Not much time has passed since the beginning of the globalization era; we must re-investigate the pertinent empirical relationships after more time has passed in order to make sure that the apparent current benefits of globalization do not induce a 'hangover' at some later time.

NOTES

1. Donnelly (1989: 69) defines a life of human dignity as one in which a person is 'an equal and autonomous member of society enjoying the full range of human rights'. We use the terms 'physical-integrity rights' and 'human rights' interchangeably in this chapter. This usage does not imply that physical-integrity rights can represent the complete range of internationally recognized human rights.
2. The World Bank defines FDI as any investment that accrues at least 10 per cent of the voting stock of a foreign enterprise.
3. Portfolio investment is defined as the purchase of stocks and bonds of less than 10 per cent of the outstanding stock of foreign enterprises.
4. Our citation for the Cross-Polity data is 1971, the latest published edition for these data. These data have been continuously updated by Arthur Banks through 1995. David Richards, among others, updated the data to 1996.
5. This indicator was updated by David Richards, among others, using the same country files for the compilation of *The Political Handbook of the World*. We thank Tom Muller at the *Handbook* for access to those materials.
6. All difference-of-mean tests reported are one-tailed.
7. These figures are in 1987 US dollars. The actual range of scores was from -0.53 (a *loss* of $362,000,000 in combined investment) to 7.88 (a level of $33,259,999,232 in combined investment inflows).
8. These small amounts of change are nevertheless statistically significant. Difference-of-means tests take into account means, Ns, and standard deviations.
9. While Asia had a larger absolute amount of growth, the region manifested very large standard deviations for both eras, resulting in the statistical insignificance of its change score.

REFERENCES

Banks, A.S. (1971), *Cross-Polity Time-Series Data* (Cambridge, MA: MIT Press).
Bergsten, C.F. and Schott, J.J. (1997), 'A Preliminary Evaluation of NAFTA', presented to the Subcommittee on Trade, Ways and Means Committee, US House of Representatives, 11 September.
Bhattacharya, A., Montiel, P. and Sharma, S. (1997), 'How Can Sub-Saharan Africa Attract More Private Capital Inflows?', *Finance & Development* 34, 3: 3–6.
Biersteker, T. (1978), *Distortion or Development* (Cambridge, MA: MIT Press).
Camp Keith, L. (1999), 'The United Nations International Covenant on Civil and Political Rights', *Journal of Peace Research* 36, 1: 95–114.
Caprio, G. and Demirguc-Kunt, A. (1998), 'The Role of Long-Term Finance: Theory and Evidence', *The World Bank Research Observer* 13, 2: 171–89.
Chang, H. (1998), 'Globalization, Transnational Corporations, and Economic Development', in D. Baker, G. Epstein, and R. Pollin (eds), *Globalization and Progressive Economic Policy* (Cambridge, Cambridge University Press), pp. 97–113.
Chase-Dunn, C., Kawano, Y., and Nikitin, D. (1998), 'Globalization: A World Systems Perspective', paper presented to the ad hoc session on the Future of Globalization at the International Sociological Association, XIV World Congress of Sociology.
Chhibber, A. (1997), 'The State in a Changing World', *Finance and Development* 34, 3: 17–20.
Chomsky, N. (1995), 'Time Bombs', in E. Katzenberger (ed.), *First World, Ha Ha Ha! The Zapatista Challenge* (San Francisco: City Lights Books), pp. 175–82.
Cingranelli, D.L. and Richards, D.L. (1999a), 'Measuring the Level, Pattern and Sequence of Government Respect for Physical Integrity Rights', *International Studies Quarterly* 43, 2: 407–17.
Cingranelli, D.L. and Richards, D.L. (1999b), 'Respect for Human Rights After the End of the Cold War', *Journal of Peace Research* 36, 5: 511–34.

Clark, C. and Clark, J. (1993), 'The Political Economy of Rapid Development in Taiwan', *Journal of Developing Societies* 9, 1: 198–211.

Courcelle, M. and de Lattre, A. (1996), 'The Enterprise Impulse in West Africa', *OECD Observer* 203: 32–4.

Dahl, R. (1989), *Democracy and its Critics* (New Haven, CT: Yale University Press).

Diebold, J. (1974), 'Why be Scared of Them?', *Foreign Policy* 3, 1: 79–95.

Donnelly, J. (1989), *Universal Human Rights in Theory and Practice* (Ithaca, NY: Cornell University Press).

Economist (2000), 'The World's View of Multinationals', 354, 8155: 21–2.

Eichengreen, B. (1997), 'The Tyranny of the Financial Markets', *Current History* 96, 622: 377–82.

Foreign and Commonwealth Office (2000), *Human Rights: Foreign and Commonwealth Office Annual Report 2000* (London: United Kingdom Foreign and Commonwealth Office).

Frundt, H. (1987), *Refreshing Pauses* (New York: Praeger).

Garrett, F. (1995), 'Capital Mobility, Trade, and the Domestic Politics of Economic Policy', *International Organization* 49, 4: 657–87.

Gilpin, R. (1987), *The Political Economy of International Relations* (Princeton, NJ: Princeton University Press).

Haggard, S. and Maxfield, S. (1996), 'The Political Economy of Financial Internationalization in the Developing World', in R. Keohane and H. Milner (eds), *Internationalization and Domestic Politics* (Cambridge: Cambridge University Press), pp. 209–42.

Helliwell, J. (1994), 'Empirical Linkages Between Democracy and Economic Growth', *British Journal of Political Science* 24, 2: 225–48.

Heredia, B. (1997), 'Prosper or Perish? Development in the Age of Global Capital', *Current History* 96, 622: 383–8.

Henderson, C. (1991), 'Conditions Affecting the Use of Political Repression', *Journal of Conflict Resolution* 35, 1: 120–42.

Henderson, C. (1993), 'Population Pressures and Political Repression', *Social Science Quarterly* 74, 2: 322–33.

Huntington, S. (1991), *The Third Wave: Democratization in the Late Twentieth Century* (Norman, OK: University of Oklahoma Press).

International Monetary Fund (various years), *Direction of Trade Statistics Yearbook* (Washington, DC).

Jaccard, J., Turrisi, R. and Wan, C.K. (1990), *Interaction Effects in Multiple Regression* (Newbury Park, CA: Sage).

Lerner, D. (1958), *The Passing of Traditional Society: Modernizing the Middle East* (Glencoe, IL: Free Press).

Lipset, S.M. (1959), 'Some Social Requisites of Democracy: Economic Development and Political Legitimacy', *American Political Science Review* 48, 1: 69–105.

Maxfield, S. (1998), 'Understanding the Political Implications of Financial Internationalization in Emerging Market Countries', *World Development* 26, 4: 1201–19.

Mitchell, N.J. and McCormick, J.M. (1988), 'Economic and Political Explanations of Human Rights Violations', *World Politics* 40, 4: 476–98.

Nelson, J.M. (1987), 'Political Participation', in M. Weiner and S. Huntington (eds), *Understanding Political Development* (London: Little, Brown), pp. 103–59.

Norton, R. (2000), 'Anti Trade/Pro Poverty', *Forbes* (10 January): 10–11.

Pill, H. and Pradhan, M. (1997), 'Financial Liberalization in Africa and Asia', *Finance & Development* 34, 2: 7–10.

Pion-Berlin, D. (1983), 'Political Repression and Economic Doctrines', *Comparative Political Studies* 16, 1: 37–66.

Poe, S.C. and Tate, C.N. (1994), 'Repression of Rights to Personal Integrity in the 1980s', *American Political Science Review* 88, 4: 853–72.

Poe, S.C., Tate, C.N., and Camp Keith, L. (1999), 'Repression of the Human Right to Personal Integrity Revisited', *International Studies Quarterly* 43, 2: 291–313.

Public Broadcasting Service, *Globalization and Human Rights* (www.pbs.org/globalization/corporations.html).

Richards, D.L. (1999a), *Death Takes A Holiday: National Elections, Political Parties, and Government Respect for Human Rights* (PhD thesis, State University of New York at Binghamton).

Richards, D.L. (1999b), 'Perilous Proxy: Human Rights and the Presence of National Elections', *Social Science Quarterly* 80, 4: 648–65.

Richards, D.L., Gelleny, R. and Sacko, D. (2001), 'Money With a Mean Streak? Foreign Economic Penetration and Government Respect for Human Rights in Developing Countries', *International Studies Quarterly* 45, 2: 219–39.

Rocard, M. (1999), 'Relaunching African Development', *OECD Observer* 216: 44–6.

Rodrik, D. (1997), *Has Globalization Gone Too Far?* (Washington, DC: Institute for International Economics).

Sachs, J. and Warner, A. (1995), 'Economic Reform and the Process of Global Integration', *Brookings Papers on Economic Activity* 5, 1: 1–118.

Schott, J. and Watal, J. (2000), 'Decision-making in the WTO,' *International Economics Policy Briefs* (Washington, DC: International Institute of Economics).

Singh, A. and Weise, B.A. (1998), 'Emerging Stock Markets, Portfolio Capital Flows and Long-term Economic Growth: Micro and Macroeconomic Perspectives', *World Development* 26, 4: 607–22.

Spar, D. (1998), 'The Spotlight and the Bottom Line: How Multinationals Export Human Rights', *Foreign Affairs* 77, 2: 7–12.

Spar, D. and Yoffie, D. (1999), 'Multinational Enterprises and the Prospects for Justice', *Journal of International Affairs* 52, 2: 557–82.

Spero, J. and Hart, J. (1997), *The Politics of International Relations* (New York: St Martin's Press).

Tamirisa, T.T. (1999), 'Exchange and Capital Controls as Barriers to Trade', *IMF Staff Papers* 46, 1: 69–88.

United Nations (1995), *World Economic and Social Survey 1995* (New York).

United Nations (1996), *World Economic and Social Survey 1996* (New York).

United Nations (1998), *World Economic and Social Survey 1998* (New York).

United Nations (1999), *World Economic and Social Survey 1999* (New York).

Vamvakidis, A. (1999), 'Regional Trade Agreements or Broad Liberalization: Which Path Leads to Faster Growth?', *IMF Staff Papers* 46, 1: 42–68.

World Bank (1995), *World Development Report: Workers in an Integrating World* (Washington, DC).

World Bank (1997a), *World Development Report 1997* (Washington, DC).

World Bank (1997b), *Global Development Finance* (Washington, DC).

World Bank (1997c), *World Development Indicators on CD-ROM* (Washington, DC).

World Bank (1999), *Global Development Finance* (Washington, DC).

World Trade Organization (1996), 'Foreign Direct Investment Seen as Primary Motor of Globalization, Says WTO Director-General', Press Release 42 (Geneva).

World Trade Organization (1999a), 'Report from G-15 Conference on Globalization and its Economic and Social Impacts', Presented to the Third Session of the World Trade Organization Ministerial Conference (Seattle).

World Trade Organization (1999b), *Annual Report 1999* (Geneva).

4

Electoral Institutions and Economic Performance in Africa, 1970–92

KAREN E. FERREE AND SMITA SINGH

INTRODUCTION

Viewing democratization solely as a globalizing process glosses over both possible regional political differences and the unique historical trajectories of democratic or partially democratic institutions in individual countries. Following what Samuel Huntington (1991) called the 'third wave of democratization', many African countries instituted more competitive processes of executive selection, allowing for candidate competition and multiparty elections (Bratton and van de Walle, 1997). Yet the economic performance of several of these countries remained lackluster or worsened after the political reforms (Ferree and Singh, 2000a, 2000b). Drawing from two recent papers by the authors, this chapter attempts to provide a richer insight into the processes producing these outcomes.

The chapter sets out to make two contributions to the debate on democratization and economic performance. It seeks first to account for the impact of changes in electoral institutions on growth performance; and second to understand how history conditions the growth effects of these political institutions. These issues are explored in the context of a data set of 45 sub-Saharan African countries from 1970 to 1992. Rather than look at the impact of democracy writ large, we focus on more precise characteristics of democratic institutions. We propose and employ a new measure – the executive scale – which captures the competitiveness of electoral mechanisms for choosing the chief executive. By using the executive scale in place of more general measures of democracy (like Freedom House or Polity III), we are able to zoom in on a dimension of democracy that is crucial for ensuring executive accountability and thus bears at least a theoretical link to economic performance.

In this chapter, we report evidence suggesting that change in the competitiveness of electoral institutions is associated with a drop in growth rates. Although both democratic and non-democratic changes in electoral systems introduce uncertainty, we found that decreases in competitiveness appear to be much more harmful to growth than reforms that increase electoral competition. We also report that stability differentially influences the growth impact of different types of electoral regimes. Countries with more competitive multiparty electoral systems, although they appear to grow more slowly initially, have progressively better growth performance over time. Endurance has the opposite effect on less competitive electoral systems. Thus, our analysis suggests that prior work that has ignored the mediating impact of institutional endurance and change on the growth effects of political institutions has missed an important dynamic in the relationship between political institutions and growth (Knack and Keefer, 1995, Przeworski and Limongi, 1993, Rodrik, 1997a).

POLITICS AND ECONOMIC GROWTH: THEORETICAL ISSUES

Perhaps because Africa has often been seen as an outlier in the literatures on democracy, political stability, and growth, the study of African economic performance has periodically attracted the attention of macro-economists (Sachs and Warner, 1997; Rodrik, 1997b). In their statistical models, African exceptionalism has found expression in the so-called Africa growth 'dummy'. The dummy term (a binary variable indicating whether or not a particular country is located in Africa) captures the residual component of African growth that remains unexplained after controlling for standard variables such as government consumption, investment, human capital, and initial per-capita income. Large negative coefficients on the dummy term imply that being located on the African continent has a sizeable growth penalty, the ultimate source of which remains uncertain (Barro, 1996; Alesina et al., 1996). The persistence of the Africa dummy into recent decades suggests that increasing globalization has not eliminated or reversed those factors responsible for differentiating African economic performance from other regions of the world. Though globalization may be an equilibrating force, regional differences such as those picked up by the Africa dummy resist erosion.

As a proximal source for the Africa dummy, researchers have looked to policy variables such as openness, social conditions such as ethno-linguistic fractionalization, and other factors such as geography and endowments (Sachs and Warner, 1997; Easterly and Levine, 1997; Bloom and Sachs, 1998). When combinations of these variables are included in growth equations, the Africa dummy evaporates (see Hoeffler, 1997 for another approach). However, as Collier and Gunning (1999: 65) point out, if 'Africa's slow growth is thus partly explicable in terms of particular variables that are globally important for the growth process, but are low in Africa ... [t]his shifts the question to why they are low'. In other words, why are growth-inhibiting policies adopted in African countries?

To unpack the dynamics of how political and economic interactions can have an impact upon the growth performance of a country, we look at the motivations of three sets of actors: investors, voters, and executives. We see investors as the relevant actors in the market environment, and voters and executives in the political one. In Africa, much investment comes from foreign sources. Thus, the international economy (and through it, forces of globalization) enters our framework through investors and is mediated by the actions of domestic political actors and institutions. We assume the following motivations: Investors desire high rates of return on their investments. Voters want to better their economic prospects, and in so far as economic growth contributes to their economic well being, they prefer higher growth rates to lower ones. Executives want to stay in power and use their office to increase their personal utility (by accumulating personal wealth, creating a political legacy, or enacting policies that further their political ideologies and aims).

In setting out our stylized understanding of the political-economic marketplace, we adopt some defensible assumptions. The market environment in which investors operate produces higher growth rates if more productive investment occurs – the more investment made and the more efficient the investment, the higher the growth rate (Barro and Sala-i-Martin, 1995). Turning to the political arena, we assume that executives choose economic policies that indirectly affect the rates of return for investment and the growth rate. Furthermore, although stochastic shocks will attenuate the relationship, we assume that certain policies are more growth enhancing than others, and that stable policy is *ceteris paribus* better for growth than unpredictable policy (see Dixit and Pindyck, 1994; Guillaumont *et al.*, 1999; Hassett and Metcalf, 1999; Serven, 1996; Brunetti, 1998b). Our account suggests the following cause–effect chain of relationships:

stable and good economic policies → improve the allocation of investment → growth

The rules (implicit or explicit) governing the relationship between citizens and the government are a key driver of the political marketplace and, through it, policy. We therefore look at how the relationship between citizens and the chief executive produces or fails to produce stable and good economic policies. We work with two types of independent variables: the competitiveness of electoral institutions and institutional instability. The former helps us pinpoint perhaps the most important aspect of the rules governing how citizens choose their executives; the latter captures changes in those rules.

Although scholars tend to assume that the institutions of executive selection can be treated as static, this is not true in many areas of the world (Easterly *et al.*, 1993). Many studies look at a country's political system in a particular year and relate that to average rates of growth in the ensuing five- or ten-year period. This type of specification ignores institutional changes that occur during the periods prior to and after the year of measurement. For example, Nigeria was a democracy in 1980. A few years earlier, it had been a military dictatorship. In 1981, it had a coup. Should we expect Nigeria's brief period as a democratic state in 1979–80 to produce a growth dividend during the 1981–85 period? Or would the instability produced by several institutional changes outweigh any positive effects of increased government accountability? Studies that relate regime type in time t with growth in time $t+1$ are likely to miss these more complex dynamics.

Why do we believe that the competitiveness of executive elections will influence policy choice and therefore economic growth? Why and how will changes in the competitiveness of selection processes for executives have an impact on growth? And conversely, does the longevity of electoral institutions (lack of change) condition growth impacts? Below, we develop our hypotheses to answer these questions.

Executive Competitiveness and Growth via Good Policy Choice

We conjecture that the competitiveness of the processes for selecting executives affects the nature of these officials' economic-policy choices. We have already stipulated that citizens prefer high growth rates to low growth rates; they therefore tend to prefer leaders who are more likely to choose policies that produce higher growth rates.[1] Scholars have proposed two types of explanations for how elections may serve to induce 'good behavior' in political agents by citizen principals: Voters can use competitive elections to select 'good types' of leaders,[2] or they can use their choice in competitive elections to vote out or punish leaders who have produced undesirable growth outcomes.[3]

Although there is a great deal of controversy about the degree to which competitive elections allow for selection or sanctioning under different information conditions, it is clear that noncompetitive elections do not provide opportunities for voter control over politicians.[4] *We expect, then, that executives elected in competitive multiparty elections are more likely to choose good policies than those who are not elected in competitive elections.* Where there is no choice there can be no selection or sanctioning mechanism – however faulty – to encourage or induce good policy choice.[5]

Institutional Change and Growth via Policy Predictability

We have considered how the competitiveness of executive elections can affect growth through policy choice. We turn now to changes in the competitiveness of selection processes for executives and their impact on growth. A change in the relationship between leaders and citizens – increasing or decreasing competitiveness – affects policy predictability or stability by changing the choice set of voters. Here we are looking not just at voters and executives, but how investors react to changes in the rules governing the relationship between voter choice and executive selection.

We explore the relative importance of *different forms* of institutional instability in explaining variation in growth outcomes.[6] Are all forms of institutional instability bad, or are changes that decrease executive contestation worse than changes that increase it?

Our priors are that *all* forms of electoral institutional instability are bad for growth – changes that decrease competition and those that increase it – because they all introduce policy uncertainty. In the eyes of an investor, the policy stances of a newly elected executive in a country where a 'strong man' such as Mobutu has ruled for decades may be just as unpredictable as those of a military cabal that has taken over from a faltering single-party state. At least initially, both may produce similar levels of uncertainty for investors. Change in the 'rules' by which leaders are chosen heighten policy uncertainty, distorting the allocation of investment until investors gain more information about the effects of such institutional changes. We therefore expect that *any* instability in executive institutions should be negatively related to short-term growth rates.

History Matters

We have hypothesized that competitive executive elections will be associated with higher growth rates, and that changes in the competitiveness of executives will depress short-term growth rates. Both arguments involve the sharing and interpretation of information – by voters in the first, and investors in the second.

In order for voters to be able to either select 'good types' or punish 'bad types', they need information about the quality (and credibility) of candidates and the performance of incumbents, respectively. The more skewed the informational asymmetry between voters and (potential) executives, the more attenuated the relationship between executive competitiveness and policy choice and, thus, growth performance. We suggest that the *duration* of a particular electoral arrangement reduces voters' informational disadvantage. They learn to critically examine party platforms and politicians' pronouncements versus actual behavior. They may learn more about actual policy choices and the relationship between policy choice and actual growth performance. As a result, *the hypothesized relationship between executive competition and growth should emerge most clearly over time.*[7]

In summary, we expect that:

1. More competitive executive elections will be associated with higher growth rates.
2. All forms of electoral institutional instability will be associated with worse growth performance.
3. The relationship between executive competition and growth will emerge more clearly over time as electoral institutions endure.

Armed with these thoughts, we move to an examination of the evidence.

DATA AND BASIC DESCRIPTIVE STATISTICS

Dependent Variable

The dependent variable in all of our models (*growth*) is the annual growth rate of per capita gross domestic product (GDP), calculated according to the chain index. We depart from the convention of using five- or ten-year average growth rates for two reasons. First, we believe that political factors such as institutional change have an immediate impact on growth that may be obscured when longer-term averages are used. Second, averaging throws away important information. African growth rates are highly erratic from year to year. While scholars interested in long-term growth patterns may prefer to even out this variability, it is central to our framework.[8]

Control Variables

We use a set of economic variables standard in the growth literature as a base for all of our regressions. Our goal is not to estimate these relationships per se, but to control for whatever effects they may have on the dependent variable. We try various permutations of them to ensure that the results for our variables of interest are robust to different configurations. In particular we use:

- Lagged log of per capita income (lngdplg): This variable captures conditional 'convergence effects' where countries at lower initial levels of income are expected to grow faster than countries at higher initial levels of income. We expect the sign on this variable to be negative.
- Lagged government consumption as a percentage of GDP (glg2): This variable is used 'to approximate the outlays that do not enhance produc-

tivity' (Barro, 1996: 9). It is considered non-productive spending and is therefore expected to reduce growth (we lag two years so that the level variable is measured at the beginning of the period covered by the change variable).

- Lagged change in government consumption as a percentage of GDP (gch2): Because we are considering short-term growth, we include a measure for changes in government consumption. We expect this variable to have a negative effect on growth.

- Lagged real investment (public and private) as a percentage of GDP (ilg2): We expect investment to be positively related to growth (lagged by two years as with glg2).

- Lagged change in real investment as a percentage of GDP (ich2): Because we are considering short-term growth, we expect changes in investment to be at least as important as the level of investment. We anticipate that increases in investment should lead to higher growth.

- Terms-of-trade shocks (trdbts) and lagged terms-of-trade shocks (trdbtslg): This variable measures unexpected changes in GDP due to changes in terms of trade.[9] We have used both contemporaneous and lagged versions. We anticipate that both will have a negative impact on growth, but expect the stronger effect to be contemporaneous.

- Lagged life expectancy (lextlg): We use this as a proxy for human capital, which is widely viewed as a necessary ingredient for growth. We opt for life expectancy instead of a schooling measure because it offers better data coverage (when we tried using average years of secondary schooling instead, we lost 250 observations), and because we suspect that it has less measurement error than other human-capital variables. We expect a positive relationship with growth.

- Lagged growth (growthlg): We initially include this measure (a lagged value of the dependent variable) to eliminate possible serial correlation. It is dropped in our final specifications.

- 1980s: A dummy variable indicating the 1980s.

- 1990s: A dummy variable indicating the 1990s.

Political Variables

All of our political variables are based on a measure of executive competitiveness that we call the 'executive scale'. Below, we describe the construction of this variable, what it means, why it improves on other measures, and its weaknesses. We then outline our measures for institutional instability and duration, both of which we created from the executive scale.

The Executive Scale (dummy variables for each level: elev1 – elev6 *):*
The executive scale measures the level of electoral competition that occurs during the selection process for executives. We define six theoretical levels: level one consists of countries without identifiable executives; level two contains countries where the executive exists but is not elected; level-three countries are those where executives are 'elected', but face no challengers during the election; level-four countries have competitively elected executives (more than one candidate contests the election) but opposition parties are banned; level-five countries have executives that are elected in competitive contests during which oppositions are legal but inactive; finally, level six consists of countries that have competitive, multiparty elections. Table 4.1 summarizes this information, which we collected for 45 sub-Saharan African countries for each year between 1970 and 1995.[10] Table 4.1 also shows the relative frequency of different categories.

We feel that the scale offers improvements over previous political indices such as Freedom House's (Gastil's) index of political rights.[11] Many of these indices measure 'democracy' by identifying aspects of a democratic system (competition, inclusion, participation, etc.) and combining them in some way to produce a ranking.[12] The method of aggregation varies in its transparency, but the weighting of different factors to develop the ranking is usually subjective.[13] This procedure maximizes the possible impact of bias due to coders' judgement and limited access to information (Bollen, 1993). It also makes precise interpretation and replication difficult. What does a '4' on Gastil's civil liberties index mean? Does it mean the same thing for every country? What is the difference between a '4' and '5'? It is impossible to know which aspects of a country's situation are being measured and how they are ranked in the final aggregation. Furthermore, changes in any number of different underlying phenomena can serve as the precipitating

TABLE 4.1
THE EXECUTIVE SCALE

Level on the executive scale	Frequency (country years)	Characteristics of electoral institutions at that level
Level 1	12	No executive exists
Level 2	374	Executive exists but was not elected
Level 3	469	Executive is elected, but was the only candidate (no competition from challenger)
Level 4	21	Executive is elected, and more than one candidate competed for the office
Level 5	0	Multiple parties were also able to contest the executive elections
Level 6	246	Candidates from more than one party competed for the executive elections

factor for a change in a country's score. The aggregate nature of the measure obscures the precise trigger for change.

In contrast, the executive scale is transparent. It is relatively easy to measure and replicate; each of the levels is clear-cut and the placement of countries can be determined from basic secondary sources.[14] A four on the scale has a precise meaning that remains the same across countries. We do not weight factors to construct the scale, nor do we rely on subjective, expert ratings to place countries into categories. We do not purport to be measuring 'democracy'. Democracy is too complex to capture in a single measure. Many aspects of democracy, such as respect for human rights, elude careful measurement. Therefore, rather than developing a poor measure of a general concept, we have focused on developing a precise measure of a specific concept. While this decision forces us to ignore many significant aspects of democracy, we feel that gains in precision outweigh losses in breadth.

It is worth highlighting a few caveats with regard to the scale. First, as Table 4.1 shows, its empirical range is more restricted than its theoretical range. Virtually all of our observations fall in categories two, three, or six: countries that had no elections, noncompetitive elections, or competitive multiparty elections. There are only a handful of cases where an executive did not exist, and categories four and five are not particularly relevant for the African data.

Second, by including countries where there is regular turnover of the executive as well as countries where a single party dominates politics and consistently wins control of the executive branch, category six potentially groups apples and oranges. If our sample were drawn from the world and not just Africa, this would present a significant complication. However, virtually all sub-Saharan African countries are single-party dominant. Therefore, in this regard at least, category six is fairly homogenous.

Perhaps a bigger question concerns the nature of single-party dominance in different African countries. In some countries, like Botswana, real popularity and support from the electorate appear to drive the long-term dominance of the ruling party. In others, like Zimbabwe during the 1990s, dominance seems to reflect coercive repression of the opposition more than popular opinion (Du Toit, 1999). Our scale does not distinguish between these two situations. In general, the scale measures competition, not the quality of competition. While capturing these distinctions would improve the scale, the quality of competition is difficult measure. Oppositions often allege that they have received unfair treatment. Losers usually claim that the election was rigged. We generally lack information to evaluate these claims – especially for elections prior to 1990. Rather than cloud the scale with uncertainty, we have chosen to leave out the quality dimension.

Given our discussion in previous sections of this paper, we expect higher levels of the scale in time t to be associated with higher rates of growth in time $t+1$.

Change Variables

We constructed three change variables out of the executive scale:

- Unsigned Change (*dlechg1p*): This variable equals one if the country's level on the scale has either increased or decreased between time t and time $t-1$, and is given a zero if there has been no change.
- Positive Change (*pechg1p*): This variable is coded one if the country's scale level increased between time t and time $t-1$, and is assigned a zero if no change or a negative change occurred.
- Negative Change (*nechg1p*): This variable is coded one if the country's level on the scale has decreased between time t and time $t-1$, and is assigned zero if there has been zero or positive change.

In our data, we had a total of 84 changes in the scale over the period covered. Thirty-one were negative changes; 53 were positive ones. Our expectation is that all forms of instability are detrimental for growth. We also experimented with a variety of other types of change variables with less clear-cut or interesting interpretations.[15]

Duration

We used the scale to generate a measure of institutional durability, along with several interaction terms:

- Duration of Executive Scale (*edur*): For each year we counted how long each country had been at its current level of the scale. (Thus, during years of institutional change, the duration variable is coded zero).
- Duration/Level Interaction (*elev2dur, elev3dur, elev4dur*): This is edur multiplied by dummy variables for each of the levels of the scale.

The average number of years of duration for executive regimes (i.e. levels of the scale) in our data set is eight and a half. For countries at level two, the average is also eight and a half years; for countries at level three, it is nine and a half years; and for countries at level six, slightly more than seven years. Though our data set only covers 25 years, the maximum value of the duration variable is actually 36 (Ethiopia at level two). This apparent contradiction occurs because the duration variable does not start at zero in 1970 for most countries, but reflects the duration of the institutions in place in 1970. We have one additional country with a duration score of 30 years or higher (Botswana at level six) and seven countries with scores of 25 years or higher. Eleven additional countries had duration spells greater than 20 years. Thus, all told, 20 countries had electoral regimes that endured for at least 20 years.

We expect duration to have a positive impact (if any) on growth. Our stronger expectations concern the interaction terms: we anticipate the relationship between scale level and growth to emerge more clearly as duration at that level increases.

Some Descriptive Statistics on the Scale

Figure 4.1 shows the movement of the mean scale over time for our sample. In the early 1970s, the mean value of the scale fell somewhat. From around 1972 until the end of the 1980s, it trended upward (very) slightly. In the early 1990s, the mean scale score began a period of rapid movement upwards.

FIGURE 4.1
AVERAGE LEVEL OF EXECUTIVE SCALE

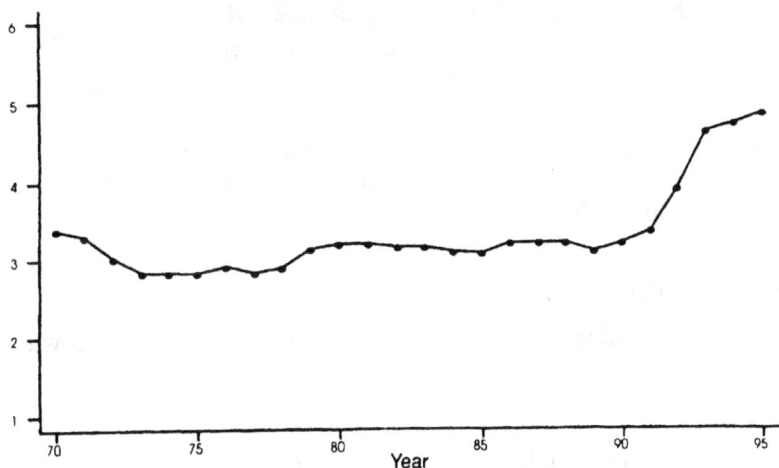

Figure 4.2 shows the total number of African countries that experienced (upward or downward) changes in their scale score for every year between 1970 and 1995. The general trend indicates a rising number of countries undergoing changes through the 1970s, with a drop off in the 1980s, and a sharp increase in the 1990s. The peak was reached in 1993 with almost one in four African nations experiencing political change as measured by their scale scores.

Figures 4.1 and 4.2 point to the 1990s as a period of widespread political

FIGURE 4.2
NUMBER OF COUNTRIES WITH ELECTORAL SYSTEM CHANGES, 1970-96

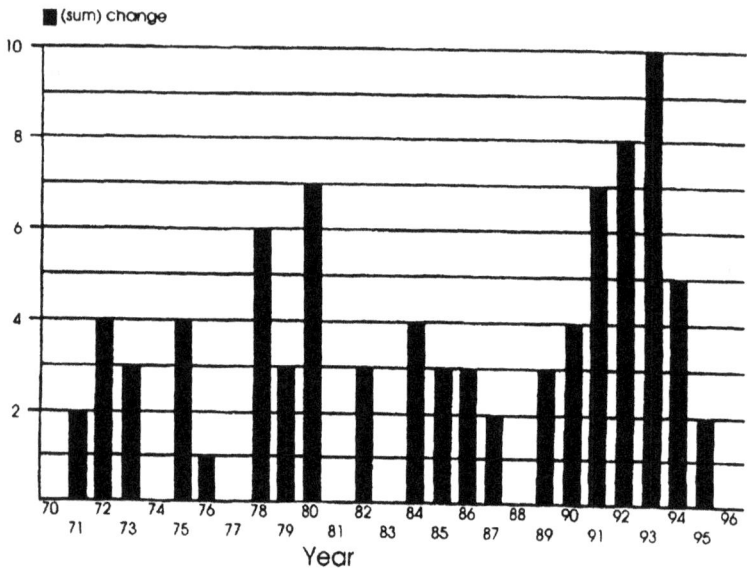

change in Africa. This trend suggests that one correlate of globalization – and concomitant internationally based demands for democratization – was domestic political change.

MODEL SPECIFICATION

We use the following pooled time-series cross-sectional model of growth:

$$\ln(Y_{i,t}) - \ln(Y_{i,t-\tau}) = \beta \ln(Y_{i,t-\tau}) + W_{i,t-\tau}\delta + Z_{i,t}\gamma + \varepsilon_{i,t}$$

where $Y_{i,t}$ is real per-capita income for country i in period t, $W_{i,t-\tau}$ is a row vector of determinants of economic growth observed in country i for period $t-1$ (a set of lagged independent variables), and $Z_{i,t}$ is a row vector of determinants observed in country i for period t (a set of contemporaneous independent variables). Our choice of independent variables for $W_{i,t-\tau}$ and $Z_{i,t}$ was outlined earlier. Our dependent variable is annual growth rates, $\tau = 1$.[16]

We employ this equation as the foundation for our specification and estimate it through ordinary least squares. Following Beck and Katz (1995), we calculate panel-corrected standard errors to deal with any problems caused by contemporaneous correlation of errors and/or panel heterogeneity. We initially included a lagged value of the dependent variable to control for serial correlation, but were able to drop this procedure as it proved to be highly insignificant across all specifications. This step did not change the coefficients on any of the other variables. Dropping the lag allowed an extra degree of freedom and allowed us to use a fixed-effects model without introducing an inconsistency problem. Consequently, all of our models are estimated in a fixed-effects framework. We estimate separate intercepts for all countries but one, as well as decade dummies for the 1980s and 1990s (the 1970s are left out). We tried yearly dummies, but this treatment had little effect on the results; we therefore stuck with the more parsimonious specification.[17]

The above specification does not allow us to control conclusively for endogeneity. The model assumes a certain causal structure by placing some variables on the right-hand side, others on the left. A different set of causal relationships is possible, however. As a partial solution, we have (in most cases) lagged our independent variables behind our dependent variables, appealing to the standard logic that an event at time t cannot cause an event at time $t-1$.

RESULTS AND DISCUSSION

Institutional Change and Growth

We begin by addressing the relationship between short-term economic performance and institutional instability. Does institutional change in executive electoral systems affect short-term growth? If so, how? We anticipate that all changes, positive and negative, are associated with drops in the growth rate.

As an initial cut on this question, we divided the 45 nations in our sample into two roughly equal groups on the basis of their median average annual growth rate. The 'slow growers' comprised all the countries with an average annual growth rate below –0.001 per cent per annum; the 'fast growers' exceeded that rate. Table 4.2 reveals the average number of scale changes for the two groups, as well as the standard deviation of the scale scores over time for each group – taken here as rough measures of political instability.[18]

TABLE 4.2
SCALE CHANGES AND SLOW VERSUS FAST GROWERS

	'Slow growers'	*'Fast growers'*
Average number of scale changes	2.35	1.13
Average standard deviation of scale scores	1.24	0.85

TABLE 4.3
AVERAGE GROWTH RATES AND POSITIVE VERSUS NEGATIVE SCALE CHANGES

	Country-years with negative change in the scales	Country-years with positive change in the scales	Country-years with no change in the scales
Average annual growth rate (%)	-5.9	-2	0.35
Average scale score	2	5	3

TABLE 4.4
REGRESSION RESULTS: CHANGE (WITH 95%-CONFIDENCE INTERVALS)

	Equation 1: Change		Equation 2: Positive vs. negative change	
Logged per capita income, lagged	-0.1918	(-0.2283, -0.1553)	-0.1911	(-0.2274, -0.1548)
Investment, lagged	0.0027	(0.0013, 0.0041)	0.0027	(0.0014, 0.0041)
Change in investment, lagged	0.0566	(0.0396, 0.0737)	0.0562	(0.0392, 0.0732)
Gov. spending, lagged	0.0002	(-0.0010, 0.0014)	0.0002	(-0.0009, 0.0014)
Change in gov. spending, lagged	0.0092	(-0.0278, 0.0461)	0.0104	(-0.0264, 0.0471)
Life expectancy, lagged	-0.0013	(-0.0044, 0.0018)	-0.0013	(-0.0043, 0.0018)
Trade income effect	0.0015	(0.0008, 0.0021)	0.0015	(0.0008, 0.0022)
1980s	-0.0178	(-0.0320, -0.0037)	-0.0182	(-0.0323, -0.0042)
1990s	-0.0244	(-0.0471, -0.0016)	-0.0262	(-0.0489, -0.0035)
All change	-0.0195	(-0.0395, 0.0005)		
Negative change			-0.0477	(-0.0775, -0.0180)
Positive change			0.0005	(-0.0248, 0.0258)
N	705		705	
K	51		52	

Country dummies not shown.

The slow growers exhibit more changes and higher standard deviations than the fast growers.

Table 4.3 slices the data from a different angle. We compared the average yearly growth rates and levels on the executive scale for country-years in which negative, positive, and no scale changes occurred. During country-years when electoral competitiveness declined, the annual growth rates averaged –5.9 per cent. During country-years of electoral reform, average yearly growth rates were –2.0 per cent. Country-years with no scale changes registered average short-term growth rates of 0.4 per cent (lackluster but at least positive!). Thus, both Table 4.2 and Table 4.3 support our initial reasoning, though there appears to be some evidence that negative changes are associated with lower growth than positive changes.

We explore this tendency further through a series of regressions (shown in Table 4.4[19]). First, we consider the relationship between growth and total change (*dlechg1p*), which is coded one if the scale has changed (in either a positive or a negative direction) and zero otherwise. Equation 1 shows that the estimated coefficient on total change is negative and implies that any change in the scale is linked with a reduction of around two percentage points in short-term per-capita GDP growth. In a continent with a mean growth rate of 0.04 per cent over the time period 1970 to 1995, this figure is sizable.

It is also worth noting that most of the economic variables perform as expected. We find evidence of convergence, with countries at lower initial per capita incomes growing at higher rates than countries at higher initial per capita incomes. Both the level of investment and changes in investment have large, well-estimated, positive relationships with growth. Neither the level of government spending nor changes in this spending were associated with lower growth (as had been predicted). When fixed effects are not controlled for, higher public expenditure does appear to have a negative relationship with growth, but this relationship goes away when country-specific effects are eliminated. Life expectancy also has no relationship with growth, contrary to our expectations. This variable is also sensitive to the fixed-effects formulation, however. When country-specific effects are not modeled, life expectancy actually has a negative relationship with growth. As expected, contemporaneous shocks in trade revenues have a large, positive, well-estimated relationship with growth. Finally, the decade dummies perform as anticipated (and are consistent across specifications), with the 1980s and 1990s associated with lower growth than the 1970s. These patterns suggest that increasing globalization has not resulted in higher growth rates in Africa.

We now refine our understanding of the relationship between scale change and growth to distinguish between changes that result in greater electoral competition versus those that reduce it. We anticipate that negative and positive changes can be pooled. However, when we separate out positive and negative changes as signed dummy variables (*pechg1p* and *nechg1p*) in Equation 2 (Table 4.4) we find the opposite to be the case. The estimated coefficient for *nechg1p* suggests that negative changes are associated with a fall of anywhere from two to eight percentage points in the annual growth rate for that year! In contrast, countries experiencing positive changes grew at rates indistinguishable from those experiencing no change. The coefficient on *pechg1p is* just slightly positive, encompassing a range of −2 and +3 within the interval of 95 per cent confidence.

Altogether, Equation 2 suggests that drops in the scale drive the negative relationship found in Equation 1. The relationship between changes in the scale and short-term growth thus appears to be asymmetric: negative changes are accompanied by a large and immediate drop in the growth rate, whereas positive changes are associated with neither a growth penalty nor a growth reward.

The results in Table 4.4 are robust to other changes: adding and deleting countries and years, dropping economic variables, and replacing economic variables with other measures. (Appendix 2 contains more details about this.) They are not robust, however, to using lagged changes instead of contemporaneous ones. When we add lagged changes in Equations 1 and 2, the coefficients on contemporaneous changes remain substantial and significant but the coefficients on lagged change become insignificant or just barely significant.

This pattern implies that the biggest 'effects' of changes in the scale are immediate. Of course, the results are also consistent with the reverse causal story: that changes in growth cause changes in the scale. However, the fact that growth rates change far more often in Africa than the scale does makes us doubt the likelihood of the latter possibility. Previous research by other authors also casts doubt on the reverse-causality hypothesis.[20] We plan to return to this issue in future work by making the scale and changes in it the subjects of analysis.

Executive Competitiveness and Growth

We now address the relationship between scale level and growth rates, leaving aside for the moment the issues of institutional change and endurance. We anticipate that those countries at levels four and six, signifying higher levels of competition, should be associated with better economic performance than those at levels two and three. However, our results do not support this hypothesis. Instead, we find that higher levels of the scale are associated with lower overall growth!

Equation 3 (in Table 4.5[21]) includes lagged dummy variables for levels two, three, and four of the scale (*elev2lg, elev3lg, and elev4lg*). Countries at

TABLE 4.5
REGRESSION RESULTS: LEVEL AND DURATION
(WITH 95%-CONFIDENCE INTERVALS)

	Equation 3: Scale level		Equation 4: Scale level and duration	
Logged per capita income, lagged	−0.1938 (−0.2317,	−0.1558)	−0.1968 (−0.2359,	−0.1576)
Investment, lagged	0.0028 (0.0014,	0.0042)	0.0027 (0.0013,	0.0041)
Change in investment, lagged	0.0574 (0.0404,	0.0744)	0.0567 (0.0396,	0.0737)
Gov. spending, lagged	0.0003 (−0.0009,	0.0015)	0.0002 (−0.0011,	0.0014)
Change in gov. spending, lagged	0.0067 (−0.0300,	0.0434)	0.0078 (−0.0290,	0.0446)
Life expectancy, lagged	−0.0009 (−0.0040,	0.0022)	−0.0009 (−0.0042,	0.0023)
Trade income effect	0.0015 (0.0008,	0.0022)	0.0015 (0.0008,	0.0022)
1980s	−0.0169 (−0.0312,	−0.0027)	−0.0152 (−0.0296,	0.0007)
1990s	−0.0245 (−0.0472,	−0.0018)	−0.0222 (−0.0453,	0.0010)
Level Two, lagged	0.0235 (−0.0027,	0.0497)	0.0330 (0.0034,	0.0621)
Level Three, lagged	0.0149 (−0.0089,	0.0388)	0.0313 (0.0038,	0.0588)
Level Four, lagged	−0.0268 (−0.0708,	0.0173)	−0.0199 (−0.0767,	0.0368)
Duration, lagged			0.0023 (−0.0008,	0.0054)
Duration at Level Two, lagged			−0.0025 (−0.0059,	0.0008)
Duration at Level Three, lagged			−0.0037 (−0.0070,	0.0004)
Duration at Level Four, lagged			−0.0020 (−0.0141,	0.0102)
N	705		705	
K	53		57	

Country dummies not shown.

level one of the scale (only a handful in our sample) were eliminated so that the intercept can be interpreted as level six. Surprisingly, the level-two and level-three dummy variables are associated with *positive* growth rates in comparison to level six. In the case of level two, the coefficient suggests that being at level two (as opposed to level six) implies an increase of two percentage points in growth rate, with 95 per cent confidence intervals just including zero on the low side and five on the high side. The coefficient on level-three countries is not as large or as well estimated (with 95 per cent confidence intervals ranging from minus one to four). The coefficient for the level-four dummy variable is indistinguishable from zero: not surprising, given the small number of cases in this category.

In view of previous work about electorates punishing governments for poor economic performance and the restraining effects of democratic institutions, these results are surprising. However, they do not take into account the longevity of different electoral regimes. Therefore, we turn to our third hypothesis to examine how these relationships change over time.

Duration and Executive Competitiveness: Interaction Effects

Our third hypothesis is that the relationship between executive competition and growth (if there is one) will emerge most clearly in the long term. Equation 4 in Table 4.5 therefore adds a term for lagged duration and three lagged duration interaction terms (for levels two, three, and four). Since relatively few countries in Africa have sustained elections over a long period of time, these results are not conclusive but are highly suggestive.

The dummy variables for levels two and three are better estimated in this specification, and both indicate that being at these lower levels of the scale is associated with a growth dividend of three percentage points. The coefficient on the dummy variable for level four remains very poorly estimated. Duration, as expected, has a positive effect on growth. Its coefficient suggests that a ten-year increase is associated with around an increase of two percentage points in the growth rate. The coefficient is not particularly well estimated, however, with a confidence interval ranging from around zero to around 0.005 (or a ten-year duration producing an increase of five percentage points).[22] It is the interaction terms that add nuance to the picture: as we conjectured, history matters, but differently for different political institutions. Each extra year at either level two or level three appears to have a dampening effect on the growth rate. This negative effect is larger and better estimated for level three, with confidence intervals spanning from a drop of half a percentage point in the growth rate to one of seven points (over ten years).[23]

Altogether, the results tell an interesting story: without taking into account duration, competition appears to *hurt* growth rates. This result, not anticipated by theory, arises perhaps because attempts to hold competitive multiparty elections are often associated with high levels of social and political upheaval. At the same time, the positive effects of competition do not kick in for several years (for the reasons already outlined). It may also be the case that multiparty elections are instituted in those countries where growth rates are at their lowest to begin with. Duration itself has a positive relationship with growth, but for level-two and -three countries, this is counteracted (or more than counteracted in the case of level three) by a negative level-specific duration effect. *That is, duration only helps level-six countries. It is at best neutral for level-two countries, and bad for those at level three.*

These relationships are best illustrated graphically. Figure 4.3 [24] plots the trajectories of level-two (no elections), -three (noncompetitive elections), and -six (competitive multiparty elections) countries. The economic variables are held at their means and the decade shown is the 1990s. As can be seen from Figure 4.3, countries with competitive multiparty elections (level six) start off well below those with no elections (level two) and noncompetitive elections (level three), but catch up over time. In contrast, countries with noncompetitive elections (level 3) deteriorate. Those with no elections (Level 2) generally stay even keel.

Simulations

The discussion so far does not include information about our certainty in the projected relationships. To obtain certainty estimates, we conducted a series of simulations.[25]

FIGURE 4.3
EFFECT OF DURATION ON GROWTH FOR LEVEL 2, LEVEL 3, AND LEVEL 6
COUNTRIES, FIXED EFFECTS MODEL, ECONOMIC VARIABLES HELD AT MEANS

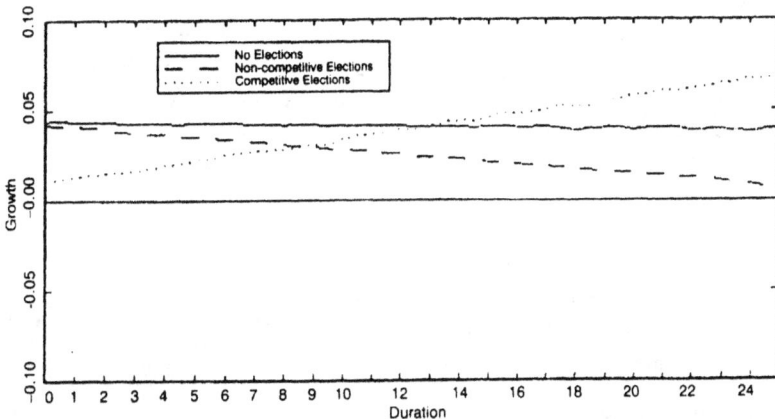

TABLE 4.6
SIMULATED COMPARISONS OF GROWTH RATES ACROSS LEVELS

One Year Out	Twenty-five Years Out
Level 6 outperformed Level 2 in 2% of the simulations	Level 6 outperformed Level 2 in 78% of the simulations
Level 6 outperformed Level 3 in 2% of the simulations	Level 6 outperformed Level 3 in 95% of the simulations

Based on 1000 simulations.

We also used simulation techniques to round out our picture of these effects. First, we compared across levels for different periods of duration. Table 4.6[26] shows the relationship between levels of the scale at one versus 25 years of duration. At one year out, countries with competitive multiparty elections (level 6) perform worse than those with no elections (level two) and noncompetitive elections (level three) in virtually all of our simulations. Twenty-five years out, the picture changes dramatically: level-six countries now grow faster than level-two countries in 78 per cent of our simulations, and faster than level-three countries in 95 per cent of them. Although, then, it seems that in the short term there is a considerable payoff to *avoiding* competitive elections, in the long term the evidence suggests the opposite.

We can also compare changes in growth impacts over time within levels. Table 4.7 shows the difference between growth twenty-five years out versus growth one year out for the three relevant levels of the scale. Across simulations, countries with noncompetitive elections (level three) are almost always doing worse twenty-five years out, while countries with competitive multiparty elections (level six) are almost always doing better. The effect of duration for states with no elections (level 2) is far more ambiguous: there is perhaps a slight tendency for them to be growing slower after twenty-five years, but this is uncertain.

The simulations intimate that political stability has a very different effect on economic performance for countries at different levels of the scale. We anticipated that duration would have a positive effect for level-six countries because it would give voters time to develop positive accountability cycles with elected executives. Our results suggest tentative support for this

TABLE 4.7
SIMULATED COMPARISON ACROSS YEARS, WITHIN LEVELS

	Level 2	Level 3	Level 6
Percentage of times growth at t=25 exceeded growth at t=5	40%	6%	93%

Based on 1000 simulations.

hypothesis. We did not anticipate, however, that duration would affect level-three countries adversely, nor did we expect a difference in the effects of duration on level-two and -three countries, both of which do not have elected executives. These results are provocative, and suggest an important job for future theoretical research – a point to which we will return in the conclusion.

Country Cases

If our results describe real patterns, we should be able to find cases that match the simulated trajectories. We find numerous cases that match the level-three pattern of declining growth over time. Gabon is a very good example: it started out at a relatively high level of per capita income at the beginning of our period (around $3,700), had a few years of good growth, but then fell for most of the years that followed and ended the period in 1992 poorer than it had been at the start (with a per capita income of around $3,600). It had had 17 unbroken years of noncompetitive elections (level three) when it transitioned in 1986 to allowing competition between candidates, although banning opposition parties (level four). Cote d'Ivoire is another example of a country that spent a long period of time at level three (23 years) and ended the period worse off than it had started. Kenya stayed at level three for a long period and had long spells of negative growth (especially after 1980) and Malawi, after 26 years at level three in 1992, was barely better off than it had been in 1970. Finally, Zaire deteriorated continually over a long period at level three. There are counter-examples, of course. Cameroon stayed at level three for 21 years and enjoyed positive growth rates for much of this period (its growth rate turning negative only at the very end). Guinea is another possible counter-example, enjoying more positive-growth years than negative ones.

Do we find countries without elections (level two) that stayed flat? Burundi was at level two for a long period (for 21 years until 1984). Its growth rate during this period bounced around quite a bit, but was positive a little less than half the time from 1970 to 1983. Burundi ended the period with a higher per capita income than it had at the beginning. Congo, Lesotho, Swaziland, and Ethiopia are additional examples of countries that spent a long time at level two without much economic deterioration although all four were quite poor to begin with. The Central African Republic, conversely, was worse off at the end of a 19-year period at level two than it had been at the beginning, and Chad is another country that deteriorated over a long period at level two. Mozambique also followed this pattern, although it was fighting a civil war, which probably influenced its pattern. Civil war was perhaps also a factor with Chad.[27]

Finally, do we have cases that match the trajectory of level-six countries (those with competitive multiparty elections)? On one hand, it is not difficult to find cases of countries that experimented briefly with competitive multiparty elections, with either a neutral or negative impact on their growth rates. Nigeria held competitive multiparty elections in 1980, experienced positive growth in 1980 and 1981, negative growth in 1982 and 1983, and then had a coup in 1984. It was considerably worse off (in terms of per capita income) in 1983 than it had been in 1980. Ghana, which also held competitive multiparty elections in 1980, followed a similar path.

We have more difficulty finding cases of countries with increasing rates of growth over a long period at level six. We have two cases (Botswana and Mauritius) of consistent growth performers over the entire period, both with considerably higher per capita incomes at the end of the period compared to their respective levels at the beginning. (Botswana's grew from $823 in 1970 to $2,198 in 1989; Mauritius grew from $2,398 to $6,167). Both countries have held competitive multiparty elections since the 1960s. The Gambia, Zimbabwe, and Senegal were the only other African countries that maintained multiparty executive elections for at least ten years, and their growth performance presents a more mixed pattern: never terrible, but never great. The Gambia and Senegal ended the period with slightly better per capita income than they had at the start; Zimbabwe's deteriorated. Altogether, the country cases suggest that short-term experiments with competitive multiparty elections are not associated with higher growth rates later on. Conversely, long-term experiments appear to pay off in more cases than not, although the picture is still mixed.

In sum, we find countries at each level that match the paths that we estimated. This is particularly true for level three. It is also true, however, that we find exceptions at each level of the scale. Finally, it is important to keep in mind that choosing case studies from simple bivariate relationships misses those complex interactions deriving from the assortment of economic, timing, and country-specific effects that we control for in our models. Although these country cases provide an intriguing lens through which to view the results, simply looking at duration and growth leaves out a number of important factors.

CONCLUSION

These results leave us with several puzzles to ponder, and open up new theoretical and empirical research directions. First, we find that institutional changes reducing electoral competition are associated with large and immediate drops in the growth rate. However, institutional reforms that increase competition do not appear to be accompanied by a growth penalty. This finding suggests an asymmetry in how investors regard political change. Although political reform does not appear to produce an immediate growth dividend, nor does it incur the same penalty as political decay. Theoretical treatments of investment under political uncertainty may be enriched by taking into account this asymmetry in response.

Second, we uncover preliminary but provocative evidence that time has a different effect on the growth impact of different types of electoral systems. Specifically, duration appears to have a positive-growth effect only for competitive multiparty systems. These results could recast the chicken-and-egg debate about economic and political development around issues of endurance. Of course, these results raise more questions than they settle. As such this chapter opens up a new set of research questions for scholars interested in democracy and growth. For example, why do countries with no elections or noncompetitive elections exhibit *higher growth rates* than countries with competitive multiparty elections *in the short run*? Is this result a by-product of the starting points for each regime – in other words, do electoral reforms tend to occur only in countries suffering from particularly poor growth performance? Or do multiparty elections themselves create a growth-dampening effect in the short run, even though investors may not initially react adversely?

Conversely, why do noncompetitive electoral regimes suffer from declining growth rates over time? And why does their long-term performance differ from states with no elections at all? It could be that these level-three states do not benefit from the electoral house-cleaning function, yet suffer over time from the entrenchment of patronage electoral politics. Alternately, we may find support for an attrition hypothesis: In the early years of competitive multiparty systems, low growth rates may result in system changes, such that only multiparty regimes (level six), where growth performance is good, survive. In other words, the level-six regimes could be the most growth sensitive. Similarly level-two states could also be more susceptible to being pushed into electoral reforms when growth performance is poor. If, then, the level-three countries' electoral systems were the most robust regarding poor growth performance, they should show a pattern of worsening growth rates over time in comparison to the other scale levels.

Finally, the results presented in this chapter suggest that the persistence and significance of the poor growth in Africa has domestic roots. Political sources of variation in growth performance across African countries include institutional instability on one hand, and the durability of the wrong type of institutions on the other. These same factors may also explain why Africa as a region has lagged behind other areas of the world in spite of increasing levels of globalization. International financial flows may have a large impact on domestic economies, but international investors take their cues from domestic events: How stable are institutions? How predictable is policy? Even as international forces tie the world ever more tightly together, the significance of such factors in shaping the economic paths of particular countries and regions is not likely to be eroded.

APPENDIX 1: CODING THE EXECUTIVE SCALE

The scale emerged from a series of questions that we asked about each country for each year: Did an executive exist? If so, was it an elected executive? If elected, did more than one candidate compete? Were multiple parties legally permitted to contest the election? Did candidates from multiple parties actually contest the election? If executives were chosen by legislatures (as in Westminster parliamentary-style systems), the answers were based on the legislature (Were seats filled via elections? Did more candidates compete than there were seats? Were parties permitted to compete? Did candidates from multiple parties actually compete?) We also noted other types of 'indirect' executive selection procedures (e.g. party congresses) but only considered these elections if the selecting body was itself elected from a national constituency.

Upon examining the responses to the five questions, we discerned an arboreal pattern in the data: if the first question is used to define an initial node, then the answers to the subsequent questions nested almost perfectly. That is, those countries that answered 'yes' to any given question, answered 'yes' to the preceding questions as well. The data therefore yield a nearly perfect Guttman scale. This allows us to collapse the answers to the five questions listed above into a single, compact measure (the scale) with almost no loss of information.

Out of over 1,100 country-years, there were only a handful of exceptions to the Guttman scale (less than 70 country-years, or around 6 per cent of the total). These were generally instances where parties were technically legal yet there was no competition between candidates (even within parties). To deal with these cases we coded 'pessimistically'. That is, we coded down to the lowest level for which the Guttman scale still applied. Thus, Comoros legally permitted parties to contest its executive elections in 1978, but only one candidate ran. We coded this as a '3' on the scale: executive elected, but not competitively.

The five questions making up the scale were coded for all years from 1970 to 1995, based on the status of the country at the end of the year. Each question refers to the executive and how he came to power. In many instances, the answer for one year will refer to events that occurred in the past. For example, the chief executive of country X was elected in a competitive multiparty election in 1976. If he is still in power in 1978 (and there have not been any coups or additional elections during the intervening years), then the answers to the 1978 executive questions will be in reference to the 1976 election. Changes in the scale refer to instances when a 'new' executive is put in place under circumstances that differ from the previous executive. This is true even if the actual identity of the individual has not changed. Thus, if a ruler seizes power in a coup in one year, and then five years later is elected in a competitive multiparty election, the scale changes during the year of the election, even though the actual person has not.

Announcements of changes and changes that do not actually affect who is in power do not affect the coding of the scale. If a leader is elected in 1976 and the country subsequently outlaws multiple parties in 1977, the answers to 1978 will still reflect the rules of 1976 because that is when the chief executive was chosen. Similarly, if a leader comes to power in a coup in 1985, then makes parties legal in 1987 and announces elections, the scale does not change until the elections actually occur.

We do this for several reasons. First, we are interested in the institutions that brought the leaders to power, not in rule-change pronouncements until they actually *apply* to the executive selection process. Second, while it is often clear when rules regarding party legality change, it is not always clear when other, more subtle rules change (like those affecting competition within parties). That is, we do not have the resources to document every constitutional (and non-constitutional) change in Africa over a 25 year period. If we changed the scale every time an obvious rule changed, we would risk measuring certain kinds of changes while ignoring others. Elections and other changeovers make many implicit rules more explicit, and therefore permit more careful measurement. Third, announcements of changes are frequent and strategic in sub-Saharan Africa: making parties legal for a time or scheduling elections for a few years out may be done with no real intention of actually allowing multiple parties to compete in an election. We prefer to adopt a 'we'll believe it when we see it' attitude to such claims. Finally, we have collected data on party legality in addition to the scale and the number of years since the last election (for elected regimes). This information can be examined separately or in conjunction with the scale if it is believed to be important.

There is one category of exceptions to the coding of changes. In a few rare instances, an executive was elected in competitive, multiparty elections but subsequently violated his terms of office in a clear and blatant fashion. For example, in 1972 the competitively elected executive of Equatorial Guinea (Nguema) declared himself 'leader for life'. We consider this an informal coup and drop Equatorial Guinea from a 6 to a 2 on the scale. Similarly, Lesotho held a legislative election in 1970. When it became clear to the incumbent executive (who had been elected previously in competitive multiparty elections) that he was losing the election, he dissolved the legislature and cancelled the election. We consider this an informal coup, and drop the coding from a 6 to a 2. These coding decisions, and any others of a similarly ad hoc nature, are fully documented in the data.

In practice, these were rare exceptions. Generally, competitively elected executives did not shut down the institutions that brought them to power. If their hold on power was shaky, they were often removed via a coup before they had a chance to abolish other parties, or abolished other parties and then held new elections to cement their rule. More frequent were executives who came to power in uncompetitive elections (level three) but never held subsequent token elections (Mobutu is one). This was not the rule for level-three countries, however. Many (Zambia, Côte d'Ivoire, Tanzania, Cameroon, and others) held elections regularly over the relevant time period. Thus, for the most part, the rules that brought leaders to power stayed intact during their tenures in power. More information about our coding decisions is available upon request.

APPENDIX 2: SENSITIVITY ANALYSIS

What countries are in? What countries are out? We coded political data for 46 sub-Saharan countries for 26 years, 1970 through 1995. This gives us a total of 1,196 potential observations. However, several of the political variables (including the scales) could not be coded for some of these years because the countries in question were still colonies – the data are not really missing, they are non-existent. Furthermore, our pool of observations dropped considerably once we began using economic data. Five countries dropped out completely: Equatorial Guinea, Tanzania, Liberia, Djibouti, and São Tomé e Principe. Equatorial Guinea lacks data on nearly all economic variables. The other four are missing terms-of-trade data. Most other countries included are missing economic data for at least a few (or in some cases, many) years. In addition, we lack economic data for years after 1992 and we lose 1970 to lags. In the end, we have a total of 705 observations. As of yet, we have not attempted multiple imputation analysis.

Robustness

We tested the sensitivity of our results to a number of changes in specification: we dropped years and countries, we used different configurations of economic variables, and we tried different human capital and terms-of-trade variables. For the most part, the results held up to these manoeuvres. The change variables were highly robust: only once did the t-statistic for negative change dip below –2.5, and this was in the extreme case of using a different human-capital variable (years of secondary schooling) with terrible coverage (the number of cases was almost halved). The level and duration variables were more fragile. They held up fine to dropping years and changing most of the economic variables (the exception was again the schooling variable), but were sensitive to case selection. This is not surprising, given the nature of the duration variables and the fixed-effects model: the historical trajectories of certain rarer cases have a big impact on the results. The results were particularly sensitive to dropping Mauritius. We suspect that this is partly because we have poor coverage of Botswana, the only other country in Africa with more than 25 years of experience with competitive multiparty elections. (Botswana's coverage is bad because of the terms-of-trade variables.) More on the particular tests follows.

Years

We tried dropping three different years: 1975, 1980, and 1985. These choices were more or less arbitrary, though important changes or events were happening during all three. The year 1975 saw a fair number of changes in political variables, many in the negative direction as African democracies ushered in at the end of independence were replaced with military rule or single-party democracy: 1980 was also a year of much change as a number of countries attempted to put in place competitive multiparty systems. (In most cases, these experiments were short lived.) 1985 was a year of political stasis and economic and climatic crises. Losing these three years resulted in dropping down to 609 observations. In spite of this, most of the results held up fine. The change results were weakened, with the coefficient on the general change variable shrinking relative to its standard error (new t-statistic is -1.136). The coefficient on negative change also shrinks relative to its standard error, but the new t-statistic is still above -2.5. The scale-level and duration variables are more or less unaffected by dropping years.

Countries

We tried dropping Botswana and Mauritius because these are the only countries with unbroken histories of competitive multiparty elections since the 1960s. We also dropped Nigeria because of its history of instability, Zaire for its long-term political stagnation and economic decline, Sierra Leone for its political deterioration, Uganda because of its rather unusual political and economic paths, and Gabon because it is an economic outlier (with much higher per capita income than most other African countries).

Dropping Botswana had only a small effect on the results: the level variables decreased in significance in the equation without the duration variables. As we only lost six cases by dropping Botswana, it seems unlikely that much of what we found has to do with this particular country. The same cannot be said for Mauritius. Dropping this country causes us to lose twenty-two cases and, because of the poor coverage on Botswana, the only real long-term democracy in Africa. The change variables survive this without a problem, but the level variables are weakened, and the duration effects more-or-less disappear. If we manipulate the specification slightly, using a contemporary value of duration instead of the lag, the duration and level results reappear. We suspect that the results are sensitive to this small change in specification because a contemporaneous duration variable captures change also. (In general, we get better results when we use the contemporaneous duration variable.)

If anything, dropping Nigeria strengthened the results. Dropping Zaire and Sierra Leone had no real impact. Dropping Uganda and Gabon weakened them slightly. On the whole, however, the results were fairly robust to excluding these countries. The main influential case therefore appears to be Mauritius.

Economic Variables

To ensure that our slightly unconventional use of both level and change economic variables (investment and public expenditure) were not driving our political results, we tried using just level variables. We also tried using just change variables. The biggest effects of these perturbations were on the other economic variables. Dropping the investment and government-spending change variables caused the coefficient on lagged investment to shrink by half, with the t-statistic dropping to 1.8. The coefficient on government spending remained the same – very small and insignificant. Dropping the investment and government-spending level variables produced no serious differences in the change variables. Importantly, the political variables were robust to all of these changes.

In addition, because our terms-of-trade variable is somewhat unusual in that it takes into account the effect of trade shocks on income, we tried a more standard terms-of-trade variable instead. The standard variable performed similarly to the variable we used, and the substitution had no appreciable effect on our results.

Finally, we tried using Barro's secondary-schooling variable ($syrxx$) instead of life expectancy as a proxy for human capital (Barro and Lee, 1993). This produced changes in all of the variables, even hardy economic ones like lagged per capita income and investment. The political variables also changed: Negative change survived but its standard error was fairly large (t-statistic was –1.5). The level variables survived, but the duration variables did not. While this seems drastic, it probably has less to do with the education variable itself, and more to do with the fact that we lose almost half of our observations (ending up with only 446) and 17 cases, many of them at level two.

NOTES

1. Because of shocks and informational asymmetries between voters and executives, voters cannot directly observe policy or discern the impact of policy choice on growth. Thus, voters have to select leaders based upon imperfectly observable indicators – policy platforms in the case of prospective models of selection, and past performance in the case of retrospective sanctioning models of selection.
2. These types of explanations fall under the category of selection models. See Fearon (1999) for a discussion of these models.
3. These are known as sanctioning models. See Barro (1973), Fiorina (1981), Ferejohn (1994, 1999), and Manin (1997).
4. In a noncompetitive election, if the voter does not like the candidate presented all he or she can do is opt out and refuse to vote. All other recourse can only be in an extra-legal context.
5. In fact, much of the literature linking regime type (democratic–authoritarian) variables to growth has been inconclusive. See Remmer (1990), Helliwell (1994), and Barro (1996).
6. It is worth noting that our approach differs significantly from previous empirical research on political instability and growth. We emphasize *institutional instability*, or more specifically, changes in the rules that bring executives to power. In contrast, prior studies looking at the link between political instability and economic growth have focused on government turnover and/or violence, not institutional instability per se. For examples, see Alesina *et al.* (1996), Londregan and Poole (1990), Alesina and Perotti (1992), Brunetti (1995, 1998a), and Knack and Keefer (1998). An exception is Clague *et al.* (1996), who consider regime duration and its effect on property rights, not economic growth rate.
7. We expect that there will probably be diminishing marginal returns to duration: we anticipate one year more of institutional stability to matter a lot more in new democratic systems, but not a lot in older systems.
8. See Pritchett (1998) for a related perspective.
9. (X/GDP) × (%change in export price index) – (M/GDP) × (%change in import price index).
10. See Appendix 1. More information on the coding of the scale is available from the authors.
11. Examples of studies that use Gastil include Helliwell (1994); Tavares and Wacziarg (1996); Barro (1996); Kormendi and Meguire (1985). Other indices and measures include Gurr's Polity III democracy/authoritarian coding (see Jaggers and Gurr 1995); and Alvarez *et al.*'s (1996) democracy indicator.
12. A notable exception is Alvarez *et al.* (1996). Their dichotomous measure of democracy and dictatorship is based on narrow, fixed, and observable characteristics. Like us, they are primarily concerned with contestation. We agree with the spirit of their work, but find that it is of limited use in Africa. Because their guidelines for classifying democracies are quite demanding, all African countries (including Botswana) are considered 'dictatorships'. Temporal variation is also obscured, as brief experiments with democratic elections (such as Nigeria's in 1980) are ignored. We have tried to capture these important differences with a more nuanced, but no less objective, measure.
13. For example, Arat (1991) constructs a 'score of democraticness' based on the following equation: Score of democraticness = [(Participation × (1 + Inclusiveness)) + Competitiveness] – Coerciveness.
14. Sources include Taylor and Jodice (1983); *Africa Research Bulletin; Africa South of the Sahara; Africa Contemporary Record;* and *Africa Confidential* for various years.
15. For example, we looked at the difference between dichotomous change variables versus actual change variables, and at a number of 'normalized' change variables (these divide actual change by potential change). However, the results showed nothing new (they were similar to dichotomous variables). Therefore, we do not present them here. All results are available from authors upon request.
16. In a few instances, outlined in the variables section, $\tau = 2$ (a two-year lag).
17. The fixed-effects framework affects some but not all of our results. The change results are unaffected by moving to fixed effects, while the level results do change somewhat (without

118 COPING WITH GLOBALIZATION

fixed effects, we tend to see level three growing slowest, level two fastest, level six in between, even in the short-term). The duration and interaction results are fairly robust.
18. For both Table 4.2 and Table 4.3, the difference in means is statistically significant at the 10 per cent level. Tables 4.2 and 4.3 are reproduced from Ferree and Singh (2000a).
19. Table 4.4 reproduces the results reported in Ferree and Singh (2000a).
20. By using a simultaneous estimation of the two equations for growth and political instability, Alesina *et al.* (1996) find that whereas leadership turnover and other measures of political change have a strongly negative effect on annual growth rates, the reverse relationship does not hold. Although they expected a significant negative effect of growth on the propensity of government change, change in the annual growth rate did not have a statistically significant impact. We cannot follow their example of using three-stage least squares because of the binary nature of the change variable.
21. Table 4.5 reproduces results reported in Ferree and Singh (2000b).
22. If we use a contemporaneous value of duration (instead of the lag), the size of the coefficient stays about the same but the standard error shrinks, making for a much better estimated effect. We suspect that this is because the contemporaneous value captures recent changes, which have a growth-depressing effect. We use the lag value because we think this specification is a more rigorous test of the importance of duration as opposed to change.
23. What about the 'Botswana' effect? That is, are these results being driven by a single country such as Botswana, which has experienced a long period of growth and happens to be one of Africa's few long-term democracies? Yes and no. Unfortunately, Botswana does not enter our sample except for six years in the mid-1980s. (This is because it lacks terms-of-trade data for all other years.) We thus lose this very important case. This means that, while the results do not hinge on Botswana, they do depend heavily on Mauritius, the only other African country with more than twenty years of experience with competitive multiparty elections in our sample. (See Appendix 2.) Although this does not negate our findings, it does point out the limitations of our data and the need to extend this work to areas of the world that include more long-term democracies.
24. Taken from Ferree and Singh (2000b).
25. We follow the prescriptions in King *et al.* (2000). All results were based on 1000 simulations with economic variables held at their means. GAUSS code available upon request.
26. Tables 4.6 and 4.7 are reproduced from Ferree and Singh (2000b).
27. We did run Equation 4 with a control variable that recorded whether political violence occurred in that year, and the results did not change for the scale levels, duration or interaction effects. Results available from authors upon request.

REFERENCES

Africa Confidential (various years from 1967) (London: Miramoor Publications).
Africa Contemporary Record (various years from 1968) (New York: Africana Publishing Co.).
Africa Research Bulletin (1965–91, various years) (Exeter: Africa Research Ltd.).
Africa Research Bulletin (various years from 1991) (Oxford: Blackwell Publishers).
Africa South of the Sahara (various years from 1971) (London: Europa Publications Ltd.).
Alesina, A. and Perotti, R. (1992), 'Income Distribution, Political Instability and Investment', Institute for Policy Reform, IPR53.
Alesina, A., Ozler, S., Roubini, N. and Swagel, P. (1996), 'Political Instability and Economic Growth', *Journal of Economic Growth* 1: 189–211.
Alvarez, M., Cheibub J., Limongi, F. and Przeworski, A. (1996), 'Classifying Political Regimes', *Studies in Comparative International Development* 31, 2: 3–36.
Arat, Z.F. (1991), *Democracy and Human Rights in Developing Countries* (Boulder, CO: Lynne Rienner).
Barro, R. (1973), 'The Control of Politicians: An Economic Model', *Public Choice* 14: 19–42.
Barro, R. (1996), 'Democracy and Growth', *Journal of Economic Growth* 1: 1–22.

Barro, R. and Lee, J.W. (1993), 'International Comparisons of Educational Attainment', National Bureau of Economic Research Working Paper, Cambridge, MA.

Barro, R. and Sala-i-Martin, X. (1995), *Economic Growth* (New York: McGraw-Hill).

Beck, N. and Katz, J. (1995), 'What to Do (and not to do) with Time-Series Cross-Section Data', *American Political Science Review* 89: 634–47.

Bloom, D.E. and Sachs, J.D. (1998), 'Geography, Demography, and Economic Growth in Africa', *Brookings Papers on Economic Activity* 2: 207–95.

Bollen, K. (1993), 'Liberal Democracy: Validity and Method Factors in Cross-National Measures', *American Journal of Political Science* 37: 1207–30.

Bratton, M. and van de Walle, N. (1997), *Democratic Experiments in Africa: Regime Transitions in Comparative Perspective* (New York: Cambridge University Press).

Brunetti, A. (1995), 'Perceived Political Instability and Economic Growth', paper presented to the Research Training Group in Positive Political Economy, Harvard University.

Brunetti, A. (1998a), 'Political Variables in Growth Regressions', in S. Borner and M. Paldam (eds), *The Political Dimension of Economic Growth* (New York: St Martin's Press), pp. 117–35.

Brunetti, A. (1998b), 'Policy Volatility and Economic Growth: A Comparative, Empirical Analysis', *European Journal of Political Economy* 14: 35–52.

Clague, C., Keefer, P., Knack, S. and Olson, M. (1996), 'Property and Contract Rights in Autocracies and Democracies', *Journal of Economic Growth* 1: 243–76.

Collier, P. and Gunning, J.W. 'Explaining African Economic Performance', *Journal of Economic Literature* 37: 64–111.

Dixit, A. and Pindyck, R. (1994), *Investment Under Uncertainty* (Princeton, NJ: Princeton University Press).

Du Toit, P. (1999), 'Bridge or Bridgehead? Comparing the Party Systems of Botswana, Namibia, Zimbabwe, Zambia, and Malawi', in H. Giliomee and C. Simkins (eds), *The Awkward Embrace: One Party Domination and Democracy* (Cape Town: Tafelberg Publishers), pp. 193–217.

Easterly, W., Kremer, M., Pritchett, L. and Summers, L. (1993), 'Good Policy or Good Luck'? Country Growth Performance and Temporary Shocks', *Journal of Monetary Economics* 32: 459–83.

Easterly, W. and Levine, R. (1997), 'Africa's Growth Tragedy: Policies and Ethnic Divisions', *Quarterly Journal of Economics* 112: 1203–50.

Fearon, J. (1999), 'Electoral Accountability and the Control of Politicians: Selecting Good Types versus Sanctioning Poor Performance', in A. Przeworski, S. Stokes and B. Manin (eds), *Democracy, Accountability, and Representation* (Cambridge: Cambridge University Press), pp. 55–97.

Ferejohn, J. (1994), 'Incumbent Performance and Electoral Control', in T. Persson and G. Tabellini (eds) *Monetary and Fiscal Policy*, vol. 2 (Cambridge, MA: MIT Press), pp. 29–45.

Ferejohn, J. (1999), 'Accountability and Authority: Toward a Theory of Political Accountability', in A. Przeworski, S. Stokes and B. Manin (eds), *Democracy, Accountability, and Representation* (Cambridge: Cambridge University Press), pp. 131–53.

Ferree, K. and Singh, S. (2000a), 'Institutional Instability and Growth in Africa, 1970–92' (unpublished manuscript, Harvard University).

Ferree, K. and Singh, S. (2000b), 'Revisiting Africa's Growth Tragedy: Electoral Competition, Institutional Duration, and Growth in Africa from Independence through the 1990s' (unpublished manuscript, Harvard University).

Fiorina, M. (1981), *Retrospective Voting in American National Elections* (New Haven, CT: Yale University Press).

Guillaumont, P., Jeanneney, S.G. and Brun, J-F. (1999), 'How Instability Lowers African Growth', *Journal of African Economies* 8: 87–107.

Hassett, K. and Metcalf, G. (1999), 'Investment with Uncertain Tax Policy: Does Random Tax Policy Discourage Investment?,' *Economic Journal* 109: 372–93.

Helliwell, J.F. (1994), 'Empirical Linkages Between Democracy and Economic Growth', *British Journal of Political Science* 24: 225–48.

Hoeffler, A. (1997), 'The Augmented Solow Model and African Growth Debate' (unpublished manuscript, Oxford University).

Huntington, S.P. (1991), *The Third Wave: Democratization in the Late Twentieth Century* (Norman, OK: University of Oklahoma Press).

Jaggers, K. and Gurr, T.R. (1995), 'Tracking Democracy's Third Wave with the Polity III Data', *Journal of Peace Research* 32: 469–82.

King, G., Tomz, M. and Wittenberg, J. (2000), 'Making the Most of Statistical Analyses: Improving Interpretation and Presentation', *American Journal of Political Science* 44: 341–55.

Knack, S. and Keefer, P. (1995), 'Institutions and Economic Performance: Cross-Country Tests Using Alternative Institutional Measures', *Economics and Politics* 7: 202–27.

Knack, S. and Keefer, P. (1998), 'Political Stability and Economic Stagnation', in S. Borner and M. Paldam (eds), *The Political Dimension of Economic Growth* (New York: St Martin's Press), pp. 136–53.

Kormendi, R. and Meguire, P. (1985), 'Macroeconomic Determinants of Growth: Cross-Country Evidence', *Journal of Monetary Economics* 16: 141–63.

Londregan, J. and Poole, K. (1990), 'Poverty, the Coup Trap, and The Seizure of Executive Power', *World Politics* 42: 151–83.

Manin, B. (1997), *Principles of Representative Government* (Cambridge: Cambridge University Press).

Pritchett, L. (1998), 'Patterns of Economic Growth: Hills, Plateaus, Mountains, and Plains', *Policy Research Working Paper* 1947 (Washington, DC: World Bank).

Przeworski, A. and Limongi, F. (1993), 'Political Regimes and Economic Growth', *Journal of Economic Perspectives* 7, 3: 51–69.

Remmer, K. (1990), 'Democracy and Economic Crisis: The Latin American Experience', *World Politics* 42: 315–35.

Rodrik, D. (1997a), 'Democracy and Economic Performance' (unpublished manuscript, Harvard University).

Rodrik, D. (1997b), 'Trade Policy and Economic Performance in Sub-Saharan Africa', National Bureau of Economic Research Working Paper 6562, Cambridge, MA.

Sachs, J. and Warner, A. (1997), 'Sources of Slow Growth in African Economies', *Journal of African Economies* 6: 335–76.

Serven, L. (1996), 'Irreversibility, Uncertainty and Private Investment: Analytical Issues and Some Lessons for Africa', unpublished manuscript, The World Bank, Washington, DC.

Tavares, J. and Wacziarg, R. (1996), 'How Democracy Fosters Growth' (unpublished manuscript, Harvard University).

Tayler, C. and Jodice, D. (1983), *World Handbook of Political and Social Indicators*, 3rd edn (New Haven, CT: Yale University Press).

5

Responses to Economic Risk in Four ASEAN Countries, 1975–97[1]

SUSAN McMILLAN

INTRODUCTION

The processes of globalization include trends toward economic integration and an ideological component supporting free markets and political democratization. Some analysts of international political economy view the processes of globalization as posing a threat to the ability of governments to make autonomous and effective macroeconomic policy (see Cerny, 1999). There is a concern that the market forces inherent in economic integration will produce a 'policy race toward the neoliberal bottom' (Garrett, 1998b: 788) in which government intervention in the economy is proscribed.

In contrast to this rather pessimistic view, a growing body of statistical studies finds that trade openness is positively associated with government size (Cameron, 1978; Quinn, 1997; Garrett, 1998b; Rodrik, 1998). The explanation given is that government consumption or spending is a domestic policy response to the risks that result from economic integration. This literature is heavily based on data from the democratic, advanced industrialized countries, and whether the same finding applies to developing countries with varying degrees of democracy is the subject of this chapter.

Specifically, I investigate two research questions. First, to what extent is government spending in developing countries influenced by participation in the international economy? Second, does democratization affect the size of government spending when controlling for the possible effects of international economic integration?

I have chosen to explore these questions using cross-sectional time-series data from four of the five original members of the Association of Southeast Asian Nations (ASEAN), for the time period 1975–97. Indonesia, Malaysia, the Philippines and Thailand are included. Singapore is excluded because as a city state and one of the original NICs (newly industrializing countries), it has a very different type of economy. The newer members of the ASEAN are excluded for reasons of data availability.

The 'ASEAN Four' countries are not necessarily representative of the entire population of developing countries, but they share characteristics that make examining them as a group reasonable. Even though there are some key differences, these countries have roughly similar economies that are rich in natural resources. They are able to earn foreign exchange and raise government revenue by exporting agricultural and mineral commodities, and they have been relatively open to the international economy (Bowie and Unger, 1997). If globalization constrains government policies, that relationship should be apparent in countries with these characteristics.

The rest of this chapter is organized in the following way. I first describe the debate about how globalization might affect the size of government, and discuss how regime type might influence spending policies. The second section presents the model to be estimated, and describes the quantitative indicators. Third, the statistical results are presented. Finally, the results and conclusions are discussed with reference to the ASEAN Four countries.

GLOBALIZATION AND RESPONSES TO ECONOMIC RISK

Globalization and Government Size

The existing literature on the relationship between globalization and domestic political and economic outcomes is large and has a history that extends back to David Hume and Adam Smith (see Evans, 1997; Quinn, 1997; Garrett, 1998b). More recent statistical studies assess the influence of globalization processes on a wide range of dependent variables, for example: income inequality (Quinn, 1997; Mahler et al., 1999), economic growth (Gasiorowski, 2000; Quinn, 1997), trade policy (Bates et al., 1991; Quinones and Gates, 1995), corporate taxation (Garrett, 1995; Quinn, 1997), welfare spending (Hicks and Swank, 1992; Huber et al., 1993), and the size of government, as measured by consumption or expenditures (Cameron, 1978; Cusack, 1997; Garrett, 1998b; Rodrik, 1997, 1998). Here, I am primarily interested in whether globalization constrains macroeconomic policies in developing countries. Therefore, I focus on the relationship between economic integration and government size.

Cameron (1978: 1243) points out that in the years following World War Two, the role of government increased to include typical welfare state policies such as transfer payments to the unemployed, the poor, the sick, and the elderly. Governments have also been expected to use fiscal and monetary policy to attempt to smooth out business cycles and manage unemployment and inflation rates. The size of government, as indicated by expenditures, consumption, or extractive capacity, is thus a reflection of efforts to pursue these sorts of policy goals.

The economic integration inherent in globalization poses risks – the potential for costs – to at least some actors within national economies (Frieden and Rogowski, 1996). For instance, there may be overall gains from liberalized trade, but there is also the risk that some businesses will not be competitive and will fail. Moreover, as capital mobility increases, investors may respond to national differences in fiscal and monetary policies by taking advantage of arbitrage profit possibilities, leading to abrupt shifts in capital and perhaps debilitating capital flight (see Quinn, 1997). Additional risks stem from the ease and speed with which economic crises elsewhere can be transmitted to national economies through global trade and finance networks.

Bates *et al.* (1991: 3–4) follow Williamson (1985) in arguing that risk-averse economic actors will want non-market institutions to make 'an effort to reduce the welfare losses incurred from variability in economic environments'. One way states can try to mitigate the risks is to follow less open trade strategies. Bates *et al.* (1991) and Quinones and Gates (1995) find statistical evidence that countries facing economic risks are more likely to pursue protectionist policies.

Another strategy is for the state to pursue a policy of compensation for those who bear the costs of economic adjustment. Macroeconomic policies, including government spending, can be used as part of a compensation plan, and governments are likely to face increasing political demands for such spending strategies. For instance, globalization of trade and finance may not necessarily create more unemployment, but it enhances sectoral and geographical mobility. These dislocations spark increasing demands for public spending on goods and services such as social insurance and education (Grunberg, 1998: 598).

Analysts differ with respect to whether, or how much, the processes of globalization constrain governments in their attempts to provide compensation for risks. One view is that because market integration increases the exit options of producers and investors, government macroeconomic policies will lose effectiveness unless they are in line with market expectations. The market logic of globalization will drive policies, causing taxation and income to become more regressive (see Quinn, 1997: 531). Since it is more difficult to maintain high corporate tax rates, it is also more difficult to continue with high levels of government spending (Grunberg, 1998; Kurzer, 1993). In short, Cooper (1972) and other observers of globalization processes have concluded that economic interdependence erodes the effectiveness of national economic policies and thus national policy autonomy (see Milner and Keohane, 1996: 16–17).

There is also an ideological component to expectations that global-ization will reduce the ability of governments to use spending policy to respond to risk. Evans (1997: 70–4) argues that, despite the history of the welfare-state model in the advanced industrialized countries, the current 'Anglo-American' ideology strongly discourages state intervention in the economy. The International Monetary Fund and the World Bank subscribed to this ideology in the 1980s, and stabilization programs for developing countries included, among other domestic adjustment measures, reductions in government spending (Walton and Seddon, 1994: 41).

The alternative point of view on the relationship between globalization and domestic policies is more optimistic regarding the ability of states to use government spending to help cover the risks of integration. In this perspective, governments have strong political incentives to meet demands for redistribution of both risk and wealth (Garrett, 1998b: 791). New theories of economic growth posit that large public economies can promote economic strength by investing in the economy in ways that support the market, and that are important for international investors (Evans, 1997; Garrett, 1998b: 801). It is possible, even likely, that globalization will make effective economic policies more difficult to implement, but, '... global-ization ... increases both the potential returns from effective state action and the costs of incompetence' (Evans, 1997: 74).

Ruggie's (1982) concept of 'embedded liberalism' explained how the advanced industrialized countries were committed to relative economic openness, while at the same time they undertook welfare policies to protect citizens from the costs of integration. Katzenstein (1985) used case studies of the small social democracies in Europe to demonstrate that adherence to market principles is not incompatible with government intervention in the economy. The experiences of government-led growth in the East Asian NICs seemed to provide further support for that conclusion.

Several statistical analyses also present evidence of a positive relation-ship between government size and trade integration (for a thorough review, see Schulze and Ursprung, 1999). The seminal work is Cameron's (1978) cross-sectional study. He found a positive correlation between trade open-ness and government revenues as a percentage of gross domestic product (GDP) in 18 advanced industrial states. Other scholars have attempted to replicate this result, as well as to control for more variables, and use additional indicators for economic integration.

Rodrik (1998) used a cross-section of more than 100 countries and found a positive relationship between trade openness and government consump-tion as a share of GDP, even when controlling for potentially confounding variables. In an effort to test whether economic risk was driving the results, he then included an indicator for terms of trade variability. When that variable was interacted with openness, the coefficient was positive and highly significant, and openness was no longer significant. He concluded that economic risk is the key international factor influencing government size.

Rodrik's analysis also included regressions using subsets of the data for developed and developing countries. His results suggest that in wealthier countries, welfare and social security spending, rather than government consumption, were significantly affected by risk. In the sample of developing countries, risk remained highly significant for explaining government consumption (Rodrik, 1998: 1021).

Rodrik focused on risk from trade, but a similar positive relationship has been found between financial integration and government size. Quinn (1997) also used cross-section regression analysis of data from 30 to 38 countries and found that change in capital mobility has a positive effect on government expenditures (minus defense and education) as a share of GDP, and on welfare and social security payments as a percentage of GDP.

Conversely, there is also some evidence that supports the contention that government spending is constrained by globalization. Employing cross-sectional data, Cusack (1997) reported a negative influence of financial integration on changes in non-defense government spending in 15 OECD (Organisation for Economic Co-operation and Development) countries. But Schulze and Ursprung (1999: 332) maintain that the finding for financial integration is not robust. In contrast with his other work, which included a much larger number of countries, Rodrik (1997) found a negative effect of both trade integration and capital market liberalization on government consumption in the OECD countries. This is consistent with his 1998 work that found significant differences for the developing and the already developed countries.

Differences in data and methodology may certainly have contributed to the different findings noted above. However, political variables may also help explain the nature of the relationship between economic risk and government size. Cusack's work (1997) included indicators for the ideological 'political center of gravity' of the government and the electorate in addition to an indicator for financial openness. He found that ideological preferences do affect government spending policies, even when controlling for the effects of international integration (Cusack, 1997: 391).

Garrett (1995) found that financial capital mobility had a negative influence on government spending. However, the relationship is more complex when political variables are taken into account. Garrett (1995 and 1998a, cited in Schulze and Ursprung, 1999) found that capital-market integration interacts significantly with his political index of 'left-labor power'. At high levels of globalization, government spending varies positively with left-labor power, and at low levels of globalization the opposite relationship holds. When political effects were included, financial capital mobility and foreign direct investment (FDI) did not have independent negative effects on government consumption (Garrett, 1998a).

The existing analyses are heavily based on data from the OECD countries, but taken together they suggest that globalization does not necessarily have the effect of constraining state macroeconomic policies. There is evidence to support the position that, for political reasons, governments respond to the risks generated by trade openness by using spending policies to help insulate actors in the domestic economies from the costs associated with globalization. The evidence from developing countries is still scarce (though see Rodrik, 1998). Therefore, whether the pattern among OECD members holds for developing countries is an open empirical question.

Some observers argue that developing countries will be especially constrained by the forces of globalization. They echo the conclusions of the dependency theorists of the 1960s and 1970s. The current argument is that, because they lack well-developed administrative capacity, the developing countries are particularly vulnerable to the risks of integration – for example, tax evasion strategies of multinational corporations (MNCs), and the consequent lost tariff and tax revenues – while they have not yet developed the institutions necessary for mitigating those risks (see Bates *et al.*, 1991: 15; Caves, 1996; Grunberg, 1998). Further, the international context, both economic and ideological, may have changed such that governments now cannot carry out the mix of welfare-state policies and progressive taxation that the already industrialized countries did (Evans, 1997; Rodrik, 1997).

Democratization and Government Size

The ability of developing countries to use government spending to mitigate risks must also be examined within the context of domestic politics. Since the existing hypotheses and empirical studies have been focused primarily on the effects of globalization in countries that were already democratic, it is not surprising that when political variables have been included in analyses, they have been related to party or ideology rather than simple regime type.

For developing countries, democratization has been a trend that has accompanied economic integration (see Diamond, 1993). Discussions of regime transitions – rather than ideology, party, and labor union structures – have dominated in the literature (e.g. Haggard and Kaufman, 1995; Huntington, 1991). It seems plausible that democracy may have different effects on macroeconomic policy in developed and developing countries because of their differences in institutions, property-rights security, and the social and cultural conditions that 'enhance democratic legitimacy and political stability' (Gasiorowski, 2000: 324).

This leads to my second research question on whether democratization affects government size when controlling for the possible effects of economic integration. There is a large body of literature relating political variables, among them regime type, to government spending patterns (e.g. Ames, 1987; Brown and Hunter, 1999; Hicks and Swank, 1992). A related question is whether democracies and authoritarian regimes are equally able to implement economic reforms that are necessary for integration into the global economy (e.g. O'Donnell, 1978).

Yet another set of research examines whether and how regime type affects the ability of governments to produce effective macroeconomic policies more generally (e.g. Gasiorowski, 2000; Olson, 1993; Cheibub, 1998). I do not review all of this literature. Rather, I extract from it two competing arguments regarding the relationship between regime type and government spending. The first argument is that democratic regimes spend more than authoritarian regimes. The second is that there is no systematic relationship between regime type and government spending.

The argument that democracies spend more than authoritarian regimes is usually based on assumptions about the processes of electoral competition (e.g. Skidmore, 1977). Politicians feel constrained to appeal to the poorer segments of society by promising and delivering policies such as increased spending that will contribute to a rise in real personal incomes (see Cameron, 1978: 1246). So, for example, Ames (1987) found that electoral competition was associated with increased social spending in Latin American countries.

In contrast, authoritarian rulers do not typically need to worry about being (re)elected. The effects of party competition, elections, and voter preferences are limited in authoritarian regimes, so the government may spend less as the leaders attempt to pursue neo-liberal macroeconomic policies (Brown and Hunter, 1999: 780). Moreover, authoritarian regimes can use repression to deal with the potential for social unrest that arises from economic integration (O'Donnell, 1978).

Some analysts are skeptical about a systematic effect of regime type on either economic policy performance, or policy choices that are reflected in the size of government budgets (e.g. Haggard and Kaufman, 1995; Przeworski and Limongi, 1993). One reason for the skepticism is that authoritarian governments may also have strong reasons to expand the public budget. Even though authoritarian leaders are not accountable to the general public in the same way as leaders in democracies, they are accountable to some constituency. They may use government spending to construct coalitions insuring their political survival (Nelson, 1990).

Another reason scholars expect no systematic difference is that democratic leaders may not feel as constrained by electoral pressures as anticipated. Some evidence suggests that economic austerity policies have more widespread democratic support than generally thought (Haggard and Kaufman, 1992: 340). The ideological component of globalization may help to increase support for neo-liberal domestic adjustment policies. If the majority of people in a democracy support difficult economic policies, electoral pressures may not necessarily lead to an expansion of the government's share in the economy.

Despite the skeptics, there is some recent evidence that regime type can be a useful variable for understanding such outcomes as social-welfare spending policies in Latin America (Brown and Hunter, 1999), and macroeconomic performance through time and among a large cross-section of countries (Gasiorowski, 2000). Given the ambiguities in the literature, I give three reasons for investigating whether democratization has an impact on government size in developing countries.

First, democratization itself can be seen as part of the ideological component of globalization (Haggard and Kaufman, 1992: 331), with adherence to market principles being another (Evans, 1997). Thus, an examination of the influence of globalization on government size ought to include the ideological aspects of democratization, as well as the effects of economic integration. Indicators for economic integration may be correlated with democratization, and this tendency may shape the relationship with government size.

Controlling for democratization is also important because authoritarian governments may react to the pressures created by economic liberalization by introducing some measure of political liberalization. In their study of countries undergoing democratization, Haggard and Webb (1997: 7) concluded that in some cases, 'Initial support for difficult programs was also secured by explicitly trading political gains for economic sacrifices.' Again, if this is the case more generally, changes in regime type might be correlated with economic integration.

Third, the effects of economic integration are mediated by domestic politics (Diamond, 1993: 58; Frieden and Rogowski, 1996; Milner and Keohane, 1996: 10), and the type of regime may be an important factor in that mediation process. In a democracy, actors facing risk, or experiencing the costs of adjustment, may have more avenues to press the government for risk-mitigating responses. As noted before, authoritarian governments may take repressive action rather than increase redistributive efforts.

RESEARCH DESIGN AND MODEL SPECIFICATION

Statistical research on developing countries is frequently hampered by missing data and/or time series that are too short to generate meaningful results. In order to try to overcome these limitations, my analysis is based on a cross-sectional time-series data set for Indonesia, Malaysia, the Philippines, and Thailand, 1975–97.

I estimate an empirical model based on previous works that have addressed the general question of whether globalization affects domestic macroeconomic policies such as government spending. I start with the premise that government size is a function of trade integration, financial integration, and a set of control variables. If globalization constrains government spending policy, trade and financial integration should be negatively related to government size. That relationship should be positive if governments are able to use spending to counter the effects of globalization. Unlike the previous studies, I include a variable to test whether government size is also a function of democratization. I operationalize this model using data from the World Bank (1999) and Freedom House.

Dependent Variable

The indicator I use for macroeconomic policies is government size, measured as total government expenditures as a percentage of GDP. This is a summary indicator of government involvement in the economy that is frequently used to show overall public sector activity (see Garrett, 1998b: 812). This indicator is too broad to allow for examining the direct effect of globalization on welfare spending or transfer payments. However, in many countries the public budget is an instrument for transferring wealth created by the private sector (Grunberg, 1998: 591). Data for this indicator were not available for the 1997 time point for Indonesia and the Philippines.

In order to present a sense of the range in the dependent variable, Figure 5.1 summarizes the time series for each of the four countries included in this analysis. Malaysia had the highest spending levels throughout the time period, peaking in 1986 and reaching its lowest point in 1997. The Philippines was at or near the bottom until an upward trend began after 1984. After that, Indonesian spending was the lowest and did not vary much from 1991 onwards. Thai spending as a per cent of GDP also peaked in the mid-1980s and then leveled off after 1990 such that the ending values were close to the starting point. Figure 5.1 demonstrates that government spending has varied both between countries, and within each country through time. It also indicates that the peaks in most countries' spending occurred during the decline of commodity prices in the mid-1980s.

FIGURE 5.1
GOVERNMENT EXPENDITURE AS PERCENTAGE OF GDP

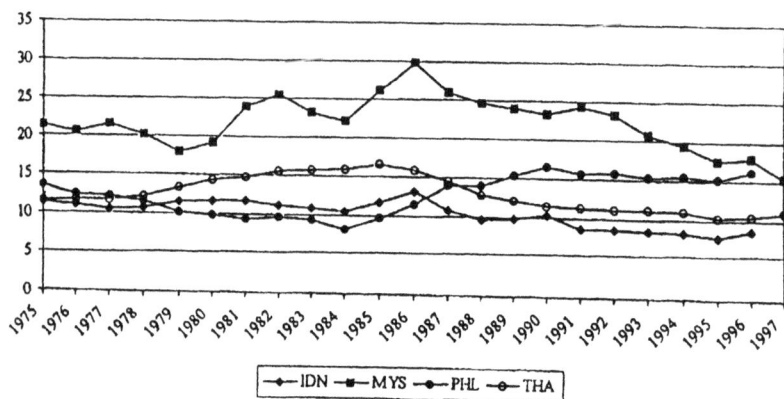

Economic Integration

Trade openness is one of the key mechanisms through which globalization affects domestic economies. The more open an economy is to trade, the more sectors of the economy are being exposed to the international economy and thus to potential risks (Cameron, 1978: 1251). My indicator for trade openness is very standard in the literature; it is the sum of exports and imports of goods and services, measured as a percentage of GDP.

Economic integration also poses risks to national economies through increasing variability in a country's terms of trade (Rodrik, 1997, 1998; Bates *et al.*, 1991; Quinones and Gates, 1995). Bates *et al.* (1991) and Rodrik (1998) used terms of trade in different ways to construct indicators to capture the risky aspect of international trade. I simply use the World Bank (1999) indicator, 'terms of trade adjustment': the capacity to import, less exports of goods and services (in constant prices).

Net flows of FDI and portfolio investment are included in my empirical model because they 'underscore the conventional views about the rise of footloose capital' (Garrett, 1998b: 806). FDI indicates how integrated a country is in the global production network, and portfolio investment is an indication of other financial links with the global economy. Of the two, portfolio investment is likely to pose more risks because it is not tied to production facilities and can thus move more rapidly. Both of these indicators are measured in millions of current US dollars, and the time series were obtained from the balance of payments in the World Bank (1999) country tables.

The data for portfolio investment present a few problems. The time series for Indonesia is shorter than for the other countries, beginning only in 1981 rather than 1975. Moreover, Indonesia had a missing data point in 1995. The data for Thailand are also missing for 1992. I used the STATA interpolation routine to fill in those two pieces of missing information. This procedure basically averages the values before and after the missing data point. The time series for Indonesia remains quite a bit shorter than for the other countries.

Democratization

Democratization may have an independent effect on government size, and I also expect it to be correlated with at least one control variable, level of development (Burkhart and Lewis-Beck, 1994). There is no standard indicator for democratization as a process, but there are several indicators for regime type that are frequently used to gauge how democratic a country is (see Bollen, 1993). I follow the work of Burkhart and Lewis-Beck (1994) and use Freedom House data to construct an index of democracy.

Freedom House uses checklists for political rights and civil liberties to construct separate 7-point scales (annually) for these components of democracy. For each country I added the scores for civil and political liberties, yielding a range from 2 (most democratic) to 14 (least democratic). The Freedom House data are reported on an annual basis, but each year is split between two calendar years. I used data beginning with 1974/75, and ending with 1996/97. I did not reverse the scale, so a positive relationship would indicate that authoritarian governments spend more than democracies. A negative relationship would indicate that democracies spend more than authoritarian regimes.

Control Variables

I include several indicators commonly suggested as determinants of government size. First, population size (in thousands) is included because there may be economies of scale and fixed costs in providing government services (Schulze and Ursprung, 1999: 337). If so, the share of government spending in the economy will be inversely related to a country's demographic size.

In addition to population, I control for the level of economic development because it is positively correlated with democracy and negatively correlated with economic growth (Mankiw *et al.*, 1992). The indicator for development is per capita GDP. I also include the annual growth rate of the economy, since economic growth may alleviate demands from the public for government spending to cover the costs of economic integration. There is also some evidence that economic growth is positively correlated with outward-oriented economic policies that support trade and financial openness (see Dollar, 1994).

Finally, in order to control for a government's ability to fund spending through borrowing, I include the proportion of total public and publicly guaranteed debt (long-term external obligations) to exports of goods and services. Debt may be correlated with both trade openness and financial integration. Trade openness may enhance the economy's ability to borrow from external sources, and thus increase government spending (Rodrik, 1998: 1008). Further, Garrett (1998b: 804) argues that financial actors focus on how government policies affect the supply of and demand for money. Since borrowing has strong implications for future inflation and thus exchange rate stability, debt is likely to be correlated with financial flows.

One final note before turning to the model estimation is that the data set is unbalanced. That is, the number of time points per country is not the same. As noted above, Indonesia and the Philippines were missing data from 1997 on the dependent variable. Also, the data for Indonesian debt begin in 1981. In the final data set, Indonesia has data for 15 time points (1981–96), and the Philippine data go from 1975 through 1996 (21 years). After interpolating the value of portfolio investment for Thailand in 1992, both Malaysia and Thailand have data for the full 1975–97 time period (22 years).

Model Estimation

Several issues must be dealt with in order to estimate a regression model using cross-sectional time-series data. First, Dickey-Fuller tests indicated that the stationarity of the time series was questionable, so I first-differenced the data to help correct this problem. Since the risks from globalization are produced by the economic changes involved in integration processes, differencing the data also makes substantive sense.

Second, with a data set that has more time points than countries, Beck and Katz (1995) have demonstrated that the error terms may be hetero-scedastic and contemporaneously correlated across the sections. I report panel-corrected standard errors to address this issue. Finally, preliminary tests indicated that autocorrelation could not be ruled out, and that the coefficient for the AR(1) process was probably different for each panel (country). I estimated a Prais-Winsten regression model, and allowed the AR(1) coefficient to vary by panel.

I used the STATA software package (version 6.0, updated July 2000) to generate the results reported here. STATA can use unbalanced panel data, estimate panel-specific AR(1) processes, and produce panel-corrected standard errors. I estimated two regression equations, the first one using differenced, non-lagged independent variables. Then, to take advantage of the time-series nature of the data, I used differenced and lagged (one year) independent variables. Using lagged data is reasonable because it may take time for economic changes to be reflected in macroeconomic policy, even in a global economy characterized by rapid information flows (see Brown and Hunter, 1999; Hicks and Swank, 1992).

ANALYSIS RESULTS

The two questions being considered are whether government spending is constrained by economic integration, and whether democracy, as part of the globalization process, is systematically related to government spending. The results of the model estimation using non-lagged data are reported in Table 5.1, and they suggest that the answer to both of these questions is no.

In contrast to the early analysis of Cameron (1978), trade openness has a negative sign, but it is significant only at the 0.20 level. Therefore, the null hypothesis of no relationship cannot be rejected. The coefficients for FDI and portfolio investment are both positive, but statistically quite insignificant. Terms of trade adjustment is the only indicator of economic integration that is statistically significant, but the coefficient is very small.

TABLE 5.1
PRAIS-WINSTEN REGRESSION: GOVERNMENT SIZE ON ECONOMIC
INTEGRATION AND DEMOCRATIZATION, ASEAN FOUR, 1975–1997

Dependent Variable: Change in Government Expenditures as a % of GDP

Independent variables	Coefficient	(s.e.*)	z	sig. z
Population	−0.1564	(0.1474)	−1.061	0.289
ΔGDP per capita	−0.0013	(0.0012)	−1.135	0.256
ΔGDP growth rate	−0.0468	(0.0492)	−0.952	0.341
ΔDebt service ratio	2.9437	(0.8316)	3.540	0.000
ΔTrade openness	−0.0429	(0.0332)	−1.292	0.196
ΔTerms of trade adjustment	9.49E-5	(4.45E-5)	2.132	0.033
ΔFDI, net flows	0.0003	(0.0003)	1.030	0.303
ΔPortfolio investment, net	0.0001	(0.0001)	0.879	0.379
ΔDemocracy index	−0.0469	(0.0485)	−0.966	0.334
Constant	0.4169	(0.4851)	0.859	0.390

IDN rho = −0.205
MYS rho = 0.084
PHL rho = 0.529
THA rho = 0.255

R^2 = 0.28
Wald chi^2(9) = 26.25
(significance = 0.002)

Number of observations = 78; Number of countries = 4.

*Numbers in parentheses are panel corrected standard errors.

This result supports the argument that trade risk increases government spending. It is consistent with Rodrik's (1998) findings.

With respect to whether democratization is systematically related to government size, the results here support the position of the skeptics. The relationship between changes in the democracy index and government size is negative, suggesting that democratic governments may spend more than authoritarian regimes. However, again, the coefficient is not statistically significant at conventional levels.

The control variables, population, per capita GDP, and economic growth all have negative signs, and the coefficients are not statistically significant. The other control variable, debt service ratio, turns out to be the most important variable in this model. It is highly significant and the sign of the relationship is positive. This finding indicates that the governments of the ASEAN Four were able to borrow in order to fund government spending plans.

It is possible that globalization effects will take some time to filter through the economy and be reflected in changes in government spending

TABLE 5.2
PRAIS-WINSTEN REGRESSION: GOVERNMENT SIZE ON ECONOMIC
INTEGRATION AND DEMOCRATIZATION, LAGGED INDEPENDENT VARIABLES

Dependent Variable: Change in Government Expenditures as a % of GDP

Independent variables	Coefficient	(s.e.*)	z	sig. z
ΔPopulation $_{t-1}$	−0.1754	(0.1691)	−1.037	0.300
ΔGDP per capita $_{t-1}$	−0.0027	(0.0016)	−1.726	0.084
ΔGDP growth rate $_{t-1}$	−0.0098	(0.0547)	−0.180	0.857
ΔDebt service ratio $_{t-1}$	−1.6058	(0.9756)	−1.646	0.100
ΔTrade openness $_{t-1}$	0.0118	(0.0374)	0.316	0.752
ΔTerms of trade adjustment $_{t-1}$	−1.19E-5	(5.84E-5)	−0.203	0.839
ΔFDI, net flows $_{t-1}$	−0.0001	(0.0004)	−0.345	0.730
ΔPortfolio investment, net $_{t-1}$	0.0004	(0.0001)	2.518	0.012
ΔDemocracy Index $_{t-1}$	0.0392	(0.0624)	0.628	0.530
Constant	0.7291	(0.5860)	1.244	0.213

IDN rho = −0.0911
MYS rho = 0.1550
PHL rho = 0.3956
THA rho = 0.2662

R^2 = 0.13
Wald chi^2(9) = 11.25
(significance = 0.259)

Number of observations = 74; Number of countries = 4.

*Numbers in parentheses are panel-corrected standard errors.

as a share of GDP. The results in Table 5.2 were produced using lagged (one year) independent variables. The overall fit of the model is not as good as in Table 5.1, but there are some interesting similarities and differences. The substantive finding for the democracy index remains the same. The sign is switched from negative to positive, but the coefficient is not even close to conventional levels of statistical significance.

The results for the indicators of economic integration present a somewhat different picture. The coefficients for lagged values of trade openness, terms of trade adjustment, and net FDI flows all have opposite signs from those shown in Table 5.1. As with non-lagged data, neither trade openness nor FDI flows is significant. However, in addition to switching from positive to negative, the parameter estimate for lagged terms of trade adjustment is not significant. Thus, prior changes in trade risks do not appear to be related to government spending.

Another difference is that changes in previous portfolio investment are positively and significantly related to changes in government size. As noted above, portfolio investment is seen as particularly risky because it can respond more quickly to market forces in a global economy. The positive relationship supports the argument that governments spend more to compensate for this risk, but there is a delay before changes in portfolio investment show up in increased government size.

For the control variables, the coefficients for population size, per capita GDP, and GDP growth rate are all still negative, but per capita GDP is now significant at the 0.10 level. Finally, the coefficient for lagged debt service ratio is negative, smaller, and significant only at the 0.10 level. The change in sign is not surprising given that debt must be repaid at.some point. Previous debt ought to constrain spending to some extent, even though current debt can finance increases in current government spending.

DISCUSSION AND CONCLUSION

Turning now to a broader discussion of the results, I begin with the finding that changes in regime type are not systematically related to government spending. The two explanations discussed earlier are that democracies are not as constrained by electoral pressures as previously expected, and that authoritarian regimes have to spend at similar levels in order to maintain support for the regime, even though they are not necessarily facing elections. Although the data cannot support a clear test of which mechanism might be a work, illustrations from these four countries suggest that leaders simply pursue spending policies in a pragmatic fashion in order to meet their needs of the moment.

In this sample of countries, Indonesia was quite authoritarian for the entire time period, shifting toward more political openness only after the 1997 financial crisis. Malaysia remained a 'soft-authoritarian' regime throughout the time period (Gomez and Jomo, 1999). Therefore, regime changes could not be related to changes in government spending. However, Dixon (1991) argues that the high levels of government expenditures were necessary to maintain enough stability for markets to operate.

The changes in democracy took place primarily in the Philippines and Thailand. In the Philippines, Marcos is credited with increasing spending both in order to get re-elected in the more or less democratic process of 1969, and to try to consolidate his authoritarian regime during the 1970s (Voss and Yap, 1996: 18). The share of government spending did increase after the 1986 transition to democracy (see Figure 5.1), but not enough to produce a significant statistical relationship.

Pei (1998) describes the Thai situation during this time period as democratic from 1973 to 1976, then authoritarian until 1988, when it gradually became more democratic until the coup of 1991. Democracy was restored again in 1992. The level of government spending as a share of GDP has not fluctuated dramatically in response to all of these changes in democracy (see Figure 5.1). It seems that, in Thailand, fairly stable economic policies tended to continue under either relatively democratic or authoritarian regimes (Bowie and Unger, 1997: 172).

These examples support the conclusion that, while the regime type may matter for how interests in society are articulated, there is no systematic effect on government spending. Since the effects of economic integration must somehow be translated into government action, one area for further research concerns how to create specific indicators and models of that process. For the advanced industrialized countries, some authors have tried to capture political variables (e.g. Garrett, 1995, 1998b). A next step for understanding the effects of globalization in developing countries would be to construct more sensitive indicators for domestic political influences.

With respect to the economic aspects of integration, the two regression models estimated here indicate that, for the ASEAN Four during the 1975–97 period, globalization was not a significant direct threat to independent government spending policies. Trade openness and current net flows of FDI and portfolio investment did not have a restraining effect on government size. The risks from terms of trade volatility and previous portfolio investment were met with greater government spending. These results are consistent with the findings from the OECD countries.

One can find country-specific examples which also support the conclusion that government intervention in the economy is not inconsistent with continued participation in the global market economy. Indonesia, because of its export earnings from oil and gas, was able to resist international pressures to dismantle its 'economic nationalist' import-substitution industrialization structures (Dixon, 1991: 200). In the 1970s, Malaysia's high government spending, which, as noted above was driven by investment in public enterprises to try to improve economic conditions for Malays, was funded in part by windfall revenues from the increases in commodity prices (Bowie and Unger, 1997: 161).

It would be too simple to conclude that developing countries are always able to respond to the risks of globalization with increased government spending. Two related factors suggest that we should use caution in making broad generalizations based on the statistical results. First, the ASEAN Four had resources for export which gave them some financial room to develop policy options. Second, in part because of their resources, and in part because they were viewed as following broadly market-oriented policies, they were able to fund higher government spending with debt.

Trade in commodities brings risks but, as the examples above suggest, it can also provide governments with export earnings with which to fund projects. Even in the Philippines, a country without oil and gas exports, the commodities prices of the 1970s provided the means to borrow in international capital markets and thus to increase government spending. Countries with fewer resource endowments may not have similar levels of export potential, and they may not have the same access to credit. In that case, they may be more constrained in their spending policies.

Even countries with access to credit must acknowledge that borrowing to increase spending may simply be putting off the adjustments required by global markets. Funding government spending through borrowing cannot go on indefinitely, as the negative relationship between prior debt and current spending indicates. One of the difficult-to-quantify aspects of the global economy is investor confidence, and it is not included explicitly in my regression equations.

Loss of confidence can lead to a crisis as investors and creditors begin to shift funds out of the economy with the perceived problems. In such a crisis, some adjustments must occur, even if they do not show up as a decrease in government spending. This can be seen dramatically in the case of the Philippines at the end of the Marcos era. The Marcos regime was able to create the illusion of sound economic policy and, despite deteriorating terms of trade in the mid-1970s, was able to borrow extensively in order to maintain government spending policies (Voss and Yap, 1996: 17). In the wake of the oil price shock of 1981, private economic actors lost confidence as they realized that this policy combination was not sustainable. Capital flight and the refusal of creditors to lend new money led to political and economic collapse.

Similarly, loss of confidence played a role in the 1997 financial crisis in

East Asia. Baer *et al.* (1999) argue that economic actors were convinced, by academic analysts as well as by selective readings of past economic growth in the region, that the leaders of the East Asian governments were being successful at limiting the role of government in the economy and at following market-conforming policies. The extensive role of the region's governments in financial markets was thus overlooked until a continuing large current-account deficit in Thailand made currency traders believe the value of the *baht* was going to fall. The Thai government was unable to convince financial markets that it could sustain the peg to the dollar and large capital outflows touched off the crisis (Baer *et al.*, 1999: 1743).

Even given the concerns about investor/creditor confidence, it is premature to conclude that macroeconomic policies in all developing countries are being driven relentlessly by market forces. As in the OECD countries, the statistical results reported here support guarded optimism concerning the ability of the ASEAN Four to use government spending policies to counter the risks that arise from participation in the global economy. These four countries were able to increase spending in response to risks from terms of trade fluctuation and from prior flows of portfolio investment, and these relationships did not depend on having either a democratic or authoritarian regime.

The optimism must be guarded, however, because the foreign borrowing that sustained government spending eventually has negative consequences for future spending. Continued access to capital depends on investor confidence that may be more difficult to maintain if government policies are perceived as creating unsustainable distortions in the domestic economy.

Further, the results from these four countries may not be generalizable to other developing countries. The ASEAN Four have resource wealth, they have followed market-oriented development strategies, and for the most part they have managed to produce strong economic growth relative to other developing countries. The features that distinguish these four countries from many other developing countries make them attractive to international capital and contribute to their high degree of interaction with the global economy. The many developing countries without these characteristics may not be able to use government spending to react to the economic risks of integration.

Despite the difficulties of extending the results here to other countries, continuing research efforts to understand the influence of globalization on domestic politics need not begin with the assumption that all developing countries will be helpless in the face of globalization. There is some evidence that governments can and do pursue policies designed to meet domestic needs, even as they participate in the economic processes of globalization.

NOTE

1. The author wishes to thank Dave Brown and Brian Pollins for helpful suggestions, and Joe McGarvey for research assistance.

REFERENCES

Ames, B. (1987), *Political Survival: Politicians and Public Policy in Latin America* (Berkeley: University of California Press).

Baer, W., Miles, W.R. and Moran, A.B. (1999), 'The End of the Asian Myth: Why Were the Experts Fooled?', *World Development* 27: 1735–47.

Bates, R.H., Brock, P. and Tiefenthaler, J. (1991), 'Risk and Trade Regimes: Another Exploration', *International Organization* 41: 1–18.

Beck, N. and Katz, J.N. (1995), 'What to Do (and Not to Do) with Time-Series Cross-Section Data', *American Political Science Review* 89: 634–47.

Bollen, K.A. (1993), 'Liberal Democracy: Validity and Source Biases in Cross-National Measures', *American Journal of Political Science* 37: 468–79.

Bowie, A. and Unger, D. (1997), *The Politics of Open Economies: Indonesia, Malaysia, the Philippines, and Thailand* (Cambridge: Cambridge University Press).

Brown, D.S. and Hunter, W. (1999), 'Democracy and Social Spending in Latin America, 1980–92', *American Political Science Review* 93: 779–90.

Burkhart, R.E. and Lewis-Beck, M.S. (1994), 'Comparative Democracy: The Economic Development Thesis', *American Political Science Review* 88: 903–10.

Cameron, D.R. (1978), 'The Expansion of the Public Economy: A Comparative Analysis'. *American Political Science Review* 72: 1243–61.

Caves, R.E. (1996), *Multinational Enterprise and Economic Analysis*, 2nd edn (Cambridge: Cambridge University Press).

Cerny, P.G. (1999), 'Globalization and the Erosion of Democracy', *European Journal of Political Research* 36: 1–26.

Cheibub, J.A. (1998), 'Political Regimes and the Extractive Capacity of Governments: Taxation in Democracies and Dictatorships', *World Politics* 50: 349–76.

Cooper, R.N. (1972), 'Economic Interdependence and Foreign Policy in the Seventies', *World Politics* 24: 159–81.

Cusack, T.R. (1997), 'Partisan Politics and Public Finance: Changes in Public Spending in the Industrialized Democracies, 1955–1989', *Public Choice* 91: 375–95.

Diamond, L. (1993), 'The Globalization of Democracy' in R.O. Slater, B.M. Schuyz and S.R. Dorr (eds), *Global Transformation and the Third World* (Boulder, CO: Lynne Rienner), pp. 31–69.

Dixon, C. (1991), *South East Asia in the World-Economy* (Cambridge: Cambridge University Press).

Dollar, D. (1992), 'Outward-Oriented Developing Economies Really Do Grow More Rapidly: Evidence from 95 LDCs, 1976–1985', *Economic Development and Cultural Change* 40: 523–44.

Evans, P. (1997), 'The Eclipse of the State? Reflections on Stateness in an Era of Globalization', *World Politics* 50: 62–87.

Freedom House, http://www.freedomhouse.org/ratings/index.htm.

Frieden, J.A. and Rogowski, R. (1996), 'The Impact of the International Economy on National Policies: An Analytic Overview' in R. Keohane and H. Milner (eds), *Internationalization and Domestic Politics* (New York: Cambridge University Press), pp. 25–47.

Garrett, G. (1995), 'Capital Mobility, Trade, and the Domestic Politics of Economic Policy', *International Organization* 49: 657–87.

Garrett, G. (1998a), 'Governing the Global Economy: Economic Policy and Market Integration Around the World', mimeo (Yale University).

Garrett, G. (1998b), 'Global Markets and National Politics: Collision Course or Virtuous

Circle?' *International Organization* 52: 787–824.

Gasiorowski, M.J. (2000), 'Democracy and Macroeconomic Performance in Underdeveloped Countries: An Empirical Analysis', *Comparative Political Studies* 33: 319–49.

Gomez, E.T. and Jomo, K.S. (1999), *Malaysia's Political Economy: Politics, Patronage and Profits*, 2nd edn (Cambridge: Cambridge University Press).

Grunberg, I. (1998), 'Double Jeopardy: Globalization, Liberalization, and the Fiscal Squeeze', *World Development* 26: 591–605.

Haggard, S. and Kaufman, R.R. (1992), *The Politics of Economic Adjustment: International Constraints, Distributive Conflicts and the State* (Princeton, NJ: Princeton University Press).

Haggard, S. and Kaufman, R.R. (1995), *The Political Economy of Democratic Transitions* (Princeton, NJ: Princeton University Press).

Haggard, S. and Webb, S.B. (1994), 'Introduction' in S. Haggard and S. Webb (eds), *Voting for Economic Reform: Democracy, Political Liberalization, and Economic Adjustment* (Oxford: Oxford University Press), pp. 1–36.

Hicks, A.M. and Swank, D.H. (1992), 'Politics, Institutions, and Welfare Spending in Industrialized Democracies', *American Political Science Review* 86: 658–74.

Huber, E., Ragin, C. and Stephens, J. (1993), 'Social Democracy, Christian Democracy, Constitutional Structure, and the Welfare State', *American Journal of Sociology* 99: 711–49.

Huntington, S.P. (1991), *The Third Wave: Democratization in the Late Twentieth Century* (Norman, OK: University of Oklahoma Press).

Katzenstein, P. (1985), *Small States in World Markets: Industrial Policy in Europe* (Ithaca, NY: Cornell University Press).

Kurzer, P. (1993), *Business and Banking: Political Change and Economic Integration in Western Europe* (Ithaca, NY: Cornell University Press).

Mahler, V.A., Jesuit, D.K., and Roscoe, D.D. (1999), 'Exploring the Impact of Trade and Investment on Income Inequality: A Cross-National Sectoral Analysis of the Developed Countries', *Comparative Political Studies* 32: 363–95.

Mankiw, N.G., Romer, D. and Weil, D.N. (1992), 'A Contribution to the Empirics of Economic Growth', *Quarterly Journal of Economics* 57: 407–37.

Milner, H.V. and Keohane, R.O. (1996), 'Internationalization and Domestic Politics: An Introduction' in R.O. Keohane and H.V. Milner (eds), *Internationalization and Domestic Politics* (New York: Cambridge University Press), pp. 3–24.

Nelson, J.N. (ed.) (1990), *Economic Crisis and Policy Choice: the Politics of Adjustment in the Third World* (Princeton, NJ: Princeton University Press).

O'Donnell, G. (1978), 'Reflections on the Pattern of Change in the Bureaucratic-Authoritarian State', *Latin American Research Review* 13: 3–38.

Olson, M. (1993), 'Dictatorship, Democracy and Development', *American Political Science Review* 87: 567–76.

Pei, M. (1998), 'The Fall and Rise of Democracy in East Asia' in L. Diamond and M.F. Plattner (eds), *Democracy in East Asia* (Baltimore: Johns Hopkins University Press), pp. 57–78.

Przeworski, A. and Limongi, F. (1993), 'Political Regimes and Economic Growth', *Journal of Economic Perspectives* 7: 51–69.

Quinn, D. (1997), 'The Correlates of Change in International Financial Regulation', *American Political Science Review* 91: 531–51.

Quinones, S.B. and Gates, S. (1995), 'Economic Risk and the Politics of Protectionism', *International Interactions* 21: 63–83.

Rodrik, D. (1997), 'Trade, Social Insurance, and the Limits to Globalization', National Bureau of Economic Research Working Paper 5905 (Cambridge, MA: NBER).

Rodrik, D. (1998), 'Why Do More Open Economies Have Bigger Governments?', *Journal of Political Economy* 106: 997–1032.

Ruggie, J.G. (1982), 'International Regimes, Transactions, and Change: Embedded Liberalism in the Postwar Economic Order', *International Organization* 36: 378–415.

Schulze, G.G. and Ursprung, H.W. (1999), 'Globalisation of the Economy and the Nation State', *World Economy* 22, 3: 295–352.

Skidmore, T. (1977), 'The Politics of Economic Stabilization in Postwar Latin America', in J. Malloy (ed.), *Authoritarianism and Corporatism in Latin America* (Pittsburgh: University of Pittsburgh Press), pp. 140–90.

Voss, R. and Yap, J.T. (1996), *The Philippine Economy: East Asia's Stray Cat? Structure, Finance and Adjustment* (London: Macmillan).

Walton, J. and Seddon, D. (1994), *Free Markets and Food Riots: The Politics of Global Adjustment* (Oxford: Blackwell).

Williamson, O. (1985), *The Economic Institutions of Capitalism* (New York: Free Press).

World Bank (1999), *World Development Indicators 1999*, CD-ROM.

6

Re-Assessing the Relationship Between Globalization and Welfare: Welfare Spending and International Competitiveness in Less Developed Countries

NITA RUDRA

INTRODUCTION

How valid is the logic of the conventional neo-liberal agenda that celebrates the efficiency effects of lower welfare spending in developing countries? The evidence in this chapter challenges the conventional wisdom that government welfare spending in this contemporary era of globalization *must* be sacrificed for the sake of improving international competitiveness. It therefore contradicts the chorus of scholars and policy-makers who claim that welfare spending is inefficient and erodes a nation's competitiveness in global markets. It agrees instead with the assertion of a growing number of researchers that the fiscal choices of the less developed countries (LDCs) do *not* in fact adversely affect their competitiveness. Rather, international market conditions and the indiscriminate behavior of foreign investors are found to be the stronger determinants of the LDCs' economic competitiveness.

Globalization is not (yet) an inexorable process, and thus it is all the more important to investigate the dynamic relationship between economic globalization and welfare spending. If the conventional neo-liberal agenda and the call for prudent fiscal policies in LDCs are valid, then lower social spending should improve economic competitiveness and promote stronger links with international markets.[1] This chapter assesses the impact of welfare spending on economic globalization among 44 LDCs during 1972–95.[2] The results of this study challenge the conventional view that reduced welfare spending increases trade competitiveness and encourages the infusion of financial or productive capital.

Conventional wisdom fails to demonstrate how a country's welfare expenditures affect its economic competitiveness. There seems instead to be an implicit agreement in the globalization literature that public spending on welfare is by definition inefficient and, consequently, hinders the competitiveness of producers of goods and services and dampens the incentives for capital investments. For example, Scholte (1997: 448) observes,

> At a time when the financing of many social security systems were coming under strain, the added pressure from global capital for reduced taxes and labor costs has driven many governments to cut back welfare programmes. In the cause of bolstering global competitiveness, governments across the planet have since 1980 rolled back social democracy and dismantled state socialism. Such shrinkages have been the cornerstone of many 'adjustment' packages in the South ... Governments have generally implemented the greatest cuts in respect of sunk costs such as unemployment benefits, old-age pensions, and untied official development assistance.

Similarly, Gill (1995: 417) remarks,

> Driven to raise operating finance on the more globalized financial markets, governments are pressured into providing a business climate judged attractive by global standards in order to win and retain foreign direct investment. Traditional forms of state intervention in the economy to promote redistribution have declined, and the socialization of risk for the majority of the population has been eroding.

There are, however, two distinct (albeit related) forces at play, one in export markets and the other in financial markets. The possibility that welfare spending can have different effects upon them is often overlooked. The separate effects of these two aspects of economic globalization must be addressed in any attempt to determine the validity of the popular view that the LDCs are caught in a 'race to the bottom'.[3] If the pertinent empirical tests fail to confirm the conventional wisdom in both respects, then the proposition that welfare spending hurts national competitiveness is seriously undermined.

This study addresses formal public programs of income maintenance and welfare services which, according to Pfaller et al. (1991), are the most visible manifestations of welfare statism.[4] These schemes are generally financed by employer, employee, and state contributions and are considered to be a component of non-wage labor costs (or social wage). Interestingly, the available data show that, on average, contributions from all three sources have fallen in the LDCs since 1972 (see Figures 6.1, 6.2, and 6.3).[5] This study focuses specifically on government spending on social welfare, since the

FIGURE 6.1
GOVERNMENT CONTRIBUTIONS TO SOCIAL SECURITY AND WELFARE 1972-95
AS PERCENTAGE OF GDP (N=44)

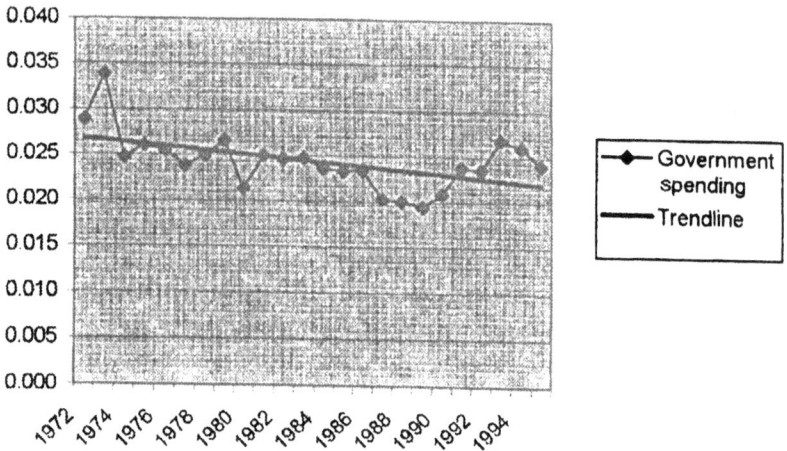

*Please see Appendix A for countries included.
Source: *Government Finance Statistics* (IMF: various editions).

FIGURE 6.2
EMPLOYER CONTRIBUTIONS TO SOCIAL SECURITY 1972-95 AS PERCENTAGE OF
GDP (N=14)

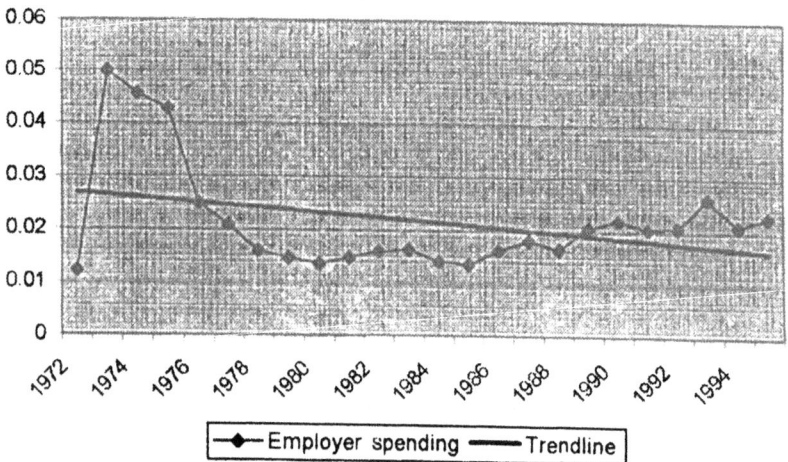

Please see Appendix A for countries included.
Source: *Government Finance Statistics* (IMF: various editions).

FIGURE 6.3
EMPLOYEE CONTRIBUTIONS TO SOCIAL SECURITY 1972–95
AS PERCENTAGE OF GDP (N=12)

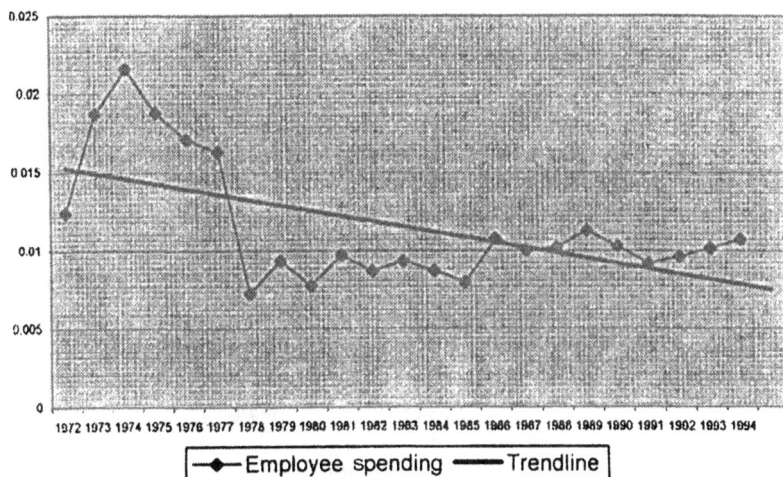

Please see Appendix A for countries included.
Source: *Government Finance Statistics* (IMF: various editions).

government is the ultimate guarantor of the size and extent of the welfare programs. It pursues two lines of inquiry. One focuses on the determinants of a country's export competitiveness, and the other addresses the forces driving capital flows. Does welfare spending necessarily raise labor costs without a corresponding gain in productivity?[6] To what extent do the fiscal policies of LDCs exercise a 'pull' on foreign capital in comparison to 'push' factors operating in the home countries of this capital?

WELFARE SPENDING AND EXPORT COMPETITIVENESS

Economists from the World Bank and the International Labor Organization (ILO) are engaged in a debate about the effects of welfare spending on export competitiveness.[7] Advocates of the World Bank perspective argue that welfare spending in the LDCs, particularly on such items as job security and mandated contributions to social funds, protects labor 'excessively' and is distortionary.[8] Such interventions interfere with the efficient allocation of resources by driving up labor costs and encouraging rent-seeking activities. According to the *World Development Report* for 1990,

> When governments intervene in the market for labor, they often exacerbate the anti-labor bias of protection. Labor market policies—

minimum wages, job security regulations, and social security—are usually intended to raise welfare or reduce exploitation. But they actually work to raise the cost of labor in the formal sector and reduce labor demand and thus depress labor incomes where most of the poor are found. (World Bank, 1990: 63)

The implication is that a state freed from such labor-market interventions would be able to devote resources to raising national output and promoting competitiveness.[9] Liberating private enterprise from such 'onerous burdens' is seen as very important for improving labor's performance (Pfaller *et al.*, 1991).[10] The World Bank perspective therefore contends that welfare spending is inversely related to export competitiveness. This is based on three supply-side arguments.

First, interventions tend to impose labor rigidities and drive up employment costs beyond equilibrium levels. The setting of labor standards causes misallocation of productive resources and prevents markets from reaching optimal conditions (Freeman, 1993). Riveros (1992) argues that the resulting level of the non-wage costs of labor significantly affects manufactured exports from LDCs. Unfettered labor markets, in contrast, set wage and employment levels that are closer to being Pareto-efficient. Thus, reducing total labor costs would lead to increased economic openness, faster economic growth and, consequently, a higher standard of living for workers.

The second argument presented by the World Bank perspective is that welfare programs indirectly influence export competitiveness by encouraging rent-seeking activities. Social welfare prompts capitalists, workers, and even governments in LDCs to devote resources to rent-seeking rather than efficiency-enhancing activities. Many critics charge that governments, in exchange for political influence, often distribute benefits to labor (Banerji and Ghanem, 1997; Pedersen, 1997). Esping-Andersen (1996) implies that traditional elites also have an interest in pressuring governments to maintain their privileges. Whether welfare programs encourage rent-seeking in the form of income transfers to workers or capitalists, they require real resources that are withdrawn from productive activities (e.g. Pedersen, 1997). The net effect is a loss in efficiency. Welfare spending hurts export competitiveness indirectly due to the 'deadweight' loss of resources which could have been put to the promotion of efficient production.

The World Bank's third argument refers to labor productivity. Simply put, interventions in the labor market create moral hazards by stifling incentives to work, save, and invest. Unemployment benefits and compensation schemes, for instance, are said to moderate the disciplinary effect of unemployment on work intensity (Marshall, 1994). The World Bank argues that early-retirement provisions reduce the supply of experienced workers, resulting in a labor force comprised mostly of relatively inexperienced employees. Thus, workers subject to market forces perform more efficiently and make a greater contribution to raising national output. The implication is that in the contemporary era, the work force should become even more 'disciplined and malleable' in order to keep up with global competition. Marshall (1994: 55) describes in the following way the alleged trade-off between welfare spending and export competitiveness faced by nations:

> A new emphasis has been placed on the alleged need for greater flexibility and less regulation of dismissal and contracts of employment. Whether expressing the more sophisticated or popular form, these views assume that for export competitiveness to improve, labor costs must go down, the workforce must become more disciplined and malleable, and individual efforts must increase. In the context of such views, labor protection and trade union intervention in the labor market and at the workplace are perceived simply as obstructions to the achievement of those aims.

In contrast, the ILO position argues that welfare programs are socially beneficial and contribute to export competitiveness and economic growth. Although the ILO perspective is 'more diffuse and less analytically grounded' than the World Bank's perspective, it nevertheless offers a potent counter-argument in favor of government programs on social welfare.

The ILO justifications for welfare programs are both economic and non-economic. Support for these programs is first and foremost based on moral imperatives. The risks and uncertainties that accompany market development require that the state provide a minimum level of economic security for all its citizens. Citizens must be compensated for the negative externalities of the market. Moreover, the ILO observers contend that government-mandated labor standards are actually Pareto improvements. Such benefits directly mitigate the principal-agent problem not considered in the World Bank assessments of the costs and benefits of welfare programs. By heightening worker motivation and workplace cooperation, labor policies can increase the employees' attachments to the firm (Kenworthy, 1999; Marshall, 1994). Therefore, higher labor benefits can actually increase productivity. The consequent reduction in per unit labor costs results in a net improvement in competitiveness.

Sengenberger (1993: 327) summarizes the net benefits of basic social-welfare programs:

> Once assured of minimum protection firms and other members of the community have an incentive to search for other, more constructive responses to competitive pressures, such as the introduction of better

products and processes, a more rational utilization of their physical and human resources and an improved infrastructure. [Minimum labor] standards can thus act as an inducement to endogenous development.

Ultimately, according to the ILO, there is no trade-off between equity and efficiency. By improving social well-being and increasing labor productivity, implementation of welfare programs makes capitalism compatible with overriding social objectives (Pfaller *et al.*, 1991).

WELFARE SPENDING AND CAPITAL FLOWS

Conventional theorists such as Grieder (1998), Nader *et al.* (1993), Strange (1997), Scholte (1997), Cerny (1995), Grunberg (1998) as well as non-conventional observers such as Rodrik (1997) base their analyses on the assumption that fiscal policies, particularly those concerning social welfare, are fundamental determinants of capital flows. These analysts adopt the position that capital flows are 'pulled' in by an attractive domestic investment climate. Lower welfare expenditures, by signaling strong fiscal discipline and a 'friendlier' tax environment, help to draw in foreign capital. This view, however, has been challenged by Maxfield (1998), Reisen (1996), and Fernandez-Arias (1996). These latter analysts question the emphasis given to domestic conditions relative to systemic ones in attracting capital inflows. Capital flows to LDCs, they argue, are more a function of the business cycle in the developed countries than conditions prevailing in the LDCs. Unfavorable conditions in the developed countries, such as low interest rates, tend to 'push' capital to the LDCs.

It is interesting to note that in the 'pull' story, capital inflows are subject to the full control of policy-makers in LDCs. In this perspective, if the goal is greater access to capital markets, governments are responsible for implementing the appropriate fiscal policies. Otherwise, bond markets, for example, will punish government policies such as welfare spending that can result in high inflation and large budget deficits. These pressures have become especially severe because the nature of capital flows to the LDCs has changed. Since the mid 1980s, most foreign capital flows to the LDCs have consisted of foreign direct investment (FDI) and investment in portfolio equity (Griffith-Jones and Stallings, 1995; Reisen, 1996; Kuczynski, 1994). This pattern is in contrast to the predominance of private loans from commercial banks in the 1970s. Thus, LDCs have become increasingly subject to the judgement of foreign investors (Baer and Hargis, 1997). The fiscal policies of LDC governments gain importance as these investors can easily signal their displeasure by pulling out their money or threatening to 'exit'.[11]

Conventional theories suggest that the relation between welfare spending and capital inflows is also influenced by the structure of domestic tax. A more favorable tax environment is attractive to capital and thus serves as an important 'pull' factor. Rodrik (1997) argues that the relative ease of capital owners to move in and out of the domestic economy and avoid higher taxes causes the tax base to become dependent upon labor. According to Rodrik (1997: 55) when globalization moves beyond a certain point, governments can no longer finance social welfare. He remarks:

> At the present ... international economic integration is taking place against the background of receding governments and diminished social obligations. The welfare state has been under attack for two decades. Moreover, the increasing mobility of capital has rendered an important segment of the tax base footloose, leaving governments with the unappetizing option of increasing tax rates disproportionately on labor income (Rodrik, 1997: 6).

Governments may lower social-insurance payroll taxes to reduce labor costs and provide a stronger lure for direct investment, particularly in labor intensive industries. Grunberg (1998) points out that this growing tax competition between nations is accompanied by fiscal degradation. Decreased tax revenues eventually mean less social spending. Relatedly, perceived pressure from abroad lowers the government's incentives to maintain a welfare state.

In contrast, the 'push' proponents argue that capital inflows are to a large extent beyond the control of LDC officials. Investors are presumed to be rational and have perfect information. Maxfield (1998) and Bertolini and Drazden (1997), however, suggest that investors tend to become less discriminatory when interest rates are low. As Maxfield (1998: 1201) states, financial markets may, in fact, be irrational and 'psychology rather than economics drives capital flows'. This tendency is intensified by the problem of information asymmetry (Reisen, 1996). Contagion effects, another systemic phenomenon, point to the phenomenon of herd behavior among international investors. Panic caused by financial conditions in one country triggers capital flight from other LDCs, usually based on incomplete information about the latter's conditions.

These scholars conclude that it is wrong to assume that international capitalists are making investment decisions according to the creditworthiness of LDCs. Thus, with some exceptions, Fernandez-Arias (1996) found that international interest rates have been the dominant factor in explaining variations in annual private net capital flows to LDCs. Domestic policy, then, is not constrained by the inability to tax capital or implement social welfare policies. Rather, it is limited by high local interest rates and by expectations to maintain stable exchange rates when global liquidity is tight (Maxfield, 1998).

ANALYTIC PROCEDURES

We employ cross-section time-series data in this study. Panel-data techniques and the fixed-effects method are applied to determine the impact of welfare spending on national competitiveness for three reasons. First, panel-data sets increase efficiency by using a large number of observation points, increasing the degrees of freedom and reducing the collinearity among explanatory variables. By following a given country over time as it changes status (e.g., from more welfare spending to less, or vice versa), panels enable a proper recursive structure to study the before–after effects (Hsiao, 1986). Second, the fixed-effects procedure allows one to control for the influence of missing or unobserved variables by utilizing information on the inter-temporal dynamics as well as the individuality of entities. Such a procedure eliminates much of the omitted-variable bias. For example, country effects capture territorial size, a variable that is highly correlated with trade and could not be used as an independent regressor for reasons of linear dependency. As another example, fixed effects are particularly important for capturing the tendency toward high inflation (especially for some Latin American countries) in the model for capital flows. Ultimately, the fixed-effects procedure controls for such country-specific differences without having to model them explicitly.

The proposed model posits that LDCs do not satisfy the conditions of perfect competition. By lagging the necessary explanatory variables, this model takes into account the time lapse involved in policy-making, economic adjustments, and the allocation of resources. Moreover, one might argue that the relevant causality is reversed and that private-capital flows affect changes in gross domestic product (GDP), foreign exchange reserves, and the amount of credit available from the International Monetary Fund (IMF). Yet it is not possible for *current* private-capital inflows to affect these same variables in the previous period. Therefore, this estimation technique mitigates the simultaneity problems by lagging some of the necessary variables such as welfare, GDP, IMF credits, and foreign-exchange reserves. Both welfare spending and IMF credits were lagged up to four years. We are limited to a lag of four years because some LDCs did not begin the process of liberalization until the early 1990s. Lags of more than four years would interfere with the analysis of the recursive effects of lower welfare spending.

Model Specification

The following equations present both the international and domestic determinants of foreign exports and capital flows. Table 6.1 offers a summary of all the variables.

TABLE 6.1
CONCEPTS, MEASUREMENTS, AND DEFINITIONS

Concepts	Measurements*	Definition
National competitiveness	The value of total exports [EXPORTS], net private capital flows [NETK] and net foreign direct investment [FDI] as a percentage of GDP–dependent variables.	Exports is the level of exports divided by GDP and as a proportion of total LDC exports (this total refers to the 44 LDCs in the full sample). Net capital flows consist of private debt and nondebt flows. Private debt flows include commercial bank lending, bonds and other private credits; nondebt private flows are foreign direct investment and portfolio equity investment (divided by GDP).
Government welfare expenditures	Social security and welfare as a percentage of GDP (+/–) [WELF]	'Social security' consists of income transfers, providing benefits in cash or in kind for old age, invalidity or death, survivors, sickness and maternity, work injury, unemployment, family allowance, and health care. 'Welfare affairs and services' are defined as assistance delivered to clients or groups of clients with special needs, such as the young, the old, or the handicapped.
Economic development	Gross domestic product (+) [GDP]	'GDP' is the total gross domestic product of a country.
Political regime	Indicator of democracy (+/–) [DEMOC]	Using scale 0–10; 10=strong democracy. This indicator is derived from the codings on the competitiveness of political participation, the openness and competitiveness of executive recruitment, and constraints on the chief executive.
Pressure from International Financial Institutions	Use of credits from International Monetary Fund (+) [IMF]	Denotes repurchase obligations to the IMF for all uses of IMF resources. Includes enlarged access resources, trust fund loans, and operations under structural adjustment facilities.
Foreign reserves	Foreign exchange reserves (+/–) [RESV]	Holdings of foreign exchange reserves minus gold as a percentage of imports.
Interest rates	Difference between international interest rates and domestic interest rates (–) [INTDIFF]	London Interbank Offer Rates represent the international interest rates. The interest rate for each developing country is represented by the 'average' annual interest rate.

*The signs in the parentheses under measurements represent the expected direction of the relationship. Multiple signs mean that there is an underlying debate regarding the expected direction of the relationship. For data sources, list of countries and years included, and more detailed definitions on some of the variables, see Appendices A and B.

Model 1

$$export = b_1 export_{i(t-1)} + b_2 welf_{i(t-1)} + b_3 netfdi_{i(t-1)} + b_j Ób_j X_{it} + Ób_k country_i + Ób_1 year_t + i_{it}$$

Model 2

$$netk = b_1 netk_{i(t-1)} + b_2 welf_{i(t-1)} + b_3 trade_{i(t-1)} + b_4 intdiff_{it} + b_j Ób_j X_{it} + Ób_k country_i + Ób_1 year_t + i_{it}$$

Model 3

$$fdi = b_1 fdi_{i(t-1)} + b_2 welf_{i(t-1)} + b_3 trade_{i(t-1)} + b_j Ób_j X_{it} + Ób_k country_i + Ób_1 year_t + i_{it}$$

The b's are the parameter estimates, while the subscripts i and t represent the country and year of the observations respectively; b_1 is the lagged rate of openness, incorporated to alleviate problems of serial correlation across error terms; and i is an error term. $ÓX$ represents the vector of control variables, or GDP, democracy, pressures from international financial institutions, and foreign-exchange reserves. The international variables are lagged in order to take the period of 'adjustments' into account. Logarithms are taken of all the variables in order to display the constant elasticities between the variables.

Models 1, 2, and 3 examine the extent to which that LDC governments are meeting the challenge of increasing competitiveness (1972–95) by reducing welfare expenditures. Model 1 assesses the conventional wisdom as it applies to competitiveness in export markets. If the World Bank's view is correct, then b_2 should be negative (thus supporting the conventional claim that lower welfare spending improves export competitiveness). However, if the ILO perspective is more valid, then b_2 should be positive (indicating that welfare expenditures actually promote export competitiveness).

Models 2 and 3 pertain to the effects of LDCs' fiscal policies on capital inflows. The net amount of incoming private capital is adopted as a proxy because it represents gross inflows minus amortization. It therefore presents an estimate of how much 'capital' remains within the country.[12] Net FDI flow, used to represent the mobility of productive capital, is the third dependent variable. While Model 2 analyzes the determinants of productive *and* financial capital flows, Model 3 addresses the effects of welfare spending on just the flows of productive capital. If the conventional logic is correct, then a negative b_2 should point to a tendency that domestic fiscal frugality helps to 'pull' in foreign capital. If, instead, 'push' factors operating at the global level, such as international interest rates, are the major determinants of capital flows to LDCs, then b_2 may be either positive or insignificant.

The possible effects of global 'push' factors on capital flows are investigated in two ways. First, we rely on an analysis of the significance levels of those dummy variables that reflect year-specific effects. This series of dummy variables captures the impact of common shocks, such as high interest rates, experienced by all the developing countries in a given year. If their coefficients are insignificant, then yearly effects do not exist and international conditions are less likely to be a determinant of capital flows to the LDCs. We also use the difference between the London Interbank Offer Rates (LIBOR) as a benchmark of the prevailing international interest rate and the domestic interest rate of developing countries to gauge the effect of global 'push' effects. If this coefficient is negative, signifying capital inflows are greater when LDCs' domestic interest rates are higher than the LIBOR, then the 'push' hypothesis will be supported.

Operational Measures

All three models measure national competitiveness by the level of exports and net (productive and financial) capital flows relative to GDP, based on Hart (1992: 7).[13] To check the robustness of our findings, the results were replicated by using an alternative measure of export competitiveness and competition for foreign capital. Both exports and net capital flows as a share of the total LDC exports (using the entire 44 country sample) and as a share of the total net capital flows, respectively, were applied as alternative indicators of competitiveness. These two corresponding measures may be related, but they are far from identical. These alternative measures did not reveal any serious differences in the findings.

Economists are quick to remind us that firms are competitive, not nations. Perry and Robertson (1998) convincingly argue, however, that political-economic systems do compete for the confidence of investors. By the same token, many scholars address the concept of trade competitiveness on an economy-wide basis. Alesina and Perotti (1997) monitor improvements in short-term competitiveness by comparing the relative unit labor costs in manufacturing in different countries. Based on this comparison, a country's actual chance of selling products in an internationally contested market is then called its performing competitiveness, defined to mean ability to sell on the work market (Pfaller *et al.*, 1991: 6). According to these authors, a country may be forced to reduce costly welfare expenditures in order to safeguard its performing competitiveness.

Significantly, although the proposed models analyze capital and trade flows independently, it cannot be denied that the two economic forces are interrelated. Net capital flows, for instance, are expected to have a negative effect on trade. Large capital inflows are often accompanied by inflationary pressures, real appreciation of the exchange rate, and deterioration in current accounts (Calvo *et al.*, 1994). Simply put, high capital inflows may adversely affect terms of trade through their direct effect on the exchange rate. It is thus expected that domestic export sectors have incentives to pressure governments for increased capital controls.

In contrast, it is plausible that high levels of trade (the sum of imports and exports as a percentage of GDP) have a positive effect on both productive and financial capital flows. A liberal trade and payments regime is often used as an indicator of a country's creditworthiness by foreign investors (Lensink and White, 1998). Moreover, the fact that production factors can be procured from the cheapest source and dividends can be repatriated helps to boost investor confidence (Asia Development Bank, 1995). Higher trade flows should then attract greater capital flows. Therefore, for both trade and capital inflows, the lagged variables of the other are used as regressors. Capital flows are lagged in Model 1 to avoid simultaneity problems, while trade flows are lagged in Models 2 and 3 since risk ratings are made on the basis of historical data.[14]

Welfare spending by LDC governments is the primary variable of interest in this study. Welfare spending, as it is measured in this analysis, provides an indication of both prudent fiscal policy and social wage. The social-wage variable is of direct relevance to the ILO–World Bank debate because it focuses on those benefits available to the working population and is therefore a component of the total labor costs. Government welfare spending in Model 2 also contributes to the push–pull debate on capital inflows. Reductions in welfare spending represent (potentially) lower inflation, less deficit spending, and a more favorable tax environment for the 'pull' proponents. Therefore, if the pull hypothesis is valid, lower levels of spending represent prudent fiscal policy and should therefore attract more foreign capital.

It should be emphasized that we are interested in *government* spending on social security and welfare. Total contributions to social security have been falling since 1972. Government, employer, and employee contributions have followed similar trends. Significantly, only government and employer contributions can affect labor costs. Governments have the option of using general revenues to compensate for a fall in employer contributions to labor. Yet the data suggest strongly that governments are following the same expenditure pattern as employers. It is not feasible to use data on employer contributions to assess the level of non-wage costs because such cross-country data are either unavailable or, when available, exist for only a few observations. Thus, for this analysis, government contributions to social security and welfare are used as a proxy for the level of social wages instead of employer contributions in LDCs (e.g. Kenworthy, 1999).

The interest-rate differential between developed and developing countries is, according to the push hypothesis, the chief determinant of capital flows to LDCs. If this differential is high, then capital flows to LDCs should be greater. Because the conventional interpretation does not place any emphasis on the push factors, it implies that INTDIFF, or b_4, should be insignificant.

The push hypothesis, however, will be supported if $b_4<0$. Three different measures of the domestic interest rate are applied alternatively to ensure the robustness of results: average interest rate, official interest rate, and private interest rate. The average interest rate is reported in this chapter because the results based on it did not differ from those based on the other two alternatives, nor did the results based on annual interest rates differ much from those based on monthly rates. As indicated before, INTDIFF is derived as:

b_4=LIBOR–domestic interest rate

If the domestic interest rate is higher than LIBOR, then b_4 should be negative as capital is expected to flow to the LDCs. Conversely, if LIBOR is higher than the domestic interest rate, then capital is expected to flow to the developed countries and away from the LDCs (b_4, of course, would still be negative).

The vector $ÓX_{it}$ represents the range of control variables. According to existing studies, the levels of democracy, pressure from international institutions, economic development, and foreign-exchange reserves all have an influence on capital and trade flows. All these control variables are expected to be positively correlated with the dependent variables.

Most of the variables and their expected signs are self-explanatory. IMF credits [IMF] should be positively related to trade and capital flows, while the GDP [GDP] coefficient is likely to be negative since larger countries tend to be more self-sufficient and, therefore, less dependent upon both trade and capital flows. Foreign-exchange reserves [RESV], however, are included only in Model 2 as they are only directly relevant to capital flows.[15]

The impact of reserves on capital flows is not as straightforward as one might expect. The traditional wisdom is that RESV is positively related to capital flows. Countries with high foreign-exchange reserves are supposedly better able to adjust to the destabilizing effects of capital inflows because these stocks can be used as 'shock absorbers'. Under such conditions, governments are less likely to restrict capital inflows and outflows. When foreign-exchange reserves are low, however, speculative attacks on a country's currency will lead governments to impose capital controls which, in turn, are supposed to discourage capital inflows, especially under regimes of fixed exchange rates (Leblang, 1997). Haggard and Maxfield (1996), however, challenge this interpretation. They argue that balance-of-payments crises lend greater bargaining power to internationally oriented sectors and thus facilitate the liberalization of capital accounts. Therefore, in this analysis, if capital inflows are positively associated with low foreign-exchange reserves (an indicator of crisis), then Haggard and Maxfield's hypothesis tends to be supported. In Model 2, a low level of foreign reserves is treated as an indication of fiscal crisis in an LDC.

The democracy variable [DEMOC] deserves a little more explanation. Scholars debate whether democratic countries will be more competitive in the global economy than their less democratic counterparts. Some argue that democratic institutions check the power of narrow interest groups. For example, Banerji and Ghanem (1997) state that democracies trade more because they are less likely to pass inefficient labor legislation for the benefit of 'insiders'. Skeptics, however, claim that democratic institutions tend to curtail trade because of the greater role and influence afforded to various interest groups in the political process (Verdier, 1998; Perry and Robertson, 1998; Destler, 1995).

A similar lack of consensus characterizes the relationship between democracy and capital flows. One might expect that democracies enjoy greater political stability and, therefore, should have an advantage in encouraging capital formation. The improved transparency and availability of information characteristic of democracies should offer a further incentive for investment. Yet Maxfield (1998) points out that soft authoritarian regimes may be better able to attract foreign capital than democracies because they are better able to accommodate foreign investors' demands relative to those of the local constituents. As P.B. Erdman and M. Brandmeyer (1994: 6), the editors of the *Columbia Journal of World Business* put it in their introduction, any 'deviation from the "Washington doctrine" [will] have a chilling affect [sic] capable of casting a pall over international investor enthusiasm'. It is thus easy to imagine why international investors may shy away from the political uncertainty still prevalent in the developing democracies.

Data and Methodological Caveats

Some obvious difficulties exist in measuring national competitiveness. Indeed, as Krugman (1994) has stressed, the success of one country in the world market does not have to be at the expense of another country. Exports as a percentage of GDP, exports as a share of LDC exports, and the magnitude of the trade balance are popular proxies of a country's general economic strength and competitiveness (Haque *et al.*, 1995; Ezeala-Harrison, 1999; Hart, 1992). Although all three measures have their drawbacks, export intensity is a better proxy of competitiveness (over time) than trade balances. It is important to emphasize that trade balance can be affected by factors other than competitiveness. For instance, South Korea is well known as a successful exporter. However, it ran a substantial trade deficit for many years because of its high imports of capital goods and technology needed for its heavy industries (Haque *et al.*, 1995). Conversely, using exports as a measure of competitiveness can be problematic because temporary currency devaluations can cause a rise in exports. Unlike trade balances, applying a fairly long time-series analysis can mitigate this shortcoming of using exports/GDP or exports/total LDC exports.

Even more limiting is the use of net capital flows as percentage of GDP to assess a country's ability to attract foreign capital. First, wealthier countries may show a low capital-inflow ratio because of the large size of their GDP. This analysis, however, is confined to the developing countries and, thus, largely avoids the tendency for extremely high GDPs to skew this ratio. Both Claessens and Naude (1993) and Fernandez-Arias (1996) have successfully applied the net capital flows/GDP measure to assess the 'competitiveness' of LDCs in recruiting foreign capital as in the case of this study. Alternatively, a country's net capital flows as a share of total LDC net capital flows can be adopted to mitigate the problem associated with using GDP ratios. A plausible argument against the use of both measures is that countries with high savings rate may 'need' less capital inflows. In fact, however, high-savings countries, such as South Korea and Singapore, have received increasing amounts of foreign capital over time.

Finally, data quality and comparability can be problematic in cross-section, time-series studies. The severity of this problem is mitigated by using mostly IMF and World Bank data, although these sources obviously do not completely eliminate all concerns (Harrison, 1996). Data definition and coverage are subject to change even for the same country over time.

DISCUSSION OF RESULTS

Altogether, there is weak support for the conventional wisdom that higher welfare spending has had an adverse effect on LDCs' international competitiveness. The results from Model 1 do not favor either the World Bank or the ILO perspective. According to this evidence, even a four-year cycle does not reveal efficiency gains due to reduced welfare expenditures (or lower social wage). Similarly, welfare spending has had no effect on a nation's competitiveness for foreign capital, either productive or financial. Instead, the results from Models 2 and 3 give very strong support to the push hypothesis, suggesting that international factors are the primary determinants of capital flows to the LDCs. In general, welfare spending has had differential effects on trade and capital flows, affecting the former more than the latter.

The effects of welfare spending on the level of exports relative to GDP and total LDC exports are reported in Table 6.2. Not much difference is evident between the two competitiveness indicators, lending confidence to the robustness of the results. The main variations in results are in the significance levels for IMF credits. Welfare spending was lagged a maximum of two years in the second measure of competitiveness, given the finding of some significant results. The convergent results from both estimation procedures suggest that welfare spending does not affect international competitiveness. They support neither the World Bank nor the ILO perspective.

The fixed-effects test revealed that country-specific differences and yearly effects account for most of the growth in trade flows (significant at the 99 per cent confidence level). This pattern suggests that historical and international conditions are the most important determinants of the LDCs' export competitiveness. It is likely that past policy choices, such as import-substitution industrialization or export-oriented industrialization, are

TABLE 6.2

REGRESSION RESULTS FOR EFFECTS OF WELFARE SPENDING ON EXPORT COMPETITIVENESS: MODEL 1 DEPENDENT VARIABLE: EXPORT COMPETITIVENESS

Independent variable	Exports as share of GDP	Exports as share of total LDC exports
exports (lagged)	0.607*** (0.031)	0.721*** (0.035)
welf[a] (lagged 4 years)	−0.007 (0.010)	−0.011 (0.013)
netfdi (lagged 1 year)	0.016* (0.009)	0.018* (0.011)
gdp (lagged 1 year)	0.127*** (0.021)	−0.462*** (0.036)
democ	0.004 (0.003)	0.003 (0.004)
imf (lagged 3 years)	0.002* (0.001)	−0.002 (0.001)
Country effects	Yes#	Yes#
Year effects	Yes#	Yes#
R^2	0.997	0.998
N	1008	
F value	10.06	

Fixed effects regression estimates. ***$p<0.01$; **$0.01<p<0.05$; *$0.05<p<0.10$.
Figures in parenthesis represent standard errors.
[a] The welfare variable in exports as a share of total LDC exports was only lagged two years before significant results emerged.
#F test for fixed effects. $p<0.01$.

important legacies affecting the current level of export success. The yearly dummies suggest that major fluctuations of the international business cycle have had an impact on trade flows. For example, the negative coefficients of the late 1970s and the early 1980s (not reported here) indicate that global recession hurt LDC exports. The LDCs' exports began to pick up again in the late 1980s when the world economy improved significantly.

The other significant determinants of trade were GDP and net FDI. It is commonly known that the larger countries tend to be more economically self-sufficient and the smaller ones more open to foreign trade. Thus, we would expect the negative coefficient for GDP in exports measured as a percentage of LDC exports. Conversely, countries with large GDPs should have more exports, thus implying a positive coefficient in column two of Table 6.2. One explanation for these divergent signs could be a sample bias resulting from the exclusion of some countries with large GDPs, such as China. Regardless, these seemingly contradictory results warrant future investigation into the effects of larger GDPs on the LDCs' trade.

The positive effect of FDI confirms the proposition that this investment raises a country's export level (Amirahmadi and Wu, 1992). The magnitude of this impact, however, should be kept in proper perspective, since the relevant coefficient suggests that an increase of 5 per cent in FDI (which is quite large) would only produce a 0.1 per cent increase in exports.

The significant effect of IMF credits for only one of the dependent variables makes it difficult to draw strong conclusions about the role of international financial institutions. After a three-year lag, this variable introduces a positive effect on export competitiveness (measured as a percentage of GDP), suggesting that Fund's programs do work. This result directly challenges those critics of international financial institutions, who are extremely critical about the effectiveness of these institutions and their 'neo-liberal crusades' in the developing countries. Lending greater credence to their arguments, however, is the second set of results reported on export competitiveness. Even with lags up to four years, there is no evidence that IMF credits helped export competitiveness measured as a share of total LDC exports.

The insignificant results produced by the democracy variable may appear surprising. Yet it is important to realize that much of the current debate about the impact of democracy on trade focuses on the already developed democracies (for an exception, see Banerji and Ghanem, 1997). The results presented in Table 6.3 suggest that for the LDCs, the effects of low GDP and high demand for capital crowd out the effects of democracy. The implication is that the poorer countries are more susceptible to the pressures of globalization, and that they are liberalizing their trade policies regardless of regime type.

TABLE 6.3
REGRESSION RESULTS FOR EFFECTS OF WELFARE SPENDING ON NET
CAPITAL FLOWS: MODEL 2 DEPENDENT VARIABLE: NET CAPITAL FLOWS
(EXCLUDING INTEREST RATE VARIABLE)

Independent variable	Parameter estimate	Standard error
netk (lagged)	0.244***	0.038
welf (lagged 3 years)	0.040	0.047
trade (lagged)	0.407**	0.180
gdp (lagged)	0.312***	0.103
democ	−0.041**	0.016
resv (lagged 2 years)	−0.154**	0.062
Country effects	Yes#	
Year effects	Yes#	
R^2	0.951	
N	1008	
F value	2.65	

Fixed effects regression estimates. ***$p<0.01$; **$0.01<p<0.05$; *$0.05<p<0.10$.
#F test for fixed effects. # $p<0.01$.

The most important lesson to be drawn from the results of this study is that lower welfare spending is not relevant for achieving export competitiveness. This 'gap' leaves much room for other alternatives to be explored in an attempt to improve labor efficiency and productivity. What stands out most is the seemingly negligible role for 'politics' in the political economy of trade (as witnessed by the insignificance of the democracy variable and the low coefficient of welfare spending). Yet this conclusion could be too hasty for two reasons. First, it is highly probable that the strong significance of the country dummies encompasses some of the country-specific political differences not captured by the democracy variable (such as the organizational strength of privileged domestic industries and/or labor unions). Second, recall that reducing welfare spending is a political choice made by LDC governments in response to the pressures of globalization. Seen in this way, governments could just as well have opted to reduce other costs such as subsidies to inefficient industries, or chosen a different strategy altogether such as currency devaluation (Pfaller et al., 1991). Nevertheless, these findings indicate that it is incorrect to associate welfare spending with a precipitous decline in export competitiveness. Welfare spending is therefore not a primary factor affecting export success and need not be discouraged in the current era of globalization.

Model 2 was first estimated in Table 6.3 without the interest-rate variable in order to disentangle the effects of the yearly dummies (in other words, it is necessary to ascertain if the yearly dummies 'swallow up' the effects of the differential in interest rates between the developed and developing countries). Inclusion of the interest-rate variable in Table 6.4 provides further and even stronger confirmation of the push hypothesis. Finally, Table 6.5 demonstrates that welfare spending is also not correlated with the inflow of productive capital. These regression results, taken together, suggest that the effects of welfare spending on productive *and* financial capital flows are clearly inconsequential. Welfare spending remains mostly insignificant even after lags up to four years are investigated, and when several different combinations of explanatory variables are explored.

Put simply, government spending on welfare does *not* encourage capital flight as alleged by conventional wisdom. In fact, it has had no effect on capital flows. On the contrary, the significance of the yearly effects (at the level of 99 per cent confidence) suggests that international factors (or the push factors) have a greater influence on the size of capital flows. Annual

TABLE 6.4

REGRESSION RESULTS FOR EFFECTS OF WELFARE SPENDING ON NET CAPITAL FLOWS (INCLUDING WORLD INTEREST RATE): MODEL 2 DEPENDENT VARIABLE: NET CAPITAL FLOWS (YEAR AND INTEREST RATE VARIABLES)

Independent variable	Dependent variable: net capital flows as share of GDP	Dependent variable: net capital flows as share of total LDC flows
netk (lagged)	0.226*** (0.038)	0.226*** (0.038)
welf (lagged 3 years)	0.022 (0.047)	0.022 (0.047)
trade (lagged)	0.407** (0.177)	0.407** (0.177)
gdp (lagged)	0.260** (0.103)	0.260** (0.103)
democ	−0.042** (0.016)	0.016** (0.016)
resv (lagged 2 years)	−0.159** (0.038)	−0.159** (0.061)
intdiff	−0.549*** (0.137)	−0.549*** (0.137)
Country effects	Yes#	Yes#
Year effects	Yes#	Yes#
R^2	0.953	0.524
N	1008	
F value	2.79	2.18

Fixed effects regression estimates. ***$p<0.01$; **$0.01<p<0.05$; *$0.05<p<0.10$.
Figures in parenthesis are standard errors.
F test for fixed effects. $p<0.01$.

TABLE 6.5
REGRESSION RESULTS FOR EFFECTS OF WELFARE SPENDING ON FDI: MODEL
3 DEPENDENT VARIABLE: NET FOREIGN DIRECT INVESTMENT

Independent variable	Parameter estimate	Standard error
fdi (lagged)	0.378***	0.041
welf (lagged 2 years)	−0.009	0.049
trade (lagged)	0.506***	0.144
gdp (lagged)	0.146*	0.084
democ	0.032**	0.015
imf (lagged 3 years)	0.014***	0.004
Country effects	Yes#	
Year effects	Yes#	
R^2	0.737	
N	1008	
F value	3.10	

Fixed effects regression estimates. ***$p<0.01$; **$0.01<p<0.05$; *$0.05<p<0.10$.
F test for fixed effects. # $p<0.01$.
Source: Global Development Finance, CD-ROM (IMF: 1999).

changes in international interest rates are more important than the domestic
variables.

The regression results in Table 6.4 indicate that capital flows to the LDCs
clearly went up during most years when international interest rates were
low. In the mid 1970s, for example, the positive signs on the yearly effects
(1974 and 1975) point to rising capital flows to the LDCs (not reported
here). The yearly coefficients are negative for the mid to late 1980s when
international conditions were improving and LIBOR was rising. Finally,
when interest rates in the developed world went down again in the early
1990s, the yearly coefficients turned up positive (see Figure 6.4).

Despite the similarities in the directions of the yearly dummies and
LIBOR, their relationship must be viewed with caution. After all, even
though the impact of interest-rate differentials may be a strong component
of the yearly effects, these dummies also capture other conditions in the
world economy that can affect capital flows (e.g. economic recession, debt
crisis).[16] Therefore, another set of regressions was undertaken in order to
capture the impact of the interest-rate differential more directly. This time,
however, the regressions were applied both ways, by including and excluding
the yearly effects, in order to avoid any multicollinearity problems. The
yearly effects remained significant even when the interest-rate variable was
included, suggesting that conditions other than interest rates had an impact
on capital flows.

FIGURE 6.4
LIBOR, ANNUAL PERIOD AVERAGES IN PERCENTAGE PER ANNUM, 1972-95

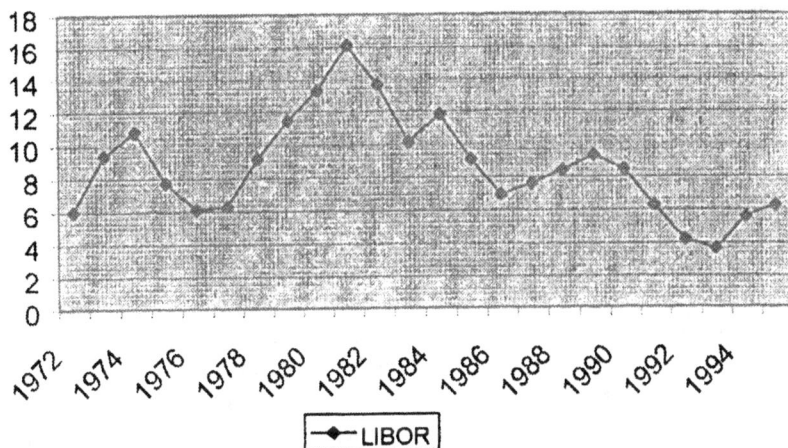

Source: *Global Development Finance* (IMF: CD-ROM: 1999).

In Table 6.5 the overall fit is very impressive. Both indicators of competitiveness (for trade and capital) reveal almost identical results, lending even greater confidence to the econometric results. Most importantly, the interest-rate variable is negative and significant at the level of 99 per cent confidence. Moreover, the impact of the push factor is quite large relative to the other variables. If interest rates in LDCs exceed those prevailing in the developed countries by, say, 2 per cent, capital flows to LDCs would increase by 3.3 per cent! These results are consistent with the studies by Maxfield (1998), Reisen (1996), and Fernandez-Arias (1996). The significance level for all of the other variables, particularly welfare spending, remained unaffected.

The remaining domestic variables, such as democracy, GDP, and foreign-exchange reserves, however, did exercise an influence on capital flows. Does this finding challenge the push hypothesis that domestic variables matter less in the competition for foreign capital? The most obvious answer is that while push factors might be the primary determinant of capital flows to LDCs in the aggregate, certain domestic differences (e.g. regime type, economic development, and foreign-exchange reserves) do still matter. For example, the results reported here suggest, contrary to Maxfield (1998), that soft authoritarian regimes are less likely to implement capital controls and attract greater capital flows.

The negative sign of foreign-exchange reserves supports Haggard and Maxfield (1996), who challenge the standard economic interpretation by arguing that a balance-of-payments crisis eventually leads to financial liberalization and thus helps to bring about more capital to LDCs. It is during a crisis that political conditions are most conducive to the removal of capital controls, since the need to reassure creditors and investors is greater under such circumstances. Haggard and Maxfield contend that the bargaining power of the proponents of liberalization in both the government and the private sector is consequently strengthened during crises. Thus, the inverse relationship between foreign-exchange reserves and capital inflows shown in Tables 6.3 and 6.4 lends strong empirical confirmation to their hypothesis.

Yet what happens when productive capital flows [FDI] are disaggregated from net capital flows? Does lower welfare spending then become an important pull factor for foreign direct investors? After all, as Schwartz (1998) points out, productive and financial capital have quite distinct effects and differing degrees of mobility. It would seem that both the social wage *and* domestic tax structure (a pull factor) would affect the investment decisions of productive capital. The driving force behind productive capital then represents a bridge between the ILO–World Bank and the push–pull debate. Table 6.5 shows that welfare spending still does not adversely affect a country's ability to attract this type of capital.

These results are interesting in that they show, except for democracy, a pattern of signs similar to those found for net capital inflows. More relevant for the purposes of this chapter, however, is that there is no evidence of a relationship between welfare spending and productive capital flows. The estimated coefficients suggest that other pull factors, besides reduced social spending, influenced the level of productive capital flows to LDCs.

To summarize, welfare spending is of minimal consequence for the international competitiveness of LDCs. The evidence in this study suggest two basic things about the political economy of trade and capital flows. First, the logic of the conventional wisdom, as represented by the World Bank perspective and the pull hypothesis, has very little empirical support. Cross-national historical differences and annual variations in international economic conditions matter more for trade and net capital flows to LDCs (although productive capital did react more to the domestic control variables). Second, our results call into question the dichotomous nature of the debate on push versus pull. It is true that international investors are not 'rational' as is commonly assumed, particularly when global interest rates are low. However, while push factors are the primary determinant of capital flows to LDCs as a whole, country-specific differences can 'pull' in more capital relative to other LDCs. In either case, this study has firmly established that government welfare spending is not a significant pull factor in the competition for either productive or financial capital.

IMPLICATIONS

The evidence presented in this chapter strongly indicates that globalization variables are not responsive to changes in domestic welfare spending. Its reassessment of the globalization–welfare nexus casts much doubt on the conventional wisdom that greater government spending on social programs creates production inefficiencies and encourages capital flight. Simply put, causality between globalization and welfare is not unidirectional. A fundamental flaw in the logic of the conventional wisdom is revealed when cause and effect are investigated separately. Thus, the dynamic nature of the globalization–welfare relationship must be understood so that more valid conclusions can be drawn. Results from the inter-temporal models used in this analysis emphasize the fact that LDC governments can make the political choice to increase social spending without affecting international competitiveness in the current era of globalization.

This analysis accomplishes three things. First, it reveals that conventional theories on globalization and welfare do not withstand more rigorous tests. Although LDCs may be lowering their welfare spending in the era of globalization, they are not consequently becoming more competitive in global markets. Second, this investigation uncovers some of the complexities behind the globalization–welfare nexus. It is ultimately *not* economic necessity but the political choice of governments that has affected the outcome of the globalization–welfare relationship in LDCs. This phenomenon is perhaps because capital generally has more institutional representation in LDCs (through international financial institutions, for instance) than does labor and other marginalized groups. Finally, this study exposes the different magnitudes of impact of domestic policy on export trade and on productive and financial capital flows. Trade flows are not affected by government spending on welfare. Similarly, capital flows are more highly correlated with international factors than with domestic political variables characterizing the LDCs.

One alternative explanation of these results could be that the average amount LDC welfare spending as a share of GDP is too low to be a source of competitiveness problems. Advocates of the conventional wisdom are wrongly expecting that welfare expenditures are inevitable casualties in the era of globalization, at least in the case of LDCs. This is all the more reason why LDC governments should be aware of their flexibility in deciding the levels of welfare spending. Increasing welfare expenditures may be incorporated with a host of other reforms leading to greater economic stability and, eventually, greater international competitiveness.

So what are these 'pressures' of globalization to which LDC governments are reacting? Why have LDC governments reduced spending on social programs in response to increased levels of globalization when LDC welfare states, in fact, do not severely affect international competitiveness? One interpretation of the empirical evidence in this study could be that the re-invigorated political faith in the efficacy of markets, combined with the underdevelopment of political institutions for labor, have created a de-emphasis on social spending. Put differently, the discourse of neo-liberalism has gained momentum in LDCs. Rodrik (1997) is on target when he argues that 'competitiveness' is too often used as an excuse for domestic reform. This analysis suggests that this tendency is particularly true for LDCs. Rodrik (1997: 80) states:

> Too often ... the need to resolve fiscal or productivity problems is presented to the electorate as the consequence of global competitive pressures. This not only makes the required policies a harder sell— why should we adjust just for the sake of becoming better competitors against the Koreans or the Mexicans?—it also erodes the domestic support for international trade—if we have to do all these painful things because of trade, maybe trade isn't such a wonderful thing anyhow!

In sum, this study reveals that the relationship between the pressures of globalization and the consequent social-policy choices is by no means deterministic. These findings provide sufficient justification for scholars and officials alike to reassess their claim that welfare spending is inefficient and erodes a nation's competitiveness in global markets. A better balance between greater exposure to international markets and addressing domestic social needs in LDCs should be set. Scholarly research has shown that greater social spending protects citizens from the risks and uncertainties of globalization. Consequently, there needs to be a growing realization on the part of LDC governments (and international finance institutions) that something more needs to be done with respect to their social programs. It is hoped that the findings in this chapter will help to convince LDC governments that they can afford to implement greater social spending in the current globalization era. In the end, international economic integration has not made national politics and policies in LDCs irrelevant.

APPENDIX A: DATA SOURCES

WELF: IMF, *Government Finance Statistics* and *International Finance Statistics.*
NETK: World Bank, *World Development Indicators* CD-ROM.
TRADE: World Bank, *World Development Indicators* CD-ROM.
FDI: World Bank, *World Development Indicators* CD-ROM.

INTDIFF: IMF, *Government Development Finance* CD-ROM.
GDP: World Bank, *World Development Indicators* CD-ROM.
DEMOC: Ted Robert Gurr and Keith Jaggar's *Polity III* (1994).
RESV: IMF: *International Finance Statistics* CD-ROM.
IMF: World Bank, *World Development Indicators* CD-ROM.

Less developed countries:
Argentina, Bangladesh, Bolivia, Brazil, Cameroon, Chile, Colombia, Costa Rica, Dominican Republic, Ecuador, Egypt, El Salvador, Fiji, Ghana, Guatemala, Guyana, Honduras, India, Indonesia, Jordan, Kenya, Lesotho, Liberia, Malawi, Malaysia, Mali, Mauritius, Mexico, Morocco, Nepal, Nicaragua, Pakistan, Panama, Paraguay, Philippines, Singapore, Sri Lanka, Tanzania, Thailand, Trinidad and Tobago, Tunisia, Turkey, Uruguay, Venezuela, Zimbabwe.

APPENDIX B: COUNTRIES INCLUDED

Government contributions to social security and welfare [Figure 6.1]:
Argentina, Bangladesh, Bolivia, Brazil, Cameroon, Chile, Colombia, Costa Rica, Dominican Republic, Ecuador, Egypt, El Salvador, Fiji, Ghana, Guatemala, Guyana, Honduras, India, Indonesia, Jordan, Kenya, Lesotho, Liberia, Malawi, Malaysia, Mali, Mauritius, Mexico, Morocco, Nepal, Nicaragua, Pakistan, Panama, Paraguay, Philippines, Singapore, Sri Lanka, Tanzania, Thailand, Trinidad and Tobago, Tunisia, Turkey, Uruguay, Venezuela, Zimbabwe.

Employer contributions to social security [Figure 6.2]:
Argentina, Brazil, Colombia, Costa Rica, Cyprus, Egypt, Honduras, Israel, Malaysia, South Korea, Thailand, Trinidad and Tobago, Uruguay, Venezuela.

Employee contributions to social security [Figure 6.3]:
Argentina, Brazil, Colombia, Costa Rica, Cyprus, Egypt, Honduras, Israel, South Korea, Thailand, Uruguay, Venezuela.

NOTES

1. Although some advocates of the conventional thesis might not directly link downsizing of the public sector to increasing international competitiveness, improving fiscal discipline and export sales have been the two primary components of structural adjustment policies in LDCs. See, for example, the Institute for International Economics study by John Williamson (1990), the *World Development Report* (World Bank, 1995, 1990), the *World*

Economic Outlook (International Monetary Fund, 1997), and *Asian Development Outlook* (Asian Development Bank, 1996).

2. The sample includes large numbers of countries from Asia, Africa, the Middle East, and Latin America, and covers most of the post-Bretton Woods era. Nine countries had to be excluded because of insufficient data. See Appendix B for more details.

3. Conventional theorists advocate the 'race to the bottom' thesis. They argue that governments compete with each other by continuously lowering their taxes and labor costs in an effort to increase capital and trade flows. See, for example, Strange (1997), Scholte (1997), Grieder (1998), and Nader *et al.* (1993).

4. These programs refer more specifically to income transfers such as pensions, unemployment benefits, and family allowances. See Table 6.1 for further descriptions.

5. Because of data limitations, this pattern could only be confirmed in a limited number of LDCs. Data on government welfare expenditures and economic globalization were collected for a total of 53 LDCs. Of these, the above pattern could only be verified in 45 per cent of the cases due to a lack of cross-national data on employer and employee contributions.

6. There is an alternative argument in the globalization literature, stating that welfare spending indirectly affects export competitiveness by causing an appreciation in the exchange rate. This effect, however, is not generalizable since currency appreciation that occurs in response to increased government spending is contingent upon several variables, such as the source of government finance (borrowing instead of taxation or money creation) and on reactions from the private sector. This analysis is based on a general definition of performing competitiveness (Pfaller *et al.*, 1991). Therefore, the direct effect of welfare spending on performing competitiveness is the focus of this chapter.

7. The attribution of views to the World Bank and ILO is, of course, stylistic. It follows the convention presented by Freeman (1993). Naturally, there are many outside these organizations who accept their respective positions. At the same time, there are members of these organizations who do not subscribe to the institutional views described here.

8. Because the World Bank views the traditional pay-as-you-go social security and welfare systems as inefficient, its policy recommendations call for the privatization of such schemes. See, for example, Holzmann (1997) and World Bank Policy Research Project (1994).

9. The idea is that better fiscal discipline will lead to lower inflation, more stable exchange rates, and more favorable export prices. Therefore, greater domestic economic stability is positively related to international economic performance. See, for example, *World Development Report* (1990) and, specifically, the discussion in Chapter 7.

10. The challenge of competitiveness can be met in several ways: by devaluing currency, reducing welfare statism, cutting other costs – most of all wages, and redistributing the costs of welfare statism away from enterprises to households. The analyses in this study focus only on the reduction of welfare statism and tests the effectiveness of this policy choice on international competitiveness.

11. Although the threat of exit is most applicable to portfolio investments, it also applies to foreign direct investment which can shift production to offshore factories with relatively low start-up costs.

12. In contrast, gross capital flows measure the degree of capital mobility (Montiel, 1994), or the cross-border transfers of capital. Capital mobility may be high, while a country's ability to attract capital relative to others may be low. The former is therefore an inadequate indicator of a country's international competitiveness for capital.

13. Hart (1992) argues that for the economy as a whole, rising real GDP, relatively mild inflation, stable or rising exports as a percentage of GDP, trade surpluses, and rising labor productivity demonstrate international competitiveness. He does not, however, specifically suggest capital flows as a percentage of GDP as a measure of this competitiveness. This latter notion is adopted from Fernandez-Arias (1996) and Claessens and Naude (1993).

14. Multicollinearity is not a problem, as the correlation between capital flows and trade was 0.28.

15. Multicollinearity involving foreign reserves and IMF credits was suspected, checked, and confirmed. Thus, Model 2 excludes the latter variable.
16. There are also some inconsistencies between the yearly effects and LIBOR. For example, in 1982 and 1983 when LIBOR was at its highest, the yearly effects for LDCs were negative.

REFERENCES

Alesina, A. and Perotti, R. (1997), 'The Welfare State and Competitiveness', *American Economic Review* 87, 5: 921–39.
Amirahmadi, H. and Wu, W. (1992), *Private Capital Flows and Developing Countries*, Working Paper #36 (New Brunswick, NJ: Center for Urban Policy Research, Rutgers University).
Asia Development Bank (1995), *Asian Development Outlook* (Oxford: Oxford University Press).
Baer, W. and Hargis, K. (1997), 'Forms of External Capital and Economic Development in Latin America: 1820–1997', *World Development* 25, 11: 1805–20.
Banerji, A. and Ghanem, H. (1997), 'Does the Political Regime Matter for Trade and Labor Market Policies?', *World Bank Economic Review* 11, 1: 171–93.
Bertolini, L. and Drazden, A. (1997), 'When Liberal Policies Reflect External Shocks, What Do We Learn?', *Journal of International Economics* 42: 249–73.
Calvo, G., Leiderman, L., and Reinhart, C. (1994), *The Capital Inflows Problem*, Occasional Papers #56 (San Francisco: International Center for Economic Growth).
Cerny, P. (1995), 'Globalization and the Changing Logic of Collective Action', *International Organization* 49, 4: 595–625.
Claessens, S. and Naude, D. (1993), *Recent Estimates of Capital Flight*, World Bank Working Paper (New York: World Bank).
Destler, I.M. (1995), *American Trade Politics* (Washington, DC: International Institute for Economics).
Esping-Andersen, G. (1996), *Welfare States in Transition* (London: Sage).
Ezeala-Harrison, F. (1999), *Theory and Policy of International Competitiveness* (New York: Praeger).
Fernandez-Arias, E. (1996), 'The New Wave of Private Capital Inflows: Push or Pull?', *Journal of Development Economics* 48: 389–418.
Freeman, R. (1992), 'Labor Market Institutions and Policies: Help or Hindrance to Economic Development?' in *Proceedings Volume of the Annual Conference on Development Economics* (Washington, DC: World Bank), pp. 117–44.
Gill, S. (1995), 'Globalization, Market Civilization, and Disciplinary Neoliberalism', *Millenium: Journal of International Studies* 24, 3: 399–423.
Grieder, W. (1998), *One World, Ready or Not* (New York: Simon and Schuster).
Griffith-Jones, S. and Stallings, B. (1995), 'New Global Financial Trends: Implications for Developing Countries' in B. Stallings (ed.), *Global Change, Regional Response* (New York: Cambridge University Press), pp. 143–73.
Grunberg, I. (1998), 'Double Jeopardy: Globalization, Liberalization and the Fiscal Squeeze', *World Development* 26, 4: 591–605.
Gurr, T.R. and Jaggars, K. (1994), *Polity III: Regime Type and Political Authority* (Ann Arbor, MI: Inter-University Consortium for Political and Social Research).
Haggard, S. and Maxfield, S. (1996), 'The Political Economy of Financial Internationalization in the Developing World', *International Organization* 50, 1: 35–68.
Haque, I.U., Bell, M., Dahlman, C., Lall, S., and Pavitt, K. (1995), *Trade, Technology, and International Competitiveness* (Washington, DC: World Bank).
Harrison, A. (1996), 'Openness and Growth: A Time-Series, Cross-Country Analysis for Developing Countries', *Journal of Development Economics* 48: 419–47.
Hart, J. (1992), *Rival Capitalists* (Ithaca, NY: Cornell University Press).
Holzmann, R. (1997), 'Pension Reform, Financial Market Development, and Economic Growth: Preliminary Evidence from Chile', *IMF Staff Papers* 2: 149–77.

Hsiao, C. (1986), *Analysis of Panel Data* (New York: Cambridge University Press).

International Monetary Fund (1997), 'Globalization and the Opportunities for Developing Countries', *World Economic Outlook*, pp. 72–92.

International Monetary Fund (1986), *A Manual on Government Finance Statistics* (New York: International Monetary Fund).

Kenworthy, L. (1999), 'Do Social Welfare Policies Reduce Poverty? A Cross-National Assessment', *Social Forces* 77: 1119–39.

Krugman, P. (1994), 'Competitiveness: A Dangerous Obsession', *Foreign Affairs* 73, 2: 28–44.

Kuczynski, P.P. (1994), 'Why Emerging Markets?', *The Columbia Journal of World Business*: 8–13.

Leblang, D. (1997), 'Domestic and Systemic Determinants of Capital Controls in the Developed and Developing World', *International Studies Quarterly* 41: 435–54.

Lensink, R. and White, H. (1998), 'Does the Revival of International Private Capital Flows Mean the End of Aid? An Analysis of Developing Countries Access to Private Capital', *World Development* 26, 7: 1221–34.

Marshall, A. (1994), 'Economic Consequences of Labour Protection Regimes in Latin America', *International Labour Review* 133, 1: 55–73.

Maxfield, S. (1998), 'Understanding the Political Implications of Financial International-ization in Emerging Market Countries', *World Development* 26, 7: 1201–19.

Montiel, P. (1994). 'Capital Mobility in Developing Countries: Some Measurement Issues and Empirical Estimates', *World Bank Economic Review* 8, 3: 311–50.

Nader, R., Grieder, W., Atwood, M., Shiva, V., Ritchie, M., Berry, W., Brown, J., Daly, H., Wallach, L., Lee, T., Khor, M., Phillips, D., Castaneda, J., Heredia, C., Morris, D. and Mander, J. (1993), *The Case Against Free Trade* (San Francisco: North Atlantic Books).

Pedersen, K. (1997), 'The Political Economy of Distribution in Developing Countries: A Rent-Seeking Approach', *Public Choice* 91: 351–73.

Perry, R. and Robertson, J. (1998), 'Political Markets, Bond Markets, and the Effects of Uncertainty: A Cross-National Analysis', *International Studies Quarterly* 42: 131–60.

Pfaller, A., Gough, I., and Therborn, G. (1991), *Can the Welfare State Compete?* (London: Macmillan).

Reisen, H. (1996), 'Managing Volatile Capital Inflows: The Experience of the 1990s', *Asian Development Review* 14, 1: 72–96.

Riveros, L. (1992), 'Labor Costs and Manufactured Exports in Developing Countries: An Econometric Analysis', *World Development* 20, 7: 991–1008.

Rodrik, D. (1997), *Has Globalization Gone Too Far?* (Washington, DC: Institute for International Economics).

Scholte, J. (1997), 'Global Capitalism and the State', *International Affairs* 73, 3: 427–53.

Schwartz, H. (1998), 'Social Democracy Going Down or Down Under', *Comparative Politics* 30: 253–72.

Sengenberger, W. (1993), 'Local Development and International Economic Competition', *International Labour Review* 132, 3: 313–29.

Strange, S. (1997), 'Erosion of the State', *Current History* 96, 613: 365–69.

Verdier, D. (1998), 'Domestic Responses to Capital Market Internationalization under the Gold Standard', *International Organization* 52, 1: 1–34.

Williamson, J. (1990), 'What Washington Means by Policy Reform', in J. Williamson (ed.), *Latin American Adjustment: How Much Has Happened?* (Washington, DC: Institute for International Economics), pp. 7–20.

World Bank (various years), *World Development Report* (New York: Oxford University Press).

World Bank Policy Research Project (1994), *Averting the Old Age Crisis* (New York: Oxford University Press).

7

Political Uncertainty and Speculative Attacks

DAVID A. LEBLANG[1]

INTRODUCTION

The devastating consequences of currency crises across the world's economies have placed issues relating to capital mobility and exchange rates squarely at the forefront of international political economy. Speculative attacks have hit industrial and industrializing countries with equal force and without prejudice. It matters not that the United Kingdom, Mexico, Thailand, and Russia are different on scores of dimensions: their currencies all came under tremendous pressure from global capital in the 1990s. Some political economists argue that domestic economic vulnerability is a result of increased economic integration and capital mobility in the world economy. This third-image, or outside-in, explanation views international capital as a 'structural characteristic of the international system, similar to anarchy' (Keohane and Milner, 1996: 257).

First-image, or inside-out, approaches to international political economy argue that the locus of change in capital flows is located within countries. Literatures from areas as diverse as dependency theory and political business-cycle theory agree that capital rewards political stability. A political change – whether via an election or a coup – causes capital to search for more stable investment arenas. Markets respond not only to actual political changes but adjust in anticipation of these changes as well. As such, political expectations on the part of speculators, traders, and other economic agents play a crucial role in the determination of a currency's value.

In this chapter, I examine the relationship between political expectations and currency markets in the developing world by focusing on speculative attacks. Speculation against a currency is a gamble on the part of economic agents: there is some probability that the government will allow its currency to depreciate. While currency speculation occurs all the time in the world economy, a speculative attack is identified when the level of speculative activity is abnormally high and the government has to either devalue the currency or expend a large portion of its foreign-exchange reserves. As such, speculative attacks are rare events. Figure 7.1 shows the number of monthly speculative attacks over 1970–96 for 87 non-OECD (Organisation for Economic Co-operation and Development) economies.

Figure 7.1 shows that the number of speculative attacks was relatively low during the 1970s, increased during the 1980s, and then declined during the 1990s. If international capital flows were the sole cause of speculative attacks then we would expect to see the number of attacks increasing over time, perhaps at a non-monotonic rate. We might also expect that capital would not discriminate between countries. This is clearly not the case. Economic explanations of speculative attacks have reasonably identified only the economic characteristics of a country that increase its vulnerability to an attack.

What is missing from these explanations is a role for politics. In no sphere of economic exchange do expectations matter as much as they do when it comes to financial relationships. The decision by an individual to hold currency depends critically on this person's belief that the relevant government will honor its obligation and continue to back the value of its currency. Similarly, the decision by actors in the international capital market to lend or to invest capital in a country is contingent on the belief or expectation that they will receive a return on their investment. I argue in this chapter

FIGURE 7.1
MONTHLY SPECULATIVE ATTACKS

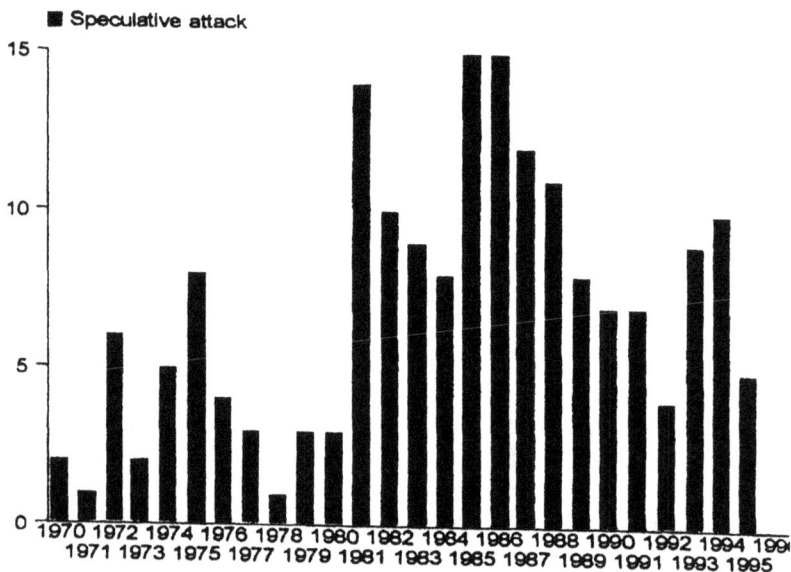

that if holders of capital are uncertain about a government's future policies, they will act on that uncertainty and speculate against its currency. I argue that economic actors acquire information and form their expectations about the government policies by observing the actions of politicians in power. A change in political leadership increases the probability that there will be an alteration in economic policy. Additionally, economic agents form expectations about the probability that leaders will leave office through constitutional and non-constitutional means. As these probabilities increase, so does the likelihood of a speculative attack.

Following this introduction, the next section develops the arguments relating political uncertainty to speculative attacks. In that section I argue that uncertainty can be operationalized in terms of the probability that a leader will lose power and leave office. Further, leaders can lose power through constitutional (e.g. election) or non-constitutional (e.g. coup) means. This discussion is followed by a presentation of a multinomial logit model of leadership change. Through this model, the probability that a leader will stay in power, leave power through constitutional means, or leave power through non-constitutional means is calculated. I then introduce the data and variables used to measure speculative attacks and the independent variables suggested by the literature. The empirical tests are carried out in the subsequent section to determine the effect of political uncertainty on the likelihood of a speculative attack for a monthly sample of 87 developing countries during 1970–96. The results support the proposition that political uncertainty increases the probability of a speculative attack. This conclusion is robust in face of alterations in the sample utilized, the control variables included, and the level of temporal aggregation employed. The concluding section discusses the implications of the present findings for future work on the political economy of international financial relations.

THE POLITICAL ECONOMY OF SPECULATIVE ATTACKS[2]

Economic Models of Currency Crises

The economics literature has generated two 'generations' of models to explain and predict currency crises. First-generation models were initially motivated by currency crises in Mexico (1973–82) and in Argentina (1978–81). Building on Salant and Henderson (1978), Krugman's (1979) model of a crisis of balance of payments argues that exchange-rate crises occur when economic fundamentals deteriorate to a level that is inconsistent with the maintenance of a currency peg. This work was subsequently extended by Flood and Garber (1984). The source of inconsistency, according to the Krugman model, is an excessive creation of domestic credit and of public-sector debt which leads to a decline in confidence in monetary stability by international capital, increased speculation against the peg, a continual loss of foreign-exchange reserves and an eventual collapse of the peg. Krugman's model implies that currency crises are predictable: market participants view government policies and identify the point below which central bank's reserves are insufficient to defend the peg.

First-generation models, however, did not adequately explain or predict either the crisis affecting the European Monetary System during 1992–93 or the one involving Mexico during 1994–95. These crises were different from those that had occurred earlier: economic fundamentals were strong and the real exchange rate was not significantly overvalued. A new round of second-generation models was therefore developed to explain these unanticipated attacks. These models argue that speculative attacks can occur even when economic fundamentals are strong and foreign-exchange reserves are adequate.

The second-generation models build on Diamond and Dybvig's (1983) model of a bank run, which shows how a bank run can occur even when a bank is solvent. In the absence of deposit insurance, depositors will withdraw their money from the bank when they believe it to be insolvent. As they see others flocking to withdraw their money, they do likewise in an attempt to salvage their deposits. The result is an equilibrium where all depositors demand to withdraw their money simultaneously and the bank is forced to default. This result is Pareto-inferior to a situation where the depositors leave their money in the bank.

Second-generation models are exemplified by Obstfeld (1994, 1996), Dornbusch et al. (1995), Krugman (1996), and Sachs et al. (1996), whose analyses attempt to endogenize government policy. In these models, economic policies are not predetermined (exogenous) but respond to changes in the economy. Economic agents in turn take these changes into account when forming their expectations. The contingent nature of expectations generates multiple equilibria. Self-fulfilling currency crises result not only from poor fundamentals, but also from speculators 'jumping' from one equilibrium to another.

This jumping occurs when private actors anticipate a currency devaluation and this anticipation in turn leads them to convert domestic currency into foreign currency before the devaluation. If a sufficient quantity of domestic currency is converted, the central bank will run out of foreign-exchange reserves and will be forced to devalue the domestic currency. In this way, the crisis is *self-fulfilling*. Self-fulfilling crises occur, according to these models, even if the central bank is not in a vulnerable position – that is, when it has sufficient reserves to carry out day-to-day operations though not enough to prevent a run on the domestic currency.[3]

First- and second-generation models identify policy credibility as a key variable in crisis prevention. If the public believes that the government is both willing and able to defend the value of a currency, then speculative pressures will either be prevented or overcome. When economic agents are uncertain about the future course of government policy, however, speculative attacks are more likely.

Political Expectations and Currency Crises

The importance of expectations regarding the future course of government policy has long been recognized by political scientists. For the most part, researchers have made arguments about the informational content of political institutions. What information is provided, however, is a question with a controversial answer. Two strands of argumentation can be identified in the literature. The first concerns differences between authoritarian and democratic regimes while the second considers differences within democracies.

When comparing authoritarian to democratic forms of government, two opposing lines of reasoning have been presented. Some scholars such as Huntington (1968) have argued that democracies are more inclined to economic volatility. Because democracies generate an increase in demand for current consumption, they reduce investment and growth in unpredictable ways. Moreover, it has been suggested that authoritarianism insulates the state from particularistic interests and thus offers more predictability in terms of policy outcomes. Others, however, have contended that when compared to authoritarian regimes, democracies provide more predictability. Arguments in this vein suggest that dictators engage in capricious and predatory behavior that are incongruous with economic development. For example, Olson's (1993) writing emphasizes that the lack of external constraints on autocrats which would prevent them acting like 'bandits' and undertaking economic expropriation. In contrast, democratic institutions provide a stable set of rules and expectations for economic agents such as through the existence of an independent judiciary and the enforcement of property rights. There is a vast literature on the empirical relationship between democracy and economic growth (e.g. Przeworski and Limongi, 1993) and that between authoritarianism and foreign direct investment (e.g. McMillan, 1995).

On its face, this debate does not settle the question of whether democracy or authoritarianism provides economic actors with a set of more stable expectations. The issues become a bit sharper when the literature on democratic institutional performance is examined. While some political economists have argued that democracy produces uncertainty, it is important to note that this uncertainty is contained within certain boundaries. For example, Freeman (1997: 13) refers to democracy as 'a source of policy uncertainty', Przeworski (1990) calls democracy a form of 'institutionalized uncertainty', and Alesina and Rosenthal (1995: 4) argue that 'partisan politics introduces uncertainty in both the polity and the economy'.

The argument that uncertainty in democracies is subject to certain institutional constraints is implicit in political economy studies of exchange rates.[4] The literature on political business cycles, for example, argues that economic agents have rational expectations and will accordingly incorporate information about political events into their expectations regarding economic policy (e.g. Alesina *et al.*, 1997). Operationally, studies in this tradition examine shifts or alterations in exchange-rate policy in a period surrounding an election. For example. Bachman (1992) uses a variant of Krasker's (1980) 'peso problem' model to assess the effect of elections on the observed bias in forward exchange rates. Assuming that 'elections provide investors with news about the country's *probability* of adopting different economic politics', Bachman (1992: 209, emphasis in original) finds that elections in the United States, Britain, France and Canada significantly influenced the forward bias. Similarly, Bloomberg and Hess (1997) show that changes in the partisan composition of a government after an election influence the level of the exchange rate. In addition, Lobo and Tufte (1998) discover that the volatility in exchange rate is higher in the four months leading up to an election in the United States than in other periods.

There are two crucial elements missing from these studies, however. First, although business-cycle models suggest that the uncertainty associated with elections can cause dramatic changes in a series of macroeconomic variables, these models assume that political information is more volatile around the time of an election and does not exist or cannot be measured at other times. Second, it is not clear how to extend this type of model to countries which do not have regularly scheduled and predictable elections. A logical extension of the existing models of political economy is to argue that uncertainty increases when leaders change or when there is a probability of leadership change.

My argument is that not only do economic agents use information about leadership succession, elections, and coups when making economic decisions, but they also price in their decisions the risk that these events will occur. Political uncertainty is the highest when there is a high likelihood of leadership change. The key point here is not that a different leader will necessarily change economic policies, but that there is uncertainty regarding the future course of government policy. This uncertainty will manifest itself in more volatile market behavior. Economic agents, for example, may invest less when they are uncertain about the future course of government policy and may be less willing to hold government debt. Uncertainty about economic policy will be evident in the behavior of the country's exchange rate. As economic agents become less certain of future policies, they will be less willing to hold that currency. Likewise, uncertainty will manifest itself in capital flight or in the reluctance of international capital to roll over short-term debt.

MODELING POLITICAL UNCERTAINTY

To estimate political uncertainty, I model the probability that a leader will leave office or remain in power. There is a vast literature on the determinants of cabinet durability in parliamentary democracies (e.g. Laver and Shepsle, 1996; Warwick, 1994), and Alt and King (1994) offer a useful review of the similarities and differences in between models of leadership and cabinet duration. Bienen and van de Walle (1991) use an event-history approach to analyze the factors that influence a leader's survival over time. Londregan and Poole (1992) and Cukierman *et al.* (1992) also seek to estimate the probability that a leader will leave power via a coup or another type of 'irregular executive transfer'. I draw on these studies and develop a discrete-time multinomial probit model to estimate both the probability of a constitutional and a non-constitutional change in government leaders. The following sections examine the methodology, variables, and the results.

Methodology: Discrete Time Hazard Model

Recent work on leadership duration uses event-history analysis. Event-history models are used both to estimate the underlying hazard of an event (e.g. a leadership change) and to analyze the influence of covariates on the length of time a leader will remain in power. Typically, scholars have estimated continuous-time survival models of leadership duration with time-constant covariates. That is, they assume that leadership duration is a function of variable values measured at the time when the leader comes to power. For example, Golda Meir became prime minister of Israel in March of 1969. Covariates used to explain the length of her tenure in power would be her age in March of 1969, the manner by which she came to power (election), and so on. This approach is similar to a set of cross-sectional data where the dependent variable is the number of months that the government has been in power.

A model with time-constant covariates, however, ignores leadership attributes that change over time. Allison (1984) and Beck *et al.* (1998) argue that discrete event-history models can be approximated by a probit model. In this specification, the hazard rate represents the probability of failure (e.g. a leader's exit from power) at a particular time given that a leader has survived to that point. A probit model also provides predicted probabilities of a leader's exit for each month included in the sample.

Given that prior literature has examined (at least) two ways in which leaders can exit power, a binary variable ignores important information. Therefore, I employ a multinomial logit model where the dependent variable can take three values corresponding to three possible states: (1) no leadership exit (the leader remains in power in that month); (2) leadership exit through constitutional means (e.g. election or other forms of legal succession); and (3) leadership exit through non-constitutional means (e.g. coup or assassination). For leaders who died in office, their departures are coded according to how their successors came to power.

Although it is straightforward to estimate duration models using a probit specification, one of the innovations of this chapter is the use of a multinomial logit model to estimate the probabilities of two different types of leadership exit. To check the compatibility of the multinomial with the binomial approach, I estimated a binary probit model where the dependent variable was leadership exit. The results from the binary probit model are similar to those presented in this chapter.

Sample, Data, Variables

The sample used in this analysis comprises 87 countries from the developing world.[5] I began with the non-OECD sample (including South Korea and Mexico) employed by Bienen and van de Walle (1991) and merged it with the data used to measure speculative attacks (described below). The sample is fairly representative of the developing world as a whole: there are countries from all continents, at all levels of income, and with varying degrees of political freedom and economic openness.

Event-history data do suffer from the problem of left censoring. To avoid this problem, for each country I identify the leader who was in power in January of 1970 and work backwards to determine when this leader came to power. For example, because Golda Meir was the leader of Israel in January 1970 but came to power in March of 1969, I include monthly observations for Israel beginning in March of 1969. Implementing this procedure for all countries eliminates left censoring. All countries do, however, have right-censored observations because they all have leaders remaining in power in December 1996. Accordingly, the data set comprises 87 countries with all of them being observed during the January 1970 to December 1996 period and with some being observed (due to the elimination of left censoring) as far back as 1938. This data set consists of 34,552 monthly observations and reports 248 leadership exits. Descriptive statistics for all the variables discussed below are contained in Appendix 1.

Dependent Variable: Leadership Exit

Leaders – whether dictators, generals, presidents, or prime ministers – leave power in various ways. I follow Bienen and van de Walle (1991) and Cukierman *et al.* (1992) and distinguish leaders who left power through 'regular' or 'constitutional' means from those that were 'removed' from power by assassination, coup, or war. Just as leaders who come to power through constitutional means can leave office via a coup, leaders who rise to power as a result of a coup can exit through constitutional means. In these cases, the constitution may give the leader the right to appoint his/her successor. The present sample has 248 instances of leadership exit: 141 left through regular means, 11 died in office, and 96 were removed by irregular means. All eleven who died were succeeded by individuals who came to power through constitutional means; as such, their exits were coded as being constitutional. The data for this variable and for all others (with noted exceptions) are from Bienen and Van de Walle (1991), *Keesing's Contemporary Archives* (various issues), and *Keesing's Contemporary Archives On-Line.*

Independent Variables

Length of Time in Power:
Studies of leadership survival test for duration dependence; that is, whether the outcome is simply a function of time. There is good reason to believe that time plays an important role in the survival of leaders, governments, and cabinets. Leaders tend to be most vulnerable to challengers when they begin their time in power. As leaders continue in power the risk of failure (or exit) declines as they acquire political capital, consolidate power, and hone leadership skills. Therefore, I include a variable called *length* that counts the number of months that the leader has been in power up to time *t*. Thus, for instance, for a leader who came to power in May 1975, the value of *length* in that month is 0, 1 for June 1975, 2 for July 1975, and so on. This variable is hypothesized to have a negative coefficient. A square of this term is also included in this analysis to capture the fact that the effect of *length* on the probability of an exit is non-monotonic. As leaders remain in power for long periods of time, the probability of their exit increases due to age, senility, or leadership fatigue (Blondel, 1980). It is also possible that the longer a leader is in power, the greater is the chance that the public at large will grow tired of him/her and desire a change (Bienen and Van de Walle, 1991: 10). I expect the squared term to be positive, indicating that the probability of exit increases the longer a leader is in power.

Leader Age:
Another way of modeling the influence of time on the survival of leaders is to include a variable measuring their age. I include *age* as a variable

and expect that as leaders get older, the probability of their exiting increases.

Political Regime:

Two variables measuring the openness of a country's political institutions are included in the multinomial logit model. The first is a dummy variable indicating whether the country has democratic electoral institutions. While Bienen and Van de Walle (1991) use a measure of constitutional entry and Cukierman *et al.* (1992) use a measure of democracy, they both argue that countries with democratic institutions are more likely to have leaders lose power through 'regular' means. I anticipate that leaders in countries with democratic electoral institutions will be more likely to leave power through 'regular' means and will be less likely to exit power via a coup. The second regime variable is a measure of democratic political institutions, for which I adopt the competitiveness of executive recruitment created by Gurr and Jaggers (1996).

A dummy variable indicating whether a *military regime* is in power is also included in the model. Because military leaders generally do not have to worry about re-election, term limits, or other legal limitations on their power, I expect that they will remain in power longer. The data for this variable are from Bienen and van de Walle (1991) and have been updated by the author.

It is important to emphasize that military leaders do not necessarily enter or leave power through irregular means and that leaders in democratic countries do not necessarily leave through regular means. In the latter case, a democratically elected leader is removed via a coup and a country experiences a transition from democratic to authoritarian government. To capture the idea that democratic and military leaders have different time-varying risks of leaving power, the *length* and *length²* variables are interacted with the democracy and military dummy variables.

Elections:

A variable that identifies the month of an election and the three months following an election is also included. I expect that, everything else being equal, elections will lead to constitutional exits. The three-month period following an election is included because leaders who lose elections usually do not leave office immediately. To code this variable, the relevant presidential or parliamentary election was identified. The data for elections come from the compilation *Voter Turnout from 1945–1997*, published by the International Institute for Democracy and Electoral Assistance (International IDEA).[6] This source contains a list of all 'legitimate' presidential and parliamentary elections from 1946 to 1997. It defines 'legitimate elections' as those where suffrage is close to universal and contestations are open and competitive. *Keesings Contemporary Archives* (various years) was used to identify the election month.

Other Controls:
Two other sets of variables are used as statistical controls. First, I include a set of region variables as suggested by Blondel (1980) and Bienen and van de Walle (1991) to capture other country-specific attributes that are constant across regions. Second, I include the number of leadership exits that a country has experienced up to time *t*. For some countries this number is as low as one, indicating that they have only had one leader since 1970. Other countries have had as many as 22 leaders. This variable helps us not only to understand the dynamics of time dependence, but also to capture unobservable variables that may influence political stability.[7]

Empirical Results
The results of the multinomial logit model of leadership duration for 87 countries are contained in Table 7.1. The log-likelihood ratio test rejects the null hypothesis that, as a whole, the model is not statistically different from zero. Maximum-likelihood parameter estimates are in column one and robust standard errors (adjusted for unequal error variance across countries) are in column two. Column three contains a set of partial effects defined as the change in the expected value for a one-standard deviation change in a continuous independent variable and a change from zero to one in a discrete independent variable.

Since the dependent variable is a comparison across three categories, the results in the top panel of Table 7.1 compare the probability of a constitutional change versus no change, and those in the bottom panel compare the probability of a non-constitutional change versus no change. As expected, in months with elections leaders are 4.7 per cent more likely to exit via constitutional means than they are to remain in power. Conversely, the probability of a non-constitutional exit is less likely when elections take place. A leader's age also has a statistically significant effect on the probability of he or she will exit power. As leaders get older, the likelihood that they exit increases.

Interpreting the *length*, *democracy* and *military regime* variables is a bit more difficult due to the fact that the inclusion of interactions creates significant collinearity. As a result, I report a series of likelihood ratio tests on the bottom of Table 7.1. These are tests for the joint statistical significance of the *military regime* (*military regime, military × length* and *military × length²*), *democracy, length* and *length²* variables. The null hypothesis of no effect can be rejected for all sets of variables at (at least) the 0.05 level of significance.

TABLE 7.1
DISCRETE-TIME HAZARD MODEL OF LEADER DURATION

	Parameter estimate	Robust standard error	Partial effect
Constitutional change v. no change			
Military regime #	−0.362	0.424	−0.0018
Democratic regime #	−0.597	0.402	−0.0035
Election #	2.367*	0.274	0.0471
Leader age	0.002*	0.0006	0.0014
Leader length in power	−0.0007	0.011	−0.0003
(Leader length in power)^2	0.00002	0.00002	0.0047
Military × (leader length in power)	0.0076	0.0097	0.0026
Military × (leader length in power)^2	−0.00002	0.00002	−0.0026
Democracy × (leader length in power)	0.0123	0.0091	0.0062
Democracy × (leader length in power)^2	−0.00003	0.00002	−0.0051
Africa #	−0.0198	0.4485	−0.0001
Asia #	0.7194	0.4961	0.0046
Latin America #	1.254*	0.472	0.0028
Number of prior leader changes	0.0839*	0.0248	0.0014
Constant	−6.632*	0.6887	
Non-constitutional change v. no change			
Military regime #	−0.3074	0.4745	−0.0007
Democratic regime #	−1.331*	0.3125	−0.0048
Election #	−28.196*	0.3219	−0.0032
Leader age	0.0019*	0.0009	0.0007
Leader length in power	−0.0106	0.0126	−0.0027
(Leader length in power)^2	0.00002	0.00002	0.0021
Military × leader length in power	0.0045	0.0102	0.0008
Military × (leader length in power)^2	−0.000006	0.00002	−0.0003
Democracy × leader length in power	0.0041	0.0085	0.0009
Democracy × (leader length in power)^2	0.000003	0.00002	0.0003
Africa #	0.864*	0.332	0.0026
Asia #	0.6558	0.443	0.0017
Latin America #	0.3125	0.3865	0.0003
Number of prior leader changes	0.0715*	0.0379	0.0006
Constant	−5.967*	0.7178	
Observations	34552		
	χ^2	Prob $> \chi^2$	
Model as a whole	47365.90	0.0000	
Military variable and interactions	18.56	0.0000	
Democracy variable and interactions	31.29	0.0000	
Length variable and interactions	23.20	0.0000	
Length^2 variable and interactions	12.74	0.0020	

Cell entries in column one are probit statistics estimated via maximum likelihood.
Cell entries in column two are standard errors which are estimated via Huber's robust standard error matrix and account for unequal variances across countries.
Cell entries in column three are effects of a one-unit change for a dummy variable and for a half of one-standard deviation change for continuous variables on the probability that a country will experience a leader change.
# indicates that the variable is a dummy variable.
*two-tailed test, p<0.05.

FIGURE 7.2
PROBABILITY OF CONSTITUTIONAL LEADER EXIT

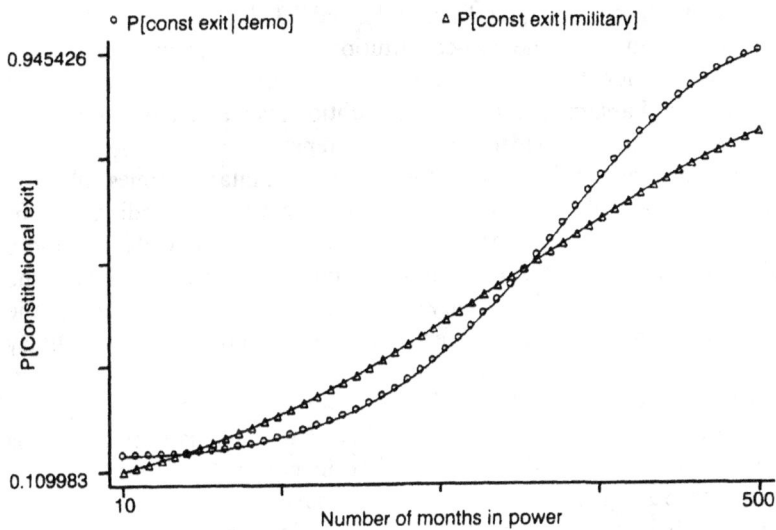

FIGURE 7.3
PROBABILITY OF NON-CONSTITUTIONAL LEADER EXIT

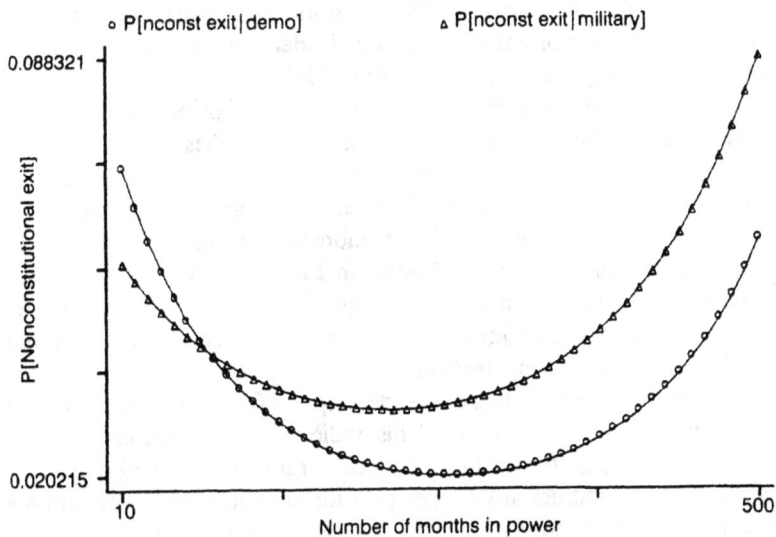

Interpretation of the interactive effects of the *democracy* and *military regime* variables with a leader's length in power is easily accomplished through graphical techniques. Figures 7.2 and 7.3 plot the predicted probability of constitutional and non-constitutional exits respectively against the monthly duration for which a leader has been in power. For ease of presentation, I assume that leadership duration reaches a maximum at 500 months. The lines plotted on Figure 7.2 represent the probability of a constitutional exit for leaders in democratic and military regimes, all other variables being held at their means. The expectation regarding a non-monotonic effect of duration in power on the probability of exit is not borne out by this figure. The probability of a constitutional exit increases the longer a leader remains in power, all other things being equal. Further, the probabilities of constitutional exit for these democratic and military regimes are not statistically different.

The results plotted in Figure 7.3, however, do conform with my prior expectations. In this figure, the probability of a non-constitutional exit is plotted against a leader's length of time in power. Leaders in military regimes face a higher risk of non-constitutional exit (e.g. coup) in the initial stages of their time in power than do leaders in democratic regimes. The probability of non-constitutional exit decreases substantially as a military leader remains in office and consolidates power. For leaders in democratic countries, the risk of a coup, assassination, or other non-constitutional exit decreases as length in office increases, but not at nearly the same rate as military leaders. For both types of leaders, the probability of leaving office through non-constitutional means increases after they have been in power for approximately 265 months. These results are consistent with prior findings that the risk of coups changes as leaders are in power for longer periods of time (e.g. Londregan and Poole, 1992).

The variable measuring the cumulative number of prior leader changes is positive and statistically significant. This finding makes sense intuitively. The number of leadership changes in the past is a good predictor of leadership turnover in the future. The regional dummies present mixed results. Leaders of African countries are more likely to leave power through non-constitutional means while leaders in Latin America have a higher likelihood of exiting via constitutional ways. This is perhaps due to the fact that many Latin America countries have recently adopted electoral laws that limit their presidents to one term in office.

The predicted probabilities of a leadership exit from this model are used to indicate political uncertainty. This indicator is continuous, easy to interpret, and straightforward to calculate. For my sample of 87 countries, the average probabilities are 7.6 per cent for constitutional exits and 4.4 per cent for non-constitutional exits. These low expected values are not surprising given that changes in leadership are very rare events. Out of over 34,000 monthly observations, approximately 1 per cent report leader exits.

Discussion

The multinomial logit model provides probability estimates that leaders will leave office through constitutional and non-constitutional means. These predicted probabilities serve as a proxy for market uncertainty. I use the predicted probabilities from the model of leadership duration as independent variables in a model for understanding speculative attacks on currencies. Changes in leadership create uncertainty about the future of economic policy. As economic agents anticipate a probable change in political leadership, they are more likely to be uncertain about economic policy. Both uncertainty variables (on constitutional and non-constitutional leadership changes), therefore, will have a positive effect on the probability of a speculative attack. However, given that policy change in democratic polities occurs within certain predictable bounds, I anticipate that the probability of a non-constitutional change will have a greater effect on the likelihood of a speculative attack than the probability of a constitutional change.

UNDERSTANDING SPECULATIVE ATTACKS

The two measures of political uncertainty are incorporated into a model of speculative attacks for a sample of 87 developing countries using monthly data. I describe below the data and the way in which the dependent and other independent variables are operationalized. All data are from the CD-ROM version of *International Financial Statistics* distributed by the International Monetary Fund (IMF). Descriptive statistics are contained Appendix 1.

Dependent Variable

Speculative Attack:
The measure of speculative attacks utilized in this analysis follows directly from that proposed by Eichengreen *et al.* (1995) and implemented by Kaminsky *et al.* (1997), Kaminsky and Reinhart (1996), Sachs *et al.* (1996), Corsetti *et al.* (1998) and others. The rationale behind the index is that a government can respond to speculation against its currency by (1) allowing the exchange rate to depreciate and/or (2) spending foreign-currency reserves in international capital markets to buy up domestic currency. Exchange-market pressure is measured as:

$$EMP_{i,t} = \frac{\Delta s_{i,t}}{\sigma_{\Delta s_i}} - \frac{\Delta r_{i,t}}{\sigma_{\Delta r_i}}$$

Here EMP is the index of exchange-market pressure, s is the bilateral exchange rate of country i with the United States at time t, and r is the non-gold international reserves held by the central bank of country i at time t. Each component of the index is weighted by its respective standard deviation to prevent one variable from swamping the others. A high index indicates that there is pressure on a nation's currency. The rationale is that an attack on a currency can be met by either a currency depreciation (an increase in s) or a loss in foreign-exchange reserves (a decrease in r) by the central bank.

Eichengreen *et al.* (1995: 278) argue that '... speculative attacks are defined as periods when this index of speculative pressure reaches extreme values'. I follow Kaminsky and Reinhart (1996) who identify the cut-off for a speculative attack as:

$$Speculative\ Attack_{i,t} = 1\ if\ EMP_{i,t} > 3\sigma_{EMPi} + \mu_{EMPi}$$
$$= 0\ otherwise$$

Here, σEMP and μEMP are the country-specific mean and standard deviation of EMP respectively. The cut-off of plus three standard deviations is selected so that extreme values of the exchange-market pressure index should be identified as a speculative attack.[8] The empirical models below are unaffected if the cut-off for EMP is set at plus two or plus three standard deviations from the mean.

Due to some data limitations, there are only 19,027 usable observations and 182 episodes of speculative attacks.

Independent Variables

In addition to the political variables, a number of control variables are included in the model of speculative attacks as suggested by the relevant theoretical and empirical literature.

Real Exchange Rate (RER) Overvaluation:
Kaminsky *et al.* (1997) and Goldfajn and Valdes (1997) found overvaluation of the real exchange rate to be the most significant indicator of currency crises in the studies they surveyed. Observers of both the Mexican and Asian financial crises have argued that these episodes were the result of a rapidly appreciating domestic currency in real terms due to dramatic capital inflows (Sachs *et al.*, 1996; Radelet and Sachs, 1998). A currency over-valuation becomes unsustainable in the long run when it results in a loss of competitiveness and in large(r) balances in currency account. In the short term, an overvaluation renders a currency vulnerable to speculative attacks as economic agents attempt to profit by forcing the exchange rate back to its perceived equilibrium.

Following Kaminsky *et al.* (1997) and Goldfajn and Valdes (1997), I measure overvaluation of the real exchange rate by using the residuals of a Hodrick-Prescott model to filter the series of real exchange rate with lambda equal to 14,400 for monthly data. The larger the residuals, the farther the real exchange rate is from its equilibrium value and the more likely is a currency crisis. The real exchange rate *s* is calculated as the local currency per US dollar adjusted for wholesale prices in both the local country and in the United States.

Foreign Interest Rates:
Currency crises are also more likely to occur when foreign interest rates are high. An increase of interest rates in OECD member countries has been identified as one of the key determinants of the debt crisis in 1982 as well as a primary reason for the flight of capital from Mexico in late 1994 and early 1995 (Frankel and Rose, 1996). As interest rates in Germany, Japan, and the United States decline, capital flows into the developing world in search of a higher return. An increase in the latter countries' interest rates triggers capital to flow out of the developing countries and back into the developed economies. In this analysis, I use the interest rate on short term (90-day) deposits in the United States to represent *foreign interest rates.* The substantive results do not differ if German or Japanese rates are used instead.

Foreign Exchange Reserves:
First-generation models of speculative attacks suggest that currency crises are likely as central banks run short of international reserves. Krugman-type models argue that the quantity of reserves is the key variable when it comes to predicting the timing of a speculative attack on a fixed exchange-rate regime. Using a variant of the Krugman-Flood-Garber model, Blanco and Garber (1986) estimate the probability that the Mexican *peso* would be devalued each quarter during the 1973–82 period. Cumby and van Wijnbergen (1989) use a similar model to explain attacks on Argentina's crawling peg in the early 1980s. These scholars, among others, find that the probability of a devaluation in each country was closely linked to that country's holdings of international reserves. Accordingly, a ratio of foreign-exchange reserves to imports is included in this study. The expectation is that the higher this ratio, the less likely are currency crises.

Banking Sector Crisis:
Recent models of speculative attacks have focused on the twin crises of banking crises and currency crises (e.g. Demirguc-Kunt and Detragiache, 1997). Sachs *et al.* (1996), for example, argue that a rapid increase in lending

by commercial banks to the private sector indicates a greater risk of loss of investor confidence. The quality of bank loans is likely to deteriorate significantly – and many of these loans are likely to become non-performing – when bank lending rises rapidly in a short period of time. Large lending means that banks are less able to effectively screen borrowers. This problem is exacerbated in the developing world where both the ability and number of regulators are limited. The increase in bank lending is measured as the growth in claims on the private sector. As private-sector claims increase, so does the likelihood of a banking and currency crisis.

Domestic Monetary Policy:
A variable indicating government monetary policy is also used as a control in this study. Calvo (1995) and Sachs *et al.* (1996) include measures of the growth of domestic credit in their models of currency crisis. The growth in domestic credit is straightforward: it indicates an increase in the domestic money supply. As the money supply increases, there is more domestic currency in circulation that can be converted into foreign assets in the event that currency holders anticipate a devaluation. The higher the rate of growth in domestic credit, the more likely it is that an (self-fulfilling) attack can be successful.

Other Controls:
I include two variables that indicate a country's vulnerability to prior crises. The first is a lagged endogenous variable to capture the fact that some speculative attacks may last longer than one month. The second, intended to capture a country's overall level of vulnerability, counts the number of prior crises it has experienced since 1970.

THE IMPACT OF POLITICAL UNCERTAINTY ON SPECULATIVE ATTACKS

I proceed to test the relationship between political uncertainty and speculative attacks in a sample of 87 countries from the developing world from February 1970 to December 1996. Since the empirical model estimated below includes a lagged endogenous variable, the analysis begins in February rather than in January of 1970. The analytic coverage ends in December 1996 with the most recent available data from the International Monetary Fund and the World Bank.

Given that the dependent variable is a dichotomous outcome – a speculative attack either occurs or it does not occur – a probit model is utilized. The pooled cross-sectional and time-series nature of the sample necessitates that the analyst account for autocorrelation and heteroscedastic disturbances. I use the technique suggested by Allison (1984) and extended by Beck *et al.* (1998). This statistical approach begins with the assumption that binary panel data are grouped-duration data. It follows that the problem of serially correlated errors can be alleviated through the inclusion of a set of linear splines that take into account the length of time since the country's last speculative attack.[9] Heteroscedasticity, or unequal variation across countries, is taken into account through the estimation of Huber's robust standard errors.[10]

The results in Table 7.2 are for models where the dependent variable is a speculative attack. For ease of presentation, cell entries in Table 7.2 are not traditional probit coefficients, but rather are measures that are more easily interpretable. These measures are the expected change in the probability of a speculative attack as the independent variable either moves from zero to one (for dummy variables) or increases by one half of one standard deviation from the mean (for continuous variables). Starred entries are statistically significant at the 0.05 level. Traditional probit coefficients and their associated robust standard errors are contained in the tables reported in Appendix 2.

Column one of Table 7.2 contains the baseline model which only includes the control variables. A likelihood ratio test allows us to reject the null hypothesis that, as a whole, the model is not statistically different from zero. The set of linear splines, not shown, is statistically significant, indicating that a degree of temporal dependence exists in the data.

Insofar as the control variables are concerned, the results conform to theoretical expectations. The lagged endogenous variable is statistically significant, indicating that speculative attacks in the prior month have a statistically discernible positive effect on the likelihood of an attack in the present period. Changes in the foreign interest rate, however, do not have a statistically significant effect on speculative attacks. This finding is not altered if German or an average of German and US interest rates is used. Prior research argues that an overvaluation of the real exchange rate increases the probability of a speculative attack. The results in Table 7.2 support this conclusion: an increase in the real exchange rate by one standard deviation from the mean of 0.0007 to 0.0902 increases the probability of a speculative attack by 3.2 per cent.

The variables measuring the growth in domestic credit and in bank lending are both statistically significant and in the positive direction. This evidence supports the arguments of Sachs *et al.* (1996) and Calvo (1995) who, among others, link the growth of domestic credit to banking crises and speculative attacks. It suggests that providing international capital with easy means to convert domestic currency into foreign assets may contribute to a monetary crash. The ratio of foreign-exchange reserves to imports is

TABLE 7.2
SPECULATIVE ATTACK MODELS: MONTHLY DATA (ENTRIES ARE MARGINAL EFFECTS)

	(1)	(2)	(3)	(4)	(5)	(6)	(7)	(8)
Speculative attack$_{t-1}$ #	0.1792*	0.1855*	0.1841*	0.1790*	0.0064	0.0063	0.0055	0.0060
Foreign interest rates	0.0079	0.0077	0.0073	0.0075	0.0015*	0.0014*	0.0012*	0.0013*
Real exchange rate overvaluation	0.0161*	0.0171*	0.0173*	0.0161*	0.0033*	0.0032*	0.0028*	0.0030*
Domestic credit growth	0.0279*	0.0289*	0.0275*	0.0275*	0.0006	0.0006	0.0004	0.0005
Growth in bank lending	0.0078*	0.0071*	0.0079*	0.0076*	0.0010*	0.0009*	0.0007*	0.0009*
Foreign reserves/imports	-0.0047*	-0.0051*	-0.0050*	-0.0046*	-0.0007	-0.0007	-0.0006	-0.0005
Number of prior attacks	-0.0018	-0.0043	-0.0050	-0.0024	-0.0002	-0.0003	-0.0005	-0.0003
P[Constitutional change]		0.0058*	0.0058*			0.0003*	0.0007*	
P[Non-constitutional change]		0.0072*	0.0097*			0.0006*	0.0008*	
Democratic electoral institutions #			0.0124	0.0004			0.0027*	0.0018
Electoral period #			-0.0135	0.0043			-0.0021	-0.0004
Non-constitutional change #			-0.0037	0.0174				
Constitutional change #			0.1638*	0.1715*			0.0162*	0.0219*
Observations	19027	19027	19027	19027	7392	7392	7392	7392
χ^2	235.89	244.99	344.79	319.60	230.00	241.03	278.96	265.51
Prob $>\chi^2$	0.0000	0.0000	0.0000	0.0000	0.0000	0.0000	0.0000	0.0000

Cell entries are effect of a one-unit change for a dummy variable and for a half of one standard-deviation change for continuous variables on the probability that a country will experience a speculative attack.
Columns 1–4 are for the entire sample; columns 5–8 are for only those country-months where the country had a pegged exchange rate.
All models are estimated with a set of five linear splines.
Standard errors for hypothesis tests are estimated via Huber's robust standard error matrix and account for unequal variances across countries.
# indicates that the variable is a dummy variable.
* two-tailed test, p<0.05.

negative and statistically significant. Countries with large holdings of foreign-exchange reserves are less vulnerable to speculative attacks than are those that have smaller holdings. Finally, the variable counting the number of prior crises is negative but statistically insignificant, indicating that past vulnerability to speculative attacks is not a good predictor of present vulnerability.

Column two addresses the central concern of this chapter. It adds two measures of political uncertainty – the estimated probabilities of constitutional and non-constitutional leadership change – to the baseline specification. Both z and likelihood-ratio test statistics ($\chi^2=9.32$, p=0.0095) reject the null hypothesis of no effect for these variables. The estimated coefficients for both variables of political uncertainty are positive as anticipated. As political uncertainty increases, so does the likelihood that a country's currency will be the target of a speculative attack. Substantively, as the probability of a constitutional change increases from the mean by one standard deviation, the probability of a speculative attack increases by 1.16 per cent. Alternatively, if the probability of a non-constitutional change increases by one standard deviation, the likelihood of an attack increases by 1.44 per cent. Although the difference between these two figures appears to be minor quantitatively, substantively they are significant. Recall that both leadership exits and speculative attacks are rare events that do not occur with great regularity. If the probability of a non-constitutional exit increases from the mean by just 1 per cent, the probability of a speculative attack rises by almost 4 per cent.

In columns three and four of Table 7.2, four additional measures of political uncertainty are added to the model specification. The inclusion of these variables does not change the statistical significance of the probability of speculative attacks. Democracy, electoral period, and non-constitutional change are not statistically significant either individually or jointly ($\chi^2=2.20$, p=0.5312). Constitutional changes in leadership do have a statistically significant and positive effect on the likelihood of speculative attacks, holding all other variables constant. A speculative attack is 16 per cent more likely in months where a constitutional change does occur than at other times. This effect becomes more pronounced in column four when the probability-based uncertainty measures are dropped.

In alternative specifications not reported here, I included *democracy, electoral period, exit mode* and the *probability of exit* separately in the analytic model in order to determine whether any of the statistical signs or significance levels reported were a function of collinearity. In no instances were the *electoral period, democracy*, or *non-constitutional exit* close to being statistically significant. This result confirms prior studies (e.g. Edwards and Santaella, 1993) which found that the probability of a devaluation increases immediately after an election. Speculative attacks are more likely not only when a leader leaves office through constitutional means, but also when economic agents anticipate a change in leadership through any means.

To determine the robustness of the relationship between political uncertainty and speculative attacks on exchange rates, in columns five through eight of Table 7.2 the sample is restricted to those countries which adopt a fixed/pegged exchange rate. In this more limited sample, there are only 51 instances of speculative attacks out of a possible 7,392 observations. Most first-generation models were explicitly concerned with the vulnerability of fixed-rate regimes to speculative attacks. In line with these expectations, the results show that countries with pegs are vulnerable to speculative attacks when (1) their exchange rate is overvalued and (2) their banks have increased lending. Surprisingly, the ratio of foreign-exchange reserves to imports is not statistically significant for this sub-sample regardless of the model specification. In addition, changes in foreign interest rates now have a statistically significant effect on the probability of a speculative attack, a finding which is in line with the prior research.

In column six, both measures of political uncertainty are statistically significant and positive. The variable for *non-constitutional leadership exit* is not included in models seven and eight because it predicts perfectly the outcome of no speculative attack. *Electoral periods* do not have a statistically significant effect on speculative attacks and *democracy* does (albeit seemingly sensitive to variations in specification). These results indicate that political uncertainty matters insofar as currency crises are concerned. As economic actors become uncertain about a country's future economic policy, they become more reluctant to hold its currency. Even more important, the results of this study show that not only political uncertainty changes over time, but also increases in uncertainty have profound effects on currency markets.

THE IMPORTANCE OF INTERNATIONAL INFLUENCES

Recently, policy-makers from the IMF and some academics have developed a 'third generation' of models on speculative attacks. The motivation behind this effort is the fact that the 'usual suspects' leading to a currency crisis were not evident in the East Asian crises during 1990–97. These analysts focus on the moral hazard faced by international lending institutions, the composition of external debt, the current account, and capital controls (e.g. Frankel and Rose, 1996; Corsetti *et al.*, 1998; Krugman, 1998; Dooley, 1997). Capital control cannot be included as a variable in these models because there has not been any instance of speculative attack when capital controls were in place.

In order to evaluate the importance of international factors, three additional variables have been included in the newer model of speculative attack. The first variable is a measure of the total stock of external debt (excluding foreign direct investment) as a share of gross national product (GNP). The second variable refers to short-term debt as a portion of foreign-exchange reserves. Short-term debt is debt that has a maturity structure of one year or less. It is useful to think of this variable as a ratio of foreign assets to foreign liabilities. The argument advanced by Frankel and Rose (1996) is that countries with high levels of debt are more vulnerable to the whims of international capital. This is especially true when the stock of short-term capital is high. The third variable measures the current account surplus or deficit as a percentage of gross national product. This variable is used in studies of sustainability of the current account and is the focus of some second-generation models. The data for these three variables come from the World Bank's *World Development Indicators* CD-ROM.

One difficulty in using these three indicators of international influences is that they are only available on an annual basis. To evaluate the importance of political uncertainty in models that incorporate foreign debt and current account, I move away from monthly data and use a data set with annual observations. The construction of all other variables is the same as described earlier with two important exceptions. The first change pertains to the index of speculative attacks for which the cut-off for determining the occurrence of an attack is now set to be beyond two rather than three standard deviations. This procedure reveals 82 attacks out of a possible 1,813 usable annual observations. A cut-off of three standard deviations would have yielded only 15 instances of attacks. The second change is obviously with the construction of the measures of political uncertainty. I construct it in exactly same manner at discussed before, except that yearly rather than monthly observations are used now. Accordingly, all political variables represent leadership exits or the probability of an exit in a given year. The model of leadership duration using yearly data is presented in Appendix 3.

Table 7.3 is organized just like Table 7.2: columns one through four are for the full sample and columns five through eight are for those countries that peg their exchange rate. Statistical tests indicate that serial correlation is not an issue; therefore, linear splines and the variable for prior number of failures were not included. The lagged dependent variable, foreign interest rates, and total debt as a share of GNP are the only variables that are statistically significant and they are in the expected direction. Countries that have heavier burdens of external debt are increasingly vulnerable to speculative attacks, as are all countries with rising foreign interest rate. The

TABLE 7.3
SPECULATIVE ATTACK MODELS: YEARLY DATA (ENTRIES ARE MARGINAL EFFECTS)

	(1)	(2)	(3)	(4)	(5)	(6)	(7)	(8)
Speculative attack$_{t-1}$ #	0.4373*	0.3926*	0.3885*	0.4252*	0.3286*	0.2902*	0.2923*	0.3174*
Foreign interest rates	0.0093*	0.0083*	0.0077*	0.0084	0.0033	0.0030	0.0028	0.0029
Real exchange rate overvaluation	0.0058	0.0052	0.0054	0.0054	0.0031	0.0033	0.0037	0.0037
Domestic credit growth	0.0034	0.0031	0.0029	0.0034	-0.0024	-0.0017	-0.0017	-0.0020
Growth in bank lending	-0.0062	-0.0061	-0.0060	-0.0060	-0.0053	-0.0049	-0.0048	-0.0049
Foreign reserves/imports	-0.0020	-0.0019	-0.0020	-0.0022	-0.0014	-0.0011	-0.0013	-0.0015
Short-term debt/total debt	-0.0166	-0.0134	-0.0128	-0.0142	-0.0119	-0.0102	0.0103	0.0111
Total external debt/GNP	0.0100*	0.0090*	0.0086*	0.0096*	0.0074*	0.0067*	0.0066*	0.0072*
Current account/GNP	0.0066	0.0062	0.0055	0.0059	0.0016	0.0014	0.0011	0.0010
P[Constitutional change]		0.0047*	0.0084*			0.0004	0.0018	
P[Non-constitutional change]		0.0067*	0.0057*			0.0059*	0.0049*	
Democratic electoral institutions #			-0.0018	0.0014			0.0005	0.0009
Election year #			-0.0192	-0.0093			-0.0087	-0.0083
Non-constitutional change #			0.0049	0.0263			0.0132	0.0387*
Constitutional change #			0.0281*	0.0497			0.0067	0.0160
Observations	1813	1813	1813	1813	1339	1339	1339	1339
χ^2	199.39	215.54	365.92	240.44	107.40	124.05	166.61	110.47
Prob >χ^2	0.0000	0.0000	0.0000	0.0000	0.0000	0.0000	0.0000	0.0000

Cell entries are effect of a one-unit change for a dummy variable and for a half of one standard-deviation change for continuous variables on the probability that a country will experience a speculative attack.
Columns 1-4 are for the entire sample; columns 5-8 are for only those country-months where the country had a pegged exchange rate.
Standard errors for hypothesis tests are estimated via Huber's robust standard error matrix and account for unequal variances across countries.
# indicates that the variable is a dummy variable.
* two-tailed test, p<0.05.

significance, magnitude and direction of these three variables are consistent with other findings in the literature (e.g. Frankel and Rose, 1996).

Columns two through four add *political uncertainty*, *leadership exit*, *democracy*, and *election mode*. Again, the z and likelihood-ratio tests favor the inclusion of the political-uncertainty measures in columns two and three and reject the statistical significance of the other variables with the exception of *constitutional leadership changes*. Substantively, an increase in the probability of a constitutional leadership change by one standard deviation increases the probability of a speculative attack by almost 1 per cent, holding all other variables at their means. An increase in the probability of a non-constitutional leadership change by one standard deviation increases the likelihood of a speculative attack by 1.34 per cent. These effects do not diminish dramatically if the discrete political measures are included as they are in column three. Interestingly, none of the discrete measures are statistically significant if the continuous measures of political uncertainty are dropped as they are in column four. I determined that this phenomenon is not a result of excessive collinearity among the political variables.

Similar results are obtained when the sample is limited to countries that peg their exchange rate. For this sub-sample, however, neither the actual nor the probability of a constitutional leadership exit has a statistically significant effect on speculative attacks. This pattern suggests that speculative attacks are more likely when the probability of leadership change through non-constitutional means increases.

A final concern pertains to the possibility of reversed causality. I checked the models in Tables 7.2 and 7.3 to make certain that political uncertainty was the cause of speculative attacks and not the other way around. To avoid an excessive number of tables, I describe rather than present the statistical findings. Complete results are, of course, available from the author. Causality was checked in two ways. First, using both the monthly and yearly sample for the period 1970–96, I included contemporaneous and lagged values of *speculative attack* in the leadership duration model. In no case was this variable statistically significant. Second, I employed a test for weak exogeneity as suggested by Hausman (1978) and Engle (1984) and described by Charemza and Deadman (1992: 255–65). The test proceeds as follows:

1. estimate a model of speculative attack,

2. compute the residuals,

3. include the residuals in the model of leadership duration,

4. use the z and likelihood-ratio tests to evaluate the null hypothesis of exogeneity.

Since the residuals were never statistically significant, I could not reject the null hypothesis of weak exogeneity.

CONCLUSION

The cause(s) of currency crises is one of the most important issues facing countries in the world political economy. Recent work in political science and in economics has advanced a myriad factors that cause or influence currency crises. The argument offered in this chapter is simple: capital reacts to expectations of political change. When there is a high probability of a change in government policies or even when there is a large degree of uncertainty regarding the future course of government, international capital will search for alternatives promising higher and more stable returns. I estimate political uncertainty using a multinomial logit model. This model allows me to estimate the probability of constitutional and non-constitutional political changes. These predicted probabilities indicate that markets care about uncertainty and they care more about the likelihood of non-constitutional than constitutional political change. The effect of political uncertainty on the probability of currency crises is robust to variations in the manner by which the dependent variable is measured, the types of control variables included in the model, and the level of temporal aggregation. Therefore, I am fairly confident that the statistical results are not a function of specification error.

The approach taken in this chapter extends prior work in the political economy of international financial relations. Prior arguments, relating static institutional differences to speculative behavior regarding exchange rates, cannot get us very far in understanding the dynamics of currency crashes and speculative attacks. While the differences between democratic and non-democratic institutional environments are informative, we need a way to measure political uncertainty and a means to understand its relationship to macroeconomic instability. A move in this direction comes from scholars who study the choice of exchange-rate regimes (Bernhard and Leblang, 1999; Collins, 1996; Edwards, 1996; Eichengreen and Frieden, 1994; and Frieden, 1991, 1998). Recognition of the importance of political uncertainty can only enhance these approaches.

Future research can fruitfully progress in at least two complementary ways. First, we need better measures of political uncertainty for developing countries. Scholars who study OECD countries utilize a myriad of measures, such as party fractionalization and political polarization, the political cohesion of government, the decisiveness of the electoral system, as indicators of political volatility. Given that democracy is becoming increasingly popular in non-OECD countries, similar variables could be constructed for developing countries. The use of such variables would help political economists capture the political dimensions of formulating and choosing economic policies in the developing world.

The second avenue for future research is more specific. Prior research has identified the conditions under which politicians devalue their country's exchange rate. The findings of this analysis identify the conditions leading to a speculative attack. A fascinating question concerns the conditions under which a politician is able and willing to defend a country's exchange rate in the face of a speculative attack. This question fits squarely into the intersection of first- and second-image approaches to international political economy and has dramatic policy relevance as well.

APPENDIX 1
DESCRIPTIVE STATISTICS

Monthly Data

Leader Duration Model (n=34,552)

Variable	Mean	Std. Dev.	Min	Max
Exit mode	0.02	0.218	0	3
Military regime	0.32	0.467	0	1
Democratic regime	0.68	0.464	0	1
Election month	0.007	0.085	0	1
Age (in months)	669.606	145.83	208	1153.
Length (in months)	96.221	93.6713	0	532
Africa	0.392	0.4883	0	1
Asia	0.183	0.387	0	1
Latin America	0.265	0.4417	0	1
# of Prior exits	1.712	2.3081	0	13

Speculative Attack Model: All Countries (n=19,027)

Variable	Mean	Std. Dev.	Min	Max
Speculative attack	0.0094	0.0968	0	1
Speculative attack $_{t-1}$	0.0094	0.0965	0	1
Foreign interest rates	7.8082	3.3941	2.92	19.1
Real exchange rate overvaluation	0.0007	0.0895	-1.7782	1.521
Domestic credit growth	7.9526	91.0012	0	4865.703
Growth in bank lending	0.0231	0.1721	-6.9106	6.983
Foreign reserves/imports	4.3614	6.3602	0.0042	258.144
P[Constitutional change]	0.0078	0.012	0.0001	0.3204
P[Non-constitutional change]	0.0043	0.004	2.78e-16	0.041
Democratic electoral institutions	0.7048	0.4561	0	1
Electoral period	0.0239	0.1527	0	1
Non-constitutional change	0.0047	0.0686	0	1
Constitutional change	0.0072	0.0848	0	1

Speculative Attack Model: Pegging Countries (n=7,392)

Variable	Mean	Std. Dev.	Min	Max
Speculative attack	0.007	0.0835	0	1
Speculative attack $_{t-1}$	0.0068	0.0827	0	1
Foreign interest rates	7.9934	3.5215	2.92	19.1
Real exchange rate overvaluation	-0.0008	0.0612	-0.7022	0.4436
Domestic credit growth	4.8838	16.5827	0	553.9
Growth in bank lending	0.0166	0.0512	-0.7257	1.0986
Foreign reserves/imports	4.1467	5.0652	0.0042	251.9163
P[Constitutional change]	0.0075	0.0109	0.0011	0.2942
P[Non-constitutional change]	0.0037	0.0036	2.78e-16	0.032
Democratic electoral institutions	0.769	0.4214	0	1
Electoral period	0.0273	0.163	0	1
Non-constitutional change	0.0033	0.058	0	1
Constitutional change	0.0066	0.0811	0	1

Yearly Data

Leader Duration Model (n=2,898)

Variable	Mean	Std. Dev.	Min	Max
Exit mode	0.2049	0.6543	0	3
Military regime	0.3374	0.4729	0	1
Leader age	681.7046	146.0329	225	1153
Democratic regime	0.7053	0.4559	0	1
Election year	0.0828	0.2756	0	1
Length in power	7.8095	7.9668	0	44
Asia	0.1832	0.3869	0	1
Latin America	0.2667	0.4423	0	1
Africa	0.3919	0.4882	0	1

Speculative Attack Model: All Countries (n=1,813)

Variable	Mean	Std. Dev.	Min	Max
Speculative attack	0.0452	0.2078	0	1
Speculative attack $_{t-1}$	0.0441	0.2051	0	1
Foreign interest rates	7.8128	3.1516	3.0255	16.3783
Real exchange rate overvaluation	0.8637	30.656	-48.0552	64.6038
Domestic credit growth	0.0167	0.2009	-1.6818	2.1567
Growth in bank lending	0.0076	0.2015	-2.5648	6.7854
Foreign reserves/imports	3.0508	3.8543	-75.1257	25.1769
Short-term debt/total debt	6.3555	42.5707	0	1524.1
Total external debt/total debt	0.6956	0.8923	0	11.9355
Current account/GDP	-5.234	8.6429	-120.599	39.5192
P[Constitutional change]	0.092	0.1572	0	0.8327
P[Non-constitutional change]	0.05	0.0591	0	0.45112
Democratic electoral institutions	0.7176	0.4502	0	1
Electoral period	0.1136	0.3174	0	1
Non-constitutional change	0.0452	0.2078	0	1
Constitutional change	0.0926	0.2901	0	1

Speculative Attack Model: All Countries (n=1,339)

Variable	Mean	Std. Dev.	Min	Max
Speculative attack	0.02912	0.1682	0	1
Speculative attack $_{t-1}$	0.02539	0.1573	0	1
Foreign interest rates	8.0734	3.1617	3.0225	16.3783
Real exchange rate overvaluation	-4.0255	29.9989	-48.0552	64.6038
Domestic credit growth	0.0163	0.1903	-1.6813	1.1818
Growth in bank lending	0.0071	0.1855	-1.6813	0.7611
Foreign reserves/imports	2.8974	4.156	-75.1257	25.1769
Short term debt/total debt	7.5149	49.3038	0	1524.05
Total external debt/total debt	0.6071	0.7168	0	11.935
Current account/GDP	-5.4129	8.8961	-120.599	39.5192
P[Constitutional change]	0.0767	0.14	0.0004	0.8196
P[Non-constitutional change]	0.0491	0.0602	0.0005	0.4511
Democratic electoral institutions	0.6945	0.4607	0	1
Electoral period	0.0985	0.2982	0	1
Non-constitutional change	0.0507	0.2196	0	1
Constitutional change	0.0694	0.2543	0	1

APPENDIX 2
SPECULATIVE ATTACK MODELS (MONTHLY DATA)

	(1)	(2)	(3)	(4)	(5)	(6)	(7)	(8)
Speculative attack $_{t-1}$ #	0.857*	0.860*	0.863*	0.862*	0.417	0.422	0.431	0.424
	(0.154)	(0.155)	(0.156)	(0.155)	(0.325)	(0.327)	(0.330)	(0.324)
Foreign interest rates	0.020	0.019	0.018	0.019	0.049*	0.049*	0.049*	0.048*
	(0.012)	(0.013)	(0.012)	(0.012)	(0.020)	(0.020)	(0.019)	(0.019)
Real exchange rate overvaluation	1.568*	1.602*	1.643*	1.599*	6.189*	6.304*	6.526*	6.288*
	(0.524)	(0.517)	(0.511)	(0.527)	(1.048)	(1.066)	(1.138)	(1.107)
Domestic credit growth	0.000*	0.000*	0.000*	0.000*	0.004	0.004	0.004	0.004
	(0.000)	(0.000)	(0.000)	(0.000)	(0.003)	(0.003)	(0.003)	(0.003)
Growth in bank lending	0.398*	0.395*	0.395*	0.394*	2.294*	2.185*	2.103*	2.317*
	(0.180)	(0.178)	(0.175)	(0.176)	(0.617)	(0.545)	(0.557)	(0.637)
Foreign reserves/imports	-0.040*	-0.041*	-0.042*	-0.040*	-0.017	-0.018	-0.017	-0.014
	(0.016)	(0.017)	(0.017)	(0.016)	(0.015)	(0.016)	(0.016)	(0.014)
Number of prior attacks	-0.010	-0.023	-0.028	-0.014	-0.023	-0.037	-0.068	-0.038
	(0.021)	(0.022)	(0.021)	(0.020)	(0.086)	(0.091)	(0.104)	(0.095)
P[Constitutional change]		3.990*	4.065*			6.422*	10.007*	
		(1.389)	(2.035)			(2.637)	(3.515)	
P[Non-constitutional change]		14.803*	20.344*			8.838*	32.091*	
		(6.800)	(8.510)			(3.049)	(14.243)	
Constitutional change #			0.795*	0.836*			0.770*	0.842*
			(0.165)	(0.168)			(0.377)	(0.375)
Democratic electoral institutions #			0.107	0.004			0.532	0.278
			(0.086)	(0.067)			(0.283)	(0.214)
Electoral period #			-0.123	0.036			-0.664	-0.057
			(0.277)	(0.193)			(0.511)	(0.381)
Non-constitutional change #			-0.031	0.136				
			(0.438)	(0.417)				
Constant	-2.286*	-2.362*	-2.463*	-2.290*	-2.951*	-3.024*	-3.584*	-3.189*
	(0.130)	(0.135)	(0.177)	(0.144)	(0.233)	(0.255)	(0.401)	(0.303)
Observations	19027	19027	19027	19027	7392	7392	7392	7392

Entries are probit estimates obtained via maximum likelihood; robust standard errors in parentheses.
Columns 1–4 are for the entire sample; columns 5–8 are for only those country-months where the country had a pegged exchange rate.
All models are estimated with a set of five linear splines.
Standard errors for hypothesis tests are estimated via Huber's robust standard error matrix and account for unequal variances across countries.
# indicates that the variable is a dummy variable.
*two-tailed test, p<0.05.

APPENDIX 3
YEARLY MODEL OF LEADERSHIP DURATION

	Const. Change versus No Change	Non-const. Change versus No Change
Military regime #	0.732	2.068*
	(1.47)	(3.87)
Democratic regime #	2.062*	0.373
	(2.43)	(0.81)
Election year #	2.623*	0.603
	(10.16)	(1.79)
Leader age	0.004*	0.004*
	(3.80)	(3.73)
Leader length in power	-0.223	-0.259*
	(1.20)	(2.07)
(Leader length in power)^2	0.006	0.004
	(1.10)	(0.84)
Democracy × leader length in power	0.176	0.113
	(0.96)	(1.06)
Democracy × (leader length in power)^2	-0.005	-0.001
	(0.92)	(0.28)
Military × leader length in power	0.181	0.121
	(1.64)	(1.14)
Military × (leader length in power)^2	-0.008	-0.003
	(1.89)	(0.85)
Latin America #	0.352	-0.351
	(1.26)	(0.65)
Middle East #	-0.624	-0.860
	(1.10)	(1.47)
Africa #	-0.832*	0.060
	(3.31)	(0.13)
Constant	-7.281*	-6.434*
	(5.92)	(5.25)
Observations	2898	
	χ^2	Prob $>\chi^2$
Model as a whole	419.31	0.0000
Military variable and interactions	140.96	0.0000
Democracy variable and interactions	85.39	0.0000
Length variable and interactions	11.53	0.0732
Length^2 variable and interactions	8.46	0.2061

Entries are multinomial logit estimates with robust z-statistics in parentheses.
# Indicates a dummy variable.
* Significant at 5% level.

APPENDIX 4

SPECULATIVE ATTACK MODELS (YEARLY DATA)

	(1)	(2)	(3)	(4)	(5)	(6)	(7)	(8)
Speculative attack$_{t-1}$ #	1.946*	1.883*	1.879*	1.936*	1.767*	1.717*	1.723*	1.756*
	(0.252)	(0.248)	(0.237)	(0.249)	(0.270)	(0.281)	(0.290)	(0.283)
Foreign interest rates	0.052*	0.052*	0.049*	0.049*	0.025	0.026	0.025	0.023
	(0.019)	(0.021)	(0.021)	(0.020)	(0.034)	(0.036)	(0.035)	(0.033)
Real exchange rate overvaluation	0.003	0.003	0.004	0.003	0.003	0.003	0.003	0.003
	(0.002)	(0.002)	(0.002)	(0.002)	(0.004)	(0.004)	(0.004)	(0.004)
Domestic credit growth	0.269	0.275	0.262	0.285	-0.268	-0.221	-0.221	-0.240
	(0.278)	(0.287)	(0.277)	(0.276)	(0.322)	(0.356)	(0.355)	(0.331)
Growth in bank lending	-0.499	-0.552	-0.554	-0.505	-0.608	-0.653	-0.641	-0.593
	(0.279)	(0.285)	(0.289)	(0.289)	(0.496)	(0.491)	(0.490)	(0.492)
Foreign reserves/imports	-0.009	-0.009	-0.010	-0.010	-0.008	-0.007	-0.008	-0.009
	(0.008)	(0.008)	(0.008)	(0.007)	(0.010)	(0.009)	(0.009)	(0.010)
Short-term debt/total debt	-0.005	-0.004	-0.004	-0.004	-0.004	-0.004	-0.004	-0.004
	(0.003)	(0.002)	(0.002)	(0.003)	(0.004)	(0.003)	(0.003)	(0.004)
Total external debt/GNP	0.194*	0.198*	0.193*	0.195*	0.251*	0.259*	0.256*	0.255*
	(0.045)	(0.046)	(0.047)	(0.047)	(0.084)	(0.080)	(0.082)	(0.086)
Current account/GNP	0.010	0.010	0.009	0.009	0.003	0.003	0.002	0.002
	(0.007)	(0.007)	(0.007)	(0.007)	(0.008)	(0.008)	(0.008)	(0.008)
P[Constitutional change]		0.678*	1.222*			0.103	0.416	
		(0.300)	(0.511)			(0.739)	(0.413)	
P[Non-constitutional change]		2.336*	2.000*			2.929*	2.411*	
		(0.780)	(0.807)			(1.001)	(1.017)	
Democratic electoral institutions #			-0.035	0.025			0.015	0.023
			(0.166)	(0.157)			(0.183)	(0.162)
Election year			-0.628	-0.210			-0.325	-0.268
			(0.458)	(0.214)			(0.591)	(0.343)
Constitutional change #			0.398	0.564*			0.159	0.303
			(0.223)	(0.188)			(0.318)	(0.311)
Non-constitutional change #			0.090	0.350			0.277	0.563*
			(0.230)	(0.241)			(0.235)	(0.247)
Constant	-2.469*	-2.681*	-2.645*	-2.529*	-2.415*	-2.619*	-2.611*	-2.465*
	(0.194)	(0.219)	(0.235)	(0.223)	(0.310)	(0.361)	(0.323)	(0.309)
Observations	1813	1813	1813	1813	1339	1339	1339	1339

Entries are probit estimates obtained via maximum likelihood; robust standard errors in parentheses. Columns 1–4 are for the entire sample; columns 5–8 are for only those country-months where the country had a pegged exchange rate. Standard errors for hypothesis tests are estimated via Huber's robust standard error matrix and account for unequal variances across countries.

# Indicates that the variable is a dummy variable.

*Two-tailed test, p<0.05.

NOTES

1. I am grateful to Bill Bernhard, Andy Sobel, Stephan Haggard, and the other seminar participants at Washington University, Yale University, and the Graduate School of International Relations and Pacific Studies at the University of California at San Diego for their helpful comments. They are, of course, not responsible for any errors and omissions in this analysis. Julie Stephens provided outstanding research assistance. Financial support from the National Science Foundation grant #SES-0096295 is gratefully acknowledged.

2. There is a voluminous literature on speculative attacks and currency crises. For a comprehensive source, see Noriel Roubini's home page on the Asian currency crisis. This page has links to recent working papers from academics, the World Bank, the International Monetary Fund, and others. Roubini's page is updated regularly and can be found at http://www.stern.nyu.edu/~nroubini/asia/AsiaHomepage.html.

3. Second-generation models have been extended to take into account 'contagion effects'. Gerlach and Smets (1994) and Eichengreen *et al.* (1997) argue that crises are transmitted from country to country through foreign-trade links. Simply, a decision to devalue by one country forces others to also devalue or to risk a loss of trade competitiveness. Calvo and Reinhart (1996) examine financial channels as avenues for contagion.

4. Aliber's (1973) work on interest parity mentions but does not explicitly model the influence of political forces. His notion of political risk, as in the work of others, is a bundle of variables that represents the probability that a government will interpose its interests ahead of those of the investor. Similarly, Bailey and Chung (1995) discuss 'political turbulence', 'political risk', and 'democratic elements' of a government in their study of the fluctuations in Mexico's exchange rate. However, they fail to operationalize and/or measure any of these three political concepts. Sobel (1995), however, does attempt to measure political risk and argues that 'politically capable governments' are able to attract foreign capital.

5. These countries are Afghanistan, Argentina, Bahrain, Bangladesh, Barbados, Belize, Benin, Bolivia, Botswana, Brazil, Burma, Burundi, Cameroon, Cape Verde, Central African Republic, Chad, Chile, China, Colombia, Comoros, Costa Rica, Côte d'Ivoire, Dominican Republic, Ecuador, Egypt, El Salvador, Equatorial Guinea, Ethiopia, Fiji, Gabon, Gambia, Ghana, Grenada, Guinea-Bissau, Israel, Jamaica, Jordan, South Kenya, Korea, Kuwait, Lebanon, Liberia, Libya, Madagascar, Malawi, Malaysia, Maldives, Mali, Mauritania, Mauritius, Mexico, Mongolia, Morocco, Nepal, Nicaragua, Nigeria, Oman, Pakistan, Panama, Paraguay, Peru, Philippines, Rwanda, Saudi Arabia, Senegal, Sierra Leone, Singapore, Solomon Islands, South Africa, Sri Lanka, St Lucia, St Vincent and Grenadines, Sudan, Suriname, Tanzania, Thailand, Togo, Tonga, Trinidad and Tobago, Tunisia, Uganda, Uruguay, Venezuela, Zaire, Zambia, and Zimbabwe.

6. International IDEA has a web site that is updated monthly (www.int-idea.se). The link for the electoral data is http://www.int-idea.se/Voter_turnout/index.html.

7. I am not able to include economic variables such as economic growth and inflation found to be important by Bienen and Van de Walle (1991) and Warwick (1994) because they are not available on a monthly basis.

8. Selecting only extreme values of the EMP index as indicators of speculative behavior may reduce the number of crises in the sample and may also decrease the correlation of crises with economic fundamentals.

9. The number of linear splines was determined through the use of sequential F-tests. The coefficients for the spline variables are not reported but are available from the author upon request.

10. All the statistical models were estimated using the probit command in STATA statistical software. The code and data necessary to replicate the analysis and diagnostics are available upon request.

REFERENCES

Alesina, A. and Rosenthal, H. (1995), *Partisan Politics, Divided Government, and the Economy* (Cambridge: Cambridge University Press).

Alesina, A. and Roubini, R., with Cohen, G.D. (1997), *Political Cycles and the Macroeconomy* (Cambridge, MA: MIT Press).

Aliber, R. (1973), 'The Interest Rate Parity Theorem', *Journal of Political Economy* 81: 1451–9.

Allison, P.D. (1984), *Event History Analysis: Regression for Longitudinal Data* (Newbury Park, CA: Sage).

Alt, J. and King, G. (1994), 'Transfers of Governmental Power: The Meaning of Time Dependence', *Comparative Political Studies* 27, 2: 190–210.

Bachman, D. (1992), 'The Effect of Political Risk on the Forward Exchange Bias: The Case of Elections', *Journal of International Money and Finance* 11: 208–19.

Bailey, W. and Chung, V.P. (1995), 'Exchange Rate Fluctuations, Political Risk, and Stock Returns: Some Evidence from an Emerging Market', *Journal of Financial and Quantitative Economics* 30: 541–61.

Beck, N., Katz, J., and Tucker, R. (1998), 'Beyond Ordinary Logit: Taking Time Seriously in Binary Time-Series-Cross-Section Models', unpublished manuscript available from ftp://weber.ucsd.edu:/pub/nbeck.

Bernhard, W. and David Leblang, D. (1999), 'Democratic Institutions and Exchange Rate Commitments', *International Organization* 53, 1: 71–97.

Bienen, H. and van de Walle, N. (1991), *Of Time and Power: Leadership Duration in the Modern World* (Stanford, CA: Stanford University Press).

Blanco, H. and Garber, P. (1986), 'Recurrent Devaluations and Speculative Attacks on the Mexican Peso', *Journal of Political Economy* 94: 148–66

Blondel, J. (1980), *World Leaders: Heads of Government in the Postwar Period* (London: Sage).

Bloomberg, S.B. and Hess, G. (1997), 'Politics and Exchange Rate Forecasts', *Journal of International Economics* 43: 189–205.

Calvo, G.A. (1995), 'Varieties of Capital-Market Crises', College Park, MD: Center for International Economics Working Paper #15, University of Maryland,.

Calvo, S. and Reinhart, C. (1996), 'Capital Flows to Latin America: Is There Evidence of Contagion Effects?,' in G. Calvo, M. Goldstein, and E. Hochreiter (eds), *Private Capital Flows to Emerging Markets after the Mexican Crisis* (Washington, DC: Institute for International Economics,), pp. 151–71.

Charemza, W.W. and Deadman, D.F. (1992), *New Directions in Econometric Practice* (Aldershot: Edward Elgar).

Collins, S. (1996), 'On Becoming More Flexible: Exchange Rate Regimes in Latin America and the Caribbean', *Journal of Development Economics* 51: 117–38.

Corsetti, G., Pesenti, P., and Roubini, N. (1998), 'Paper Tigers? A Model of the Asian Crisis', New York: Manuscript, Department of Economics, New York University.

Cukierman, A., Edwards, S., and Tabellini, G. (1992), 'Seigniorage and Political Instability', *American Economic Review* 82: 537–55.

Cumby, R. and van Wijnbergen, S. (1989), 'Financial Policy and Speculative Runs with a Crawling Peg', *Journal of International Economics* 27: 111–27.

Demirguc-Kunt, A. and Detragiache, E. (1997), 'The Determinants of Banking Crises: Evidence from the Industrial and Developing Countries', Washington, DC: International Monetary Fund Working Paper #97–106.

Diamond, D. and Dybvig, P. (1983), 'Bank Runs, Deposit Insurance, and Liquidity', *Journal of Political Economy* 91: 401–19.

Dooley, M. (1997), 'A Model of Crises in Emerging Markets', Washington, DC: International Finance Discussion Papers, #1998-630, Board of Governors, Federal Reserve Bank.

Dornbusch, R., Goldfajn, I., and Valdes, R. (1995), 'Currency Crises and Collapses', *Brookings Papers on Economic Activity* 2: 219–95.

Edwards, S. (1996), 'The Determinants of the Choice Between Fixed and Flexible Exchange

Rate Regimes', Washington, DC: National Bureau of Economic Research Working Paper #5576,.

Edwards, S. and Santaella, J. (1993), 'Devaluation Controversies in the Developing Countries: Lessons from the Bretton Woods Era', in M. Bordo and B. Eichengreen (eds), *A Retrospective on the Bretton Woods System* (Chicago: University of Chicago Press), pp. 405–60.

Eichengreen, B. and Frieden, J. (eds) (1994), *The Political Economy of European Monetary Unification* (Boulder, CO: Westview Press).

Eichengreen, B., Rose, A., and Wyplosz, C. (1995), 'Exchange Market Mayhem: The Antecedents and Aftermath of Speculative Attacks', *Economic Policy* 21: 249–312.

Eichengreen, B., Rose, A., and Wyplosz, C. (1997), 'Contagious Currency Crises', unpublished manuscript, Berkeley, CA: Department of Economics, University of California.

Engle, R. (1984), 'Wald, Likelihood Ratio, and Lagrange Multiplier Tests in Econometrics', in Z. Griliches and M. Intriligator (eds), *Handbook of Econometrics*, Vol. 2 (Amsterdam: North-Holland), pp. 775–826.

Flood, R. and Garber, P. (1984), 'Collapsing Exchange Rate Regimes: Some Linear Examples', *Journal of International Economics* 17 : 1–13.

Frankel, J. and Rose, A. (1996), 'Currency Crashes in Emerging Markets: An Empirical Treatment', *Journal of International Economics* 41: 351–66.

Freeman, J. (1997), 'Democracy and Markets: The Case of Exchange Rates', unpublished manuscript, Minneapolis: Department of Political Science, University of Minnesota.

Frieden, J. (1991), 'Invested Interests: The Politics of National Economic Policies in a World of Global Finance', *International Organization* 45: 425–51.

Frieden, J. (1998), 'The Political Economy of European Exchange Rates: An Empirical Assessment', unpublished manuscript, Cambridge, MA: Department of Government, Harvard University.

Gerlach, S. and Smets, F. (1994), 'Contagious Speculative Attacks', London: Centre for Economic Policy Research, Discussion Paper #1055.

Goldfajn, I. and Valdes, R. (1997), 'Are Currency Crises Predictable?' Washington, DC: International Monetary Fund Working Paper # 97–159.

Gurr, T.R. and Jaggers, K. (1994), *Polity III: Regime Type and Political Authority* (Ann Arbor, MI: Inter-University Consortium for Political and Social Research).

Hausman, J. (1978), 'Specification Tests in Econometrics', *Econometrica* 46: 1251–71.

Huntingdon, S. (1968), *Political Order in Changing Societies* (New Haven: Yale University Press).

Kaminsky, G. and Reinhart, C. (1996), 'The Twin Crises: The Causes of Banking and Balance-of-Payments Problems', Washington, DC: Board of Governors of the Federal Reserve, International Finance Discussion Paper #544.

Kaminsky, G., Lizondo, S. and Reinhart, C. (1997), 'Leading Indicators of Currency Crises', Washington, DC: International Monetary Fund, Working Paper #97–79.

Keohane, R. and Milner, H. (eds) (1996), *Internationalization and Domestic Politics* (New York: Cambridge University Press).

Klein, M. and Marion, N. (1997), 'Explaining the Duration of Exchange-Rate Pegs', *Journal of Development Economics* 54: 387–404.

Krasker, W. (1980), 'The "Peso Problem" in Testing the Efficiency of Forward Exchange Markets', *Journal of Monetary Economics* 6: 269–76.

Krugman, P. (1979), 'A Model of Balance of Payments Crises', *Journal of Money, Credit and Banking* 11: 311–25.

Krugman, P. (1996), 'Are Currency Crises Self-Fulfilling?' Cambridge, MA: Manuscript, Department of Economics, Massachusetts Institute of Technology.

Krugman, P. (1998) 'What Happened to Asia?' http://web.mit.edu/krugman/www/DISINTER.html.

Laver, M. and Shepsle, K. (1996), *Making and Breaking Governments* (New York: Cambridge University Press).

Lobo, B. and Tufte, D. (1998), 'Exchange Rate Volatility: Does Politics Matter?' *Journal of*

Macroeconomics 20: 351–65.

Londregan, J. and Poole, K. (1992), 'The Seizure of Executive Power and Economic Growth: Some Additional Evidence' in Cukierman, A., Hercowitz, Z. and Leiderman, L. (eds), *Political Economy, Growth, and Business Cycles* (Cambridge, MA: MIT Press), pp. 51–79.

McMillan, S. (1995), 'Foreign Direct Investment in Ghana and Côte d'Ivoire', in S. Chan (ed.), *Foreign Direct Investment in a Changing Global Economy* (New York: St. Martin's Press), pp. 150–65.

Obstfeld, M. (1994), 'The Logic of Currency Crises', Washington, DC: National Bureau of Economics Working Paper #4640.

Obstfeld, M. (1996), 'Models of Currency Crises with Self-Fulfilling Features', *European Economic Review* 40: 1037–47.

Olson, M. (1993), 'Dictatorship, Democracy and Development', *American Political Science Review* 87, 3: 567–76.

Przeworski, A. (1990), *The State and the Economy Under Capitalism: Fundamentals of Pure and Applied Economics* 40 (Chur: Harwood).

Przeworski, A. and Limongi, F. (1993), 'Political Regimes and Economic Growth', *Journal of Economic Perspectives* 7: 51–69.

Quinn, D. (1997), 'The Correlates of Change in International Financial Regulation', *American Political Science Review* 91,3: 531–52.

Radelet, S. and Sachs, J. (1998), 'The Onset of the East Asian Financial Crisis', Cambridge, MA: Institute for International Development, Harvard University.

Sachs, J., Tornell, A. and Velasco, A. (1996), 'Financial Crises in Emerging Markets: The Lessons from 1995', *Brookings Papers on Economic Activity* 1: 147–215.

Salant, S. and Henderson, D. (1978), 'Market Anticipation of Government Policy and the Price of Gold', *Journal of Political Economy* 86: 627–48.

Sobel, A. (1995), 'The Capital Pool: Sink or Swim? Political Institutions and International Capital Markets', Paper presented at the 1995 Annual Meeting of the Midwest Political Science Association, Chicago.

Warwick, P. (1994), *Government Survival in Parliamentary Democracies* (New York: Cambridge University Press).

Index

For Product Safety Concerns and Information please contact our EU
representative GPSR@taylorandfrancis.com
Taylor & Francis Verlag GmbH, Kaufingerstraße 24, 80331 München, Germany

www.ingramcontent.com/pod-product-compliance
Lightning Source LLC
Chambersburg PA
CBHW070408270326
41926CB00014B/2752